WILL OLDHAM ON
BONNIE "PRINCE" BILLY

Will Oldham is a singer songwriter and actor, and a native of Louisville, Kentucky.

Alan Licht, guitarist, has appeared on over seventy-five recordings that range from indie rock to free improvisation to minimalist compositions. He is the author of *Sound Art: Beyond Music, Between Categories*, and a frequent contributor to *Artforum*, *Wire*, and many other publications. He lives with his partner, vocalist Angela Jaeger, in New York.

WILL OLDHAM ON
BONNIE "PRINCE" BILLY

edited by Alan Licht

W. W. NORTON & COMPANY
NEW YORK · LONDON

First published in 2012 by Faber and Faber Limited

First American Edition 2012

Manufacturing by Courier Westford
Book design by Chris Welch
Production manager: Louise Mattarelliano

Library of Congress Cataloging-in-Publication Data

Oldham, Will.
Will Oldham on Bonnie "Prince" Billy / edited by Alan Licht. — 1st American ed.
p. cm.
Includes index.
ISBN 978-0-393-34433-2 (pbk.)
1. Bonnie "Prince" Billy—Interviews. 2. Singers—United States—Interviews.
3. Rock musicians—United States—Interviews. 4. Rock musicians—United States—
Biography. I. Licht, Alan. II. Title.
ML420.B6854A5 2012
782.42166092—dc23
[B]

2012017023

W. W. Norton & Company, Inc.
500 Fifth Avenue, New York, N.Y. 10110
www.wwnorton.com

W. W. Norton & Company Ltd.
Castle House, 75/76 Wells Street, London W1T 3QT

1 2 3 4 5 6 7 8 9 0

CONTENTS

INTRODUCTION

"They [interviews] have nothing to do with the music. It's usually people asking a bunch of weird questions like, 'Why are the songs so slow?' Well, maybe because they are. Because that's how we play them. Because I wrote them at a less rapid pace. It's always why, why, why? Why everything? And the answer to 'why' is because it just is. Things just are."

—*Will Oldham,* Observer, *November 17, 2002*

To longtime followers of the media's encounters with Bonnie "Prince" Billy/Will Oldham/Palace, the appearance of this book may come as something of a surprise. Look at almost any article about the singer/songwriter/actor from the last two decades and you will find words to the effect that its subject is an elusive, puzzling, and obfuscating artist who does not like to be interviewed, and is often evasive when he is. So, why would Oldham agree to do a book-length interview? One reason is to answer questions about his past in a single volume, to provide a basic information source for future interlocutors to consult— and maybe so he won't have to do so many interviews.

The facts are these: Will was born in Louisville, Kentucky, on

January 15, 1970 (not December 24, as some profiles would have it), the second of three sons. Up until the age of nineteen he pursued acting vigorously, appearing in local productions and a few television movies (*Umbrella Jack*, starring John Carradine [1984]; *Everybody's Baby: The Rescue of Jessica McClure* [1988]) and feature films (*What Goes Around*, directed by Jerry Reed [1982]; *Matewan*, directed by John Sayles [1987]; *A Thousand Pieces of Gold*, directed by Nancy Kelly [1989]). Suddenly disillusioned with acting, but a lifelong fan of music, he was encouraged to sing and make songs by friends and, particularly, his older brother Ned, and initiated an ad hoc group called Palace Flophouse (after the locale in John Steinbeck's novel *Cannery Row*). This turned into Palace Brothers, and as the Chicago indie-rock label Drag City began to release their records the name would change with each one—Palace Music, Palace Songs, or simply Palace—as would the participants involved (who, until 1994's *Hope* EP, were generally uncredited). There were also no songwriting credits at first, and as little information given as possible on each release—which, combined with Oldham's reluctance to tour or to give interviews, is how he started to get tagged as an enigma.

The first four Palace albums that originally brought him attention—*There Is No One What Will Take Care of You*, *Days in the Wake*, *Viva Last Blues*, and *Arise Therefore*—remain a vital, high-contrast body of work. In the aftermath of *Arise Therefore*, Oldham retired the Palace moniker and seemed to be at a low ebb; one record made in collaboration with the Dirty Three was scrapped, and *Joya*, a reworking of some of the same mate-

rial released in 1997 under his own name, almost went unre-
corded entirely. The next year Bonnie Prince Billy was created,
an appellation that Will has used for recording and performing
ever since, and the following album, *I See a Darkness*, yielded
some of his strongest material (the title track was later covered
by Johnny Cash). Subsequent releases—*Ease Down the Road,
Master and Everyone, The Letting Go, Lie Down in the Light*, and
Beware—have retained the light-and-dark thematic concerns of
the Palace records, each building on its predecessor in terms
of recording, performances, and songwriting (2004's *Bonnie
"Prince" Billy Sings Greatest Palace Music*, which re-dressed old
Palace songs as straight country material with a crack Nashville
session band, is a particularly intriguing recent disc).

In some ways the moniker "Bonnie" could be viewed as an
accommodation with Oldham's growing success: rather than
sign with a major label or settle on one backup band or sound,
the decision to stick with one name *does* provide a certain stability lacking in the Palace era. But this remains the exception
rather than the rule: Will questions and usually outright rejects
any and all accepted record-industry wisdom with regard to
virtually every aspect of the production, merchandising, and
promotion of his music and himself. As much as, if not more
than, long-standing rock-industry mavericks like Neil Young,
Bob Dylan, or Lou Reed, Oldham is a law unto himself.

Emerging from the indie-rock scene of the early 1990s, Palace was at times lumped in with the "No Depression" alternative country-rock bands like Son Volt or Uncle Tupelo, or with
the lo-fi movement identified with Sebadoh, Daniel Johnston,

Guided by Voices, or Drag City labelmate Smog, and later Bonnie Prince Billy was occasionally held up as a forebear of the "freak-folk" scene of the past decade. Yet the music is too slippery for such simple categorizations. It touches on—refracts, really—rock, pop, folk, country, bluegrass, and ethnic music without hybridizing any of them. Like Oldham's vocal delivery itself, which has deepened and developed from cracked and adenoidal to idiosyncratic but assured, the music is continually evolving, and in concert the old songs are reworked from tour to tour and often from night to night. The music is sometimes characterized as dark, which it can be, but it can also be—even in the same song—bright, fun-loving, sly, bawdy, or cockeyed. The lyrics speak both to the joy (and struggles) of community and the pleasures (and struggles) of solitude.

Another part of the press's codification problem is that Oldham has never fit the singer-songwriter mold. As a mutual acquaintance put it in an email to me, "I still see Will more as a film-maker without film than a musician." Which is not to say that the music conjures up sweeping CinemaScope vistas or resembles a movie soundtrack (although Oldham has scored some short independent films), but each album and tour is written, directed, and cast (or produced, as he will note herein) by Oldham. He has referred to his songs as "little scripts" that he hands out to the players and engineers during recording sessions, and has lamented that he'd like his records to be filed in a record store by name, as a DVD would be in a video store, rather than by artist (hence the numerous iterations of the Palace name on early releases).

He is also often confused with the voice on the record or the figure onstage. The songs are not confessional; when religion, animals, royalty, family, travel, death, sex, riding, friends, or the wind keep reappearing in the lyrics, it's like a painter returning to the same subjects, not another scene from the life of Will Oldham. In reading past Palace/Bonnie press coverage, I was reminded of soap-opera stars recalling people approaching them in an airport or a restaurant and chastising them for something their character did in the show, and having to explain to them, "That's not me." Indeed, there was one Bonnie show in Belgium where two fans came up to Oldham afterwards and said, "You looked like you were having fun up there, and that's not what we came to see."

My own association with Will goes back to the early 1990s. A fellow named Ken Katkin released a single by my band, Love Child, in 1990. Ken was (then) a New Yorker, but a big fan, and friend, of Louisville indie-rock bands, also releasing singles by the Babylon Dance Band and King Kong. Love Child played in Louisville several times, and on a stop there during a US tour in spring 1993 we stayed with Ethan Buckler, King Kong's leader, who took us to a party at a house shared by Will, Pavement's Bob Nastanovich, and Britt Walford (a veteran of both King Kong and of Slint, a band Ethan had once played bass in). Ken had mentioned Will to me a few times as someone who was not a musician but who was involved in the Louisville music scene, renowned, he said, for having appeared in John Sayles's *Matewan* (a movie I had, at the time, never seen), taking the cover photo of Slint's album *Spiderland*, and opening for Steve Albini's just-post–Big Black outfit Rapeman at CBGB—not playing music, but making "anal breathing" sounds with his butt. Will was a fan of Love Child, and we had previously spoken briefly at one or more of our shows. At one point during the party Will and I found ourselves in the kitchen, and he asked me if I had a job besides music. I did, working at Kino International, a foreign- and independent-film distribution company in New York (ironically, a dozen years later, after I had left, Kino would distribute Kelly Reichardt's *Old Joy*, Oldham's return to acting). This proved to be of great interest to him, and for the next hour we talked, mostly about film distribution and movies in general. Later, as I was walking out the door, he handed me a 7" record—"Ohio River Boat Song," the first Palace single. This was a surprise—neither he nor anyone else had said anything about it.

When Palace began to tour, I caught three shows within a year (1994). The first one, at Threadwaxing Space on lower Broadway, was a fairly shambling affair; the next one I saw, a few months later and also at Threadwaxing Space, was solo, and riveting; the third took place at Maxwell's, where Will was backed up by Ned's band, the Anomoanon, a much more cohesive ensemble sometimes compared to the Grateful Dead. These shows were each so different, and unique, that going forward I made a point of seeing him play, knowing that whatever he was doing would not be repeated the next time he appeared. Oldham's sets were so compelling, in fact, that I found it shocking when he mentioned to me that he didn't care for live playing and that the records were his real focus.

In late 1995 Will invited me to open a few shows in the Midwest as a solo act. I agreed, developing a set where I would play guitar against a backing tape of hollering contests from South Carolina, drastically reharmonizing the a cappella originals. A year and a half later, my next band, Run On, was going on tour and I asked Will if he'd like to share some of the bills. He fashioned his own solo show using a backing tape of his songs played on a Roland sequencer, karaoke-style. After these two tours, we did a few concerts in New York playing together, including a Halloween show at Tonic in 1998 (early in the Bonnie Prince Billy phase: Britt played drums under the name "The Sheik," wearing a makeshift Arab headdress; I was "Hung Lucifer," clad in a body-length skeleton costume; and Bonnie was in whiteface, with black circles around his eyes, and wearing a crown), a benefit concert for Anthology Film Archives where we played movie-themed songs (including King Kong's "Movie Star" and Bob Seger's "Hollywood Nights"), and an all-improvised show at Tonic with vocalist Catherine Jauniaux and turntablist Erik M (allegedly attended by Rick Rubin, who supposedly wondered aloud, "Where are the songs?" and left after a few minutes).

In early 2002 I ran into Will at Joe's Pub, and he asked me to play on his next record, which was ultimately released as *Master and Everyone*. The next year I invited him to perform in a two-person dance piece as part of a night I was asked to curate for Jutta Koether and Kim Gordon's "Club in the Shadow" series at the Kenny Schachter Gallery. We've stayed in touch, but this book marks our first collaboration since then.

We agreed to meet for a week of extensive interviews. Oldham is nothing if not prolific, and we went over every tour and concert, every release and credit, every role. The website The Royal Stable (http://users.bart.nl/~ljmeijer/oldham/) proved to be an invaluable resource for assembling a timeline of Oldham's professional life, as well as the discography that appears at the end of the book.

Laurence Bell approached me about doing this book, at Will's suggestion. I am grateful to Laurence for providing back-catalog releases and acting as a liaison between Faber & Faber, Will, and myself; to Lee Brackstone, my editor at Faber & Faber; to Tom Mayer, my editor at W. W. Norton; to Dan Koretzky and Sara Hays at Drag City for aid with research materials; to Kevin Scott; to Ian Bahrami; to Richard King; to Ian Bahrami; to Paul Cronin and Michael Chaiken; and to Will for his time and his generous hospitality.

Alan Licht

New York, 2011

1

THE WOLF MAN MEETS
ABBOTT AND COSTELLO

ALAN LICHT: How comfortable are you with life at its most turbulent or unexpected?

WILL OLDHAM: When I was a kid, long before I saw the movie, I heard the *Zorba the Greek* soundtrack, with Anthony Quinn saying Zorba's lines in between the songs. One of the lines he says is, "Life is trouble, only death is not." And I thought, "Yeah, that sounds good." On some level there's a degree of comfort in the most intimate or most challenging or most demanding situations, because I can almost relax; I know it's not going to get worse or stronger or more intense than that.

A lot of people like to watch movies or read books where they know what's going on, but I like the opposite—I don't like to know what's going on. Not to the point where reality is obliterated; I like a strange situation where you don't know what's going to happen, but there are one or two parts that are familiar to you. Because to me, that's what the course of any given day is like. There's no predetermination my tiny brain can comprehend. It's dealing with conflict in conjunction with time. The bulk of surprises is reason to get out of bed and touch your toes.

I've done a couple of in-store and radio-station tours, and *anything* can happen if you're traveling alone in those situations. 'Cause usually you play in the afternoon, so that means mornings and nights you don't know what's going to happen—don't know where you're gonna sleep, don't know anything about

3

what life is going to be like. *Then* it's fully 24/7 Bonnie; there is no other identity. It's pretty exciting.

Identity seems to be a recurring theme in your records, especially in *Beware*; and identity is involved in acting, where you're taking on a role for the duration of the play or movie. Is identity something you're consciously thinking about?

At the time I started to make Bonnie Prince Billy records, there was an acceptance that something that would be on the table then would be—I didn't necessarily know what it meant—a relationship to identity. That having your person and/or your work absorbed by people who had no access to any other part of you was inherent in being involved in the arts and the natural tendency for people, whether or not they wanted or needed to, to fill out the character, fill out the person, fill out the life. It wasn't a moment of saying, "That's cool," or "That's great," or "That's fine"; it was, "Oh, that *is*." And it doesn't have to be bad—it will be bad, in a lot of ways, but there can be good things about that. On some level there's the relationship of the audience to the identity, but I didn't want that to be the theme, to where it's super-reflexive and that's what the content is about—it seemed like that would be a dead end—but to understand that I could have the relationship and see if it translated or not.

It has to do with resembling a working life like Humphrey Bogart's, where there's no substantial reason to identify a person like him with anything his characters have done. I don't think there's any direct relation, necessarily, between his characterizations and who he was outside his work. It's harder in music for audiences to make that kind of association; there's always this idea that the person *is* what the person seems to represent. Because of my inability to work with liaisons most of the time—and also because of my low-maintenance way, especially in the first ten years of making records, where there was a lot of direct contact with people—I didn't want to feel I was accountable every moment of every day for the content of the songs, as much as for making them available or interpreting them. People will take content first and foremost. When you make a song or a movie or a piece of art, the idea is to put forward something that does not have the process completely visible, to make something someone can have a clean emotional experience with. But then people don't know how to get from what they see through the art to the life of the person on the other side—that's too many steps for a human being to have to make.

These are songs, and people like to listen to songs with personal subject matter in them. If it were a screenplay, no one would ask those questions. I don't think when James Cameron writes and directs a movie, people confuse him with the Terminator. Writing songs is a profession; so it's not an attempt to take things from my interactions with other people and for some reason give them to a total stranger to listen to. I find it offensive to hear other people do that. I basically use other things that have touched me as examples, which I know share nothing with the person who was involved, and I know I'm sharing something that has nothing to do with anything specific at all. There's something to be said about your emotional palette coming from your personal experience, but music is about changing things, like a book or a movie—you take a situation and construct a new one. The songs are not meant to be real life. They're meant to have a psychic, rather than factual, bearing on the listener. Songs are made to exist in and of themselves, like a great James Jones or Robert Louis Stevenson novel. They're not autobiographical, and yet there's reality on every single page. It's real life of the imagination. I will always rewrite a song that seems like it is too connected to a real event, because the intention is always to create the hyperreal event, so that, ideally, more people can relate to it.

The writer just has to use language that allows others in. Then if people want to connect on some level, they will. There are a lot of things I'm using to represent love, although there's no single tangible object of desire. Magic words like "love" or "God" or "death" could mean a thousand different things, and if you want to write a song that's about more than a thousand things, you can begin by assuming that every way of jamming words together can be as literal as you desire and still be taken in a different way by every listener. It doesn't matter if you're singing about a basement or Jeffrey Dahmer or Bruce Lee. I've always loved "Bat out of Hell." Have you ever had a motorcycle wreck? Has Meat Loaf? I don't think so. But I feel like it's probably a translation of something that he knows. Maybe because he's crazy, but people like Daniel Johnston can translate something literally from his life and put it into a song and have it be as weird and surreal and beautiful and powerful as Jim Steinman can with his motorcycle accident.

Sometimes with Nick Cave and Tom Waits—say, the first

eight Nick Cave and the Bad Seeds records—it's fun to think of their songs as descriptions of a personal experience that have been given character shadings. Most of the songs on that first Palace Brothers record [*There Is No One What Will Take Care of You*] are full-on character things. Singing and doing music the way I do is related to the idea of personifying a text of some sort, and looking for my idols in text personification. It's as if Elvis Presley is a written, created character like Stanley Kowalski.

Any first-person lyric, and just the use of the voice, is very tricky, not just for the listener but also probably for most performers, because one of the main reasons one does it is because of the appeal of inhabiting a persona and a voice. But once you commit to that, you don't know the effect it's gonna have. What does it do to your psyche, to sing any lyric? I'll never know for sure, but you know that every time it has some kind of effect. Assuming that people have all sorts of feelings or issues about their own relationship to identity and multiple identities, the issue of the singer's identity is not what people come to the records for, but hopefully somehow it resonates.

At the best of times, in the past, I've consciously thought irrational things, like that there would be a gradual transition from human form to musical form, a transformation that would occur if I allowed it to occur. And because those moments have existed, identity themes remain strong [*laughs*]. Because then there are times when it seems like that's not happening, when you're very earthbound. There was a John Woo movie based on a Philip K. Dick story called *Paycheck* that wasn't very good, with Ben Affleck, where his character knows that he is going to travel into the future and have his mind erased. So he assembles a set of clues and puts them in a manila envelope and leaves them for himself in the future so that he can reconstruct what happened to him. And in some ways, there's a little bit of that going on in the songs: knowing that I am going to be basically giving myself into Bonnie's way of being, that that will be kind of OK, and that there will be little reminders of what real physical humanity is like hidden in there, hidden in amongst the songs as I'm singing them. So the reentry back into the world of physical bleeding will not be as difficult as it has sometimes been in the past.

While we're on the subject of transformation to and from human form, let's talk about the Wolf Man and the Incredible Hulk.
All right!

Was there something about monsters that you could relate to as a kid?
I'm not sure why I felt such sympathy for the Lon Chaney Jr. Wolf Man character. As it turns out, as an adult I can have a very unpleasant, fierce, and unforgiving temper at times. But I don't think I had that when I was a kid. These days, at least, when I enter into any friendship, relationship, or collaboration, I try either to establish enough private space to allow for the monster to exist without the awareness of the other person or without affecting them, or I try to be upfront about giving warnings. Both were survival tactics of Larry Talbot in those movies; it

seemed like he tried to keep his distance and to be forthcoming about telling people to be careful. More than most movie characters, that was one that I connected with.

Did you like that it was part man, part animal?
It was visceral. I think when he became the wolf creature, he wasn't becoming a monster, he wasn't becoming something that was scary; for the most part, it was actually liberating. When you watched him transform, you could actually breathe again, seeing that he was no longer burdened with a conscience, for example, or with the need to be considerate or responsible [*laughs*]. He could just *be*.

The Incredible Hulk was like that, but the Hulk wasn't furry, and fur is really welcoming and good and also . . . I wonder if Lon Chaney Jr. played the Wolf Man once the makeup was on—was that still him? [It was.] 'Cause I didn't care about the Hulk in the comics, but you knew that Bill Bixby and Lou Ferrigno [the actors in the 1970s TV series] were different people. So part of that was even more frightening, because I didn't feel like it was a release when Bruce Banner became the Hulk. I felt like he was trapped all of a sudden in this weird, pervert, deaf body-builder's body, with green makeup all over him—which was a *bad* place to be. It was kind of the reverse, where he seemed like he knew he was one thing, and the other side was a mutation, and bad, but it was imposed upon him and forced him to not be able to have any constants in his life.

The great thing about the Wolf Man was that he got to be in a movie with Abbott and Costello. He's not just in this weird horror world, he's also in this great comedy world. He gets to branch out. Even though he's got this weird personality limitation, it doesn't cross the possibilities off the list of what he can do with his life: he gets to hang out with Bud and Lou.

I remember Ned [Oldham, older brother] getting us to watch the Specials on *Saturday Night Live* doing "Gangsters." There was some sort of Ramones clip that I'd seen around that time as well, and the Ramones and the Specials were very frightening to me, just the way they looked and the way they moved. The Specials seemed like an extension of the Universal horror movies—*The Wolf Man, Frankenstein, The Mummy* movies—but playing music. I don't know if they were trying to do that, be scary in a horror-movie kind of way, or if they were just trying to be aggressive and threatening. I think the singer, specifically, his whole complexion and makeup, looked like the Bride of Frankenstein, except with short hair.

So was there a lot of music in the house when you were growing up?
My folks had records. When I was young, my two or three favorite records that they had were probably *West Side Story*, the Broadway *Hair* record and *The Very Best of the Everly Brothers*—that was a record that I claimed and listened to over and over and over and over. They had two Leonard Cohen records, *The Best of Leonard Cohen* and *Death of a Ladies' Man*, and I remember "Paper Thin Hotel" being on a mix tape my dad made for when we would go on family vacations. That's easily the first Leonard Cohen song that I grew to know and love, but just as a

soundtrack in the background. I thought it was a wild song, but I had no idea of anything about it.

My older brother had records. Those that I remember liking were the Fall, specifically the *Slates* EP, and Lou Reed's *Transformer* and the Ramones' *Rocket to Russia*. I also remember him listening to things like James White and the Blacks, Skafish, Bauhaus, X, Minor Threat, the Meatmen—just an amazing array of stuff. And then I had records. That's what I listened to.

The first record you bought was a compilation of novelty songs called *Dumb Ditties*.
First record I bought with my own money, for myself. I saw commercials for it on TV, over and over again, and then I bought it with money that I got for my birthday. It was sold at a drugstore in a cardboard stand that said, "As Seen on TV. $4.99." And then, of course, lots of kids records, like [Marlo Thomas's] *Free to Be . . . You and Me* and [Carole King's] *Really Rosie*, which is a good record. I'm sure I know all the words to both those records. The first music I bought when I was nine or ten was pop from the 1950s and 1960s, like Elvis, Del Shannon, the Flamingos, Dion, the Platters—whatever I could get my hands on.

You started acting as a child too. What made you want to act?
I wanted to act in order to be Gene Kelly's peer. When I was really little and saw *Singing in the Rain* for the first time, knowing that that doesn't really happen in real life, that you can put music together with lyrics and a plot and a rainstorm . . . it just doesn't seem to happen every day. Well, if I want that to happen

I have to be involved in these fabricated existences that aren't fabricated because they're real while you're watching them. Some people have difficulty communicating, especially when they're young, and that was definitely something I had a hard time with. I had zero difficulty communicating with myself, but how do you communicate an idea to somebody else? You can translate it through a constructed and written text.

I found [acting] classes near where I lived and did more and more of them. My folks looked around and found this theater called Walden Theatre; that was more hard-core training for after school, so I went there and stayed until I was eighteen, when I graduated. I was probably one of the youngest people in the company at that point. The first semester I was there they did an improv performance one Saturday morning at the Water Tower, the old Louisville water company that's now moved up the hill, that's on the river. I was asked to participate in that, so it was my first performance with them. I totally shit my pants all morning with nerves, but it was amazing.

Even when I was doing theater stuff, the least pleasant part of any of that was live performance. It was exciting, the challenge of working with other people on the spot, where you can't stop, but it was an imposition that there was a room full of people. That was not a cool thing, except for the fact that they made you do it straight through and try to do it really well. But I realized early on that I didn't understand the live audience's reaction, that they weren't the best judges of whether you were doing it well. That also made the idea of film acting or recording more exciting than live theater or live performing. You don't have that mysterious group of people doing whatever it is they do in their seats.

This is a shortcoming of my own, in some ways, but at the end of the night it's no fun to play a good or bad show and realize that it doesn't relate to the audience's perception, to feel like you didn't share something with the audience, essentially. 'Cause there are better ways of spending your time than being in a room with people you don't have anything to do with, when you're supposed to have something to do with them.

In other words, you played a bad show and the audience reacted as if it was a good one?
That's what I mean. It didn't bother me as much to have a good show that people thought was bad, 'cause whether or not people liked it at least you had the satisfaction of having played a good show, but it really bothered me when it was a bad show and people thought it was good. Very confusing, very upsetting.

I feel correct in saying so, but it feels dubious on other levels that I happened to fall in love with movies and records, but my personality is not one that appreciates the public aspect of those things. And I think I always assumed that it wasn't an issue, because, especially as a kid, when you listen to David Bowie records, de facto there is no such person as David Bowie. You're not going to see him in Louisville, Kentucky, in a coffee shop, you're not going to see him in New York City on the street—someone might, some time, but essentially he doesn't exist. You're not going to have mutual friends, especially as a kid. In the same way, Rock Hudson, he's not a person—never will be, it's not an issue. So I thought, if I want to do this work, I assume it can work the same way—that I can act in a movie and it doesn't relate to anybody else. If they see that person, they don't see that person here. And that's not the way that it works, a lot of the time. But it's something I often have to relearn, and then refigure out where to stand in relation to that step.

A funny thing happened in Prague in 1989. Every Tuesday night they showed a Shirley Temple movie on TV. And usually I watched it, but one night I didn't, and the next day I was walking around and people were looking at me really funny, and I started to get paranoid, thinking my fly was down or I had done something wrong . . . And it turned out that they'd shown the *Jessica McClure* movie instead of a Shirley Temple movie the night before, and everyone was recognizing me in the street.

Did studying acting prepare you for delivering lines in a song?
I know that it did, but it also helped me understand better what some of my teachers were telling me, which I didn't understand at the time. There's so much more to work with when you have the word and rhythm and melody rather than just having the word. A great actor treats the word and has a sense for rhythm and melody, but I had to start making songs to understand that that was part of what makes a great acting performance. I think before that, if any performance of mine ever came off, it was all due to the ability of the writer and the director, 'cause I wasn't giving it the attention it could have been given. I had had so many lessons drilled into me, and all of a sudden they started to make more and more sense, the more I got into making songs.

I need to encounter my main theater instructor, whom I haven't spoken to since 1988 or 1989, partly because she was an intense force that was very intimidating. She was hard-core, and part of me has just [*laughs*] never wanted to see her again. But I was talking with a guy a couple of weeks ago about her, and he was like, "We should take her out to lunch." I realized it would probably be a healthy thing to do, to see her as an adult, 'cause I know I couldn't have done most of the things I've done in my life without her. It would be like somebody reuniting with an abusive parent, or something like that. She pushed those lessons in.

Did you socialize with other theater people?
By the time I was thirteen, I was starting to hang out with Britt [Walford], Brian [McMahan], Dave [Grubbs], and Clark [Johnson],* so that was my social life. I did theater, I did school, then hung out with these other people, a couple of whom I went to school with, but most of them I didn't. I never socialized with people at the theater or the school, except for these two or three people. I was trying to learn acting and all that, and whatever free time I had was devoted to music: listening to music and photographing music and going to my friends' band practices, with

* All four were members of Squirrel Bait, a post-hardcore punk band that existed from 1983 to 1988. Walford and McMahan went on to play in Slint and King Kong, McMahan in the For Carnation, and Grubbs in Bastro (with Johnson, initially, and later Bundy K. Brown and John McEntire) and Gastr Del Sol, plus numerous solo activities.

no interest *at all* in playing in a band or making music. I think I was probably at two out of three Maurice practices, this kind of math-y, metal thing, with Britt and Brian and Dave [Pajo],* just listening, taking pictures. I could only make two out of three practices, 'cause the theater [schedule] was like: get out of school at 2:40, Monday writing class was 4 to 6, Tuesday would be like an acting class from 4 to 6, rehearsal from 6:30 to 8:30, Thursday the same, Friday voice and movement class 4 to 6, and then 6:30 to 8:30 rehearsal, and then Saturday morning improv class, and Saturday afternoon rehearsal, so it was a lot of time.

You were going to see shows too.
I think I saw Samhain around '84, at the Jockey Club. That would have been [the tour for] *Unholy Passion*. It was an amazing night, the first time I stayed up all night. Then the tour with Maurice [opening for Samhain] was for *November-Coming-Fire*. I went along for the trip, taking pictures. *So* exciting. We were all huge Misfits fans. Sean Garrison, the singer for Maurice and then later Kinghorse, had a correspondence with Glenn [Danzig],†

---

* Pajo went on to play alongside Walford and McMahan in Slint and King Kong, and since then has done stints touring and/or recording with Tortoise, Stereolab, Royal Trux, Zwan, the Yeah Yeah Yeahs, and Interpol, as well as his own projects, variously named M / Aerial M / Papa M / PAJO.

† Danzig formed the Misfits, one of the crucial post-Ramones US punk bands, in 1977. The Misfits broke up in 1983 and Danzig launched the more heavy-metal-oriented Samhain, which he retooled and renamed Danzig upon signing to Def American in 1987. Samhain officially reunited for one tour, opening for Danzig, in 1999.

and then I developed a correspondence with Glenn, just fan correspondence, but I'd send him a cow skull or make him a collage out of an encyclopedia set from the school called *Man, Myth and Magic*, in hopes of getting 7"s that were out of print. And he did—he sent me "Cough/Cool." He would never write a letter or anything like that, but a month later I would get a package from Lodi [New Jersey, where Danzig was then based], and it would have amazing shit in it. And I would never know— I would send these gifts and, like, ten bucks, and just wait and see what happened. He would send back, like, an amazing pale-yellow Samhain T-shirt. I've never seen another like it.

Just seeing five or six Samhain shows in a row in small places and eating at Denny's with them . . . I remember specifically Bloomington and Detroit, 'cause Detroit was at the Greystone, which was Corey [Rusk]'s place. I remember being there and after the soundcheck wondering where Glenn was, and some-one says, "He's upstairs with Corey and Tesco Vee," and my mind was blown.* Although I never saw Tesco Vee there that night, that's just what somebody said. In Bloomington there was a party afterwards, and Glenn drank a beer, which appar-ently was very unusual, and he started fooling around with an

---

* Vee was the leader of the Meatmen and launched a seminal fanzine, *Touch and Go*, which begat the equally seminal US indie-rock label of the same name. Rusk was the bassist of the Necros and has run Touch and Go Records from 1981 to the present, initially with Vee and, since 1983, with his wife Lisa, releasing albums by Big Black, the Butthole Surfers, Jesus Lizard, Slint, and Urge Overkill, among many others. Until 2009 T&G also did manufacturing and distribution for Drag City and several other labels.

acoustic guitar on the front porch of the house, singing John Mellencamp's "Small Town" but with comedic lyrics, completely cracking himself up: [*sings*] "I was born with no dick," then laughing, laughing, "and I am a lesbian," and just laughing his head off, which again was so mind-blowing. He liked to goof around some, but that was an extreme. Just seeing him with a guitar was amazing. I remember Pajo remarking on some way that Glenn made a chord, saying, "Wow, I've never seen that chord made that way."

There was a story about going to a Big Black show, after you had ordered a T-shirt from Steve Albini . . .

Actually I had ordered a record—*Lungs*. They played in Newport [Kentucky], at the Jockey Club, to twenty people or something like that, after *Racer X* came out [1984]. Rich Schuler was in art school in Cincinnati, and we all stayed in his apartment.[*]
I loved *Racer X*, but that's all that I had. But yeah, across the room, Steve just lays back on the couch, pulls his fedora down, with all his clothes on, and that was him for the night. In the morning, getting up, he was like, "What did you say your name was?" I said, "Will Oldham," and he says, "I owe you a record." He had a *Lungs* there, which was amazing because even at that point I think they were essentially out of print, even though

---

* Schuler had played drums in an early incarnation of Squirrel Bait, and would also occupy the drum chair in King Kong. He played live with Palace in 1992 and 1995, as well as on the Rian Murphy / Will Oldham EP *All Most Heaven*.

they had some on tour that they were selling, and then he gave me a shirt as a late bonus.

It was mind-blowing to be able to be a fan of Samhain or Big Black or Dinosaur Jr. and then to run into them in the course of either just going to shows or going to see friends play on bills with them, and being able to communicate as a kind of a peer. Even though I wasn't making music, the conversation wasn't like, "Oh, I love your record." It was more like, "Where are you guys sleeping?" "I don't know, where are you guys going to sleep?" I didn't like the music *because* I met those people; I liked the music *and* met those people, and then didn't necessarily like them because of the music—I either liked them or I didn't. And seeing a community grow between Louisville and Chicago, musically, and then between Louisville and New York . . . When Squirrel Bait got on Homestead [Records], that opened up, by proxy, the community to Dinosaur Jr. or Sonic Youth, who did at least one record on Homestead; even Nick Cave and the Bad Seeds had a record or two licensed to Homestead. So it was incredible, really exciting; you felt like you were connected to it in some way. It was just a couple of people removed between me and, like, Mike Watt.* And he was still, you know, an icon.

So how did you reconcile this sort of access to these people with the idea of never running into David Bowie in the street?

---

* Bassist Watt was a founding member of the legendary Californian hardcore band the Minutemen, soldiered on in fIREHOSE and various solo projects, and now is part of the reformed Iggy and the Stooges.

It helped to reinforce the idea of the distance of these other people, and made me begin to wonder about how and why the David Bowies, or whoever, were different. I don't know, that's a good question. You know, I remember meeting Lou Reed, I remember meeting Iggy Pop, I remember meeting or being in close contact with Leonard Cohen—in dreams, during that time—and having interactions with them. I still, for the most part, don't like playing, but I also don't like seeing big shows, and partly it's probably because I've seen too many great small shows and think, "Why would I see a big show?" I think that was the beginning of understanding that you could do both, that you could be some kind of human being and make records that meant something to somebody. And that was very valuable, and very affirming. It was also affirming to not become friends with them; I became friends with Albini later, but then it was just like this minimal, served-a-purpose but great contact, and I didn't wanna hang out or anything like that.

It was an observation period. Which was great. This was something that I loved, and I didn't relate it to anything that I was doing, which was, essentially, professional training to be a part of this world . . . but from another angle. Only later did I find that it was equally important to all the other training I was going through, that it was its own preparation, so much better than any college I could ever have gone to. I was essentially preparing for my work from the age of eight, starting with acting, and then starting to go to shows and band practices when I was twelve. And from then on I was, like, in a guild system, as an apprentice. Which is pretty radical.

An underlying factor is the different economies that are at play with a Big Black tour as opposed to a David Bowie tour. There is so much more money invested in Bowie that more people are glomming onto Bowie to get a piece of the action, and this then creates, in effect, a buffer between David Bowie and the rest of the world. Whereas when Big Black go on tour in 1985, there's virtually no money at all, and no entourage, so someone in that position has nowhere to run or hide.

Yeah. But there's also knowing *Racer X* backwards and forwards when I first see Big Black, and then seeing them in a big club— I don't remember what the capacity was, maybe six hundred, something like that—with twenty other people . . . that was incredible because it felt like an extension of listening at home. It's like, "This is still a private experience, this is still a very powerful, private experience"—much to the chagrin, probably, of Big Black at the time. But *I* didn't realize that, because the show was so good, to me, that it seemed like they were doing exactly what they wanted or planned to do. And maybe they would say that even now.

When you had these major-label records . . . I mean, essentially it was like Hollywood, it was all a fiction. All records were just fictional space. None of it seemed real, anyway: nobody ever came to Louisville, so the idea of a David Bowie show, or a Lou Reed show, or a Leonard Cohen show, or a Jonathan Richman show, whatever, didn't seem like even the remotest of possibilities. And at the same time, when I would hear about the Who playing nearby, it sounded like hell, you know. Going to a place with thousands and thousands of people never has been and never will be my idea of fun.

That was actually my first concert, the Who at an arena in 1982—and we walked out after three songs for that exact reason. We were like, "What are we doing here?"
I think I saw my older brother's band play once or twice, when I was eleven or twelve. I think they were called Some Boody Pudding, and I think it was Sean Mulhall who actually grabbed me and raised me above his head—affectionately and aggressively at the same time—and hauled me into the [mosh] pit, mostly high above the heads of the pogoers.[*] And I went to the Jockey Club, with Britt and Brian [to see Hüsker Dü in 1983], and then Prince was on his *Purple Rain* tour, and I went and saw him in Lexington [Kentucky], a huge arena show, at the very height of his popularity.

And yeah, it was a huge moment in listening to music because it made me feel kind of like I had no business in listening to the music. Listening to old records or records where the distance still seemed obvious made sense to me; but listening to something where that was a part of the experience . . . Being a fan, I thought, "Huh. I don't belong listening to this kind of music." This experience is not good, it's not satisfying at all, being in a stadium where his mouth is moving a fraction of a second before you hear the sound—what's the point, you know? I don't

---

[*] Mulhall was the drummer in the Babylon Dance Band, one of the first—and best—Louisville punk bands, which existed from 1978 to 1983.

get it at all. And from then on, I only liked to listen to music
where I felt like it was OK to listen to the records. You never had
to talk to anybody about going to the shows, you didn't have to
go to these big shows; *or* you could go to the small shows, get up
close and listen, or watch them play the song in a way that was
surprising or new, or feel like they were playing the song with
the people that were onstage and with the audience that was in
the room.

**In a big stadium show, even though there are so many people,
there's actually no sense of community at all.**
None. Sometimes when I go to shows now, or when I play a
show, where I feel like it's a thing to do rather than people
into what's going on, it feels almost the same. I love going to
shows where the room is full of people that know the music.
Especially if *I* don't know the music, it's so much fun. Or if
I've never met anybody else that likes a certain kind of music,
and I love it, then going to a show and being like, "Wow, here
we are, this group of people. We like this music"—and there's
nobody else there besides people who like the music. Then
you leave the show and you can't talk to anybody about it, but
you *know* that for an hour and a half or two hours you were
in a room with a bunch of people that you had something in
common with.

Going to that ethnomusicology conference [Society for Ethnomusicology 54th annual conference, in Mexico City, 2009]
. . . That's something I had never found people I could talk to
about. Since I was a kid, I was getting music out of the library

or going to record stores, and I would go to their world and folk section and look for things, and I never learned how to talk about it. But all of a sudden being in a hotel with two or three hundred other people where it was second nature for them to talk about this stuff was like, wow. It was like being on crack—but I've never been on crack. It was like being on Dexedrine.

Ben Chasny [aka Six Organs of Admittance] was playing a house show [in Louisville], which I went to, and it turned out the house was owned and operated by a guy named Claude Stevens, who worked as a naturalist out at Bernheim Forest, which my dad had a lot to do with. Ben's set was acoustic, by himself, in a room about the same size as this, about eight to ten people sitting on the floor. And it made me so happy. It was such a great set, such a good show; you were in a small room with people who were there to see the show, and it didn't matter how many were paying attention—that was the exciting thing. Because if I can go to a show like that Six Organs show or hear a record like those first two Baby Dee records [*Little Window* (2000) and *Love's Small Song* (2002)] say every three or six months of my life, or be involved with making a record like those, then that's all I need. Everything else that everyone else pushes on you about how records could sell and should sell, how shows should be and could be . . . these were proof that most people, when they tell you how to make a good show, how to make a good tour, how to make a good record, they're just wrong. And you make a good show or a good tour or a good record by paying attention to the content of the show, and where it is *is* content—where the show is *is* part of the content of the show. So you *can't* have a good show at some venues, and you *can't* have a good tour by doing it in certain ways; you have to make up the ways for doing the tour, and you have to make up the ways for recording the record and putting it out.

You were still in your teens when you acted in John Sayles's film *Matewan* (1987). How did you get cast in it?
This guy Gary Leon Hill did a play I was in in 1982 or '83, *Food from Trash*, here at the Humana Festival of New American Plays [an annual festival organized and hosted by Actors Theatre]. That was very exciting. It was one of my first paying jobs. I got paying gigs through Actors Theatre every couple of years throughout my teens. Working at Actors Theatre was really great. Around 1979 or '80 it got a Tony Award for its quality as a repertory theater. It was Louisville's heyday culturally, because the ballet, the symphony, the newspaper, and the theater were all really strong. In that time, people would come from all over the country, all over the world to see the Humana Festival, and that's where a casting agent saw me in *Food from Trash,* and that's what got John Sayles and his folks interested in giving me a call [for *Matewan*]. I also remember meeting Sigourney Weaver, 'cause she was attending [the festival], and seeing Mary McDonnell, who was later in *Matewan,* as well as *Battlestar Galactica* and *Dances with Wolves,* and Chris Cooper, who's in all sorts of shit now. I saw him there when I was a kid, in *Grapes of Wrath,* and loved him and remembered him for years, and then he was in *Matewan,* of course. I remember

seeing Holly Hunter in a play by a guy named Murphy Guyer called *Eden Court* and just being head over heels in love with her; she was my size, or shorter, and gave me the time of day as well 'cause I was a fellow actor in this festival, which was amazing, and she was so *good*.

They called me: "We're putting this movie together. This woman saw you—would you be interested in auditioning?" They sent me the screenplay, and I didn't read it; I put it on the kitchen counter, in the corner, and it sat there I don't know how long . . . a year and a half. Then they called again: "Remember we called you a long, long time ago? Well, we lost the money at that point"—and then they made *Brother from Another Planet*—"but we're gonna make it now. Would you be interested in auditioning?" That was probably spring or early summer of 1986. We had kind of planned a family mini-vacation to New York City, 'cause Ned was gonna go to some overseas farming program with Willie MacLean [later of Anomoanon and King Kong] in Greece, and we were gonna go up and see him off, so I said, "We're gonna be up there in New York in two weeks," and they said, "OK, that's fine." It turned out our hotel was a block and a half from where the audition was going to be held. I auditioned and got cast in it, and totaled my car and broke my foot right before we were supposed to shoot. I had a broken foot for at least the first month of the shoot, which they had to kind of shoot around, because I was limping and on crutches.

Legally they had to hire a tutor/guardian, who was an amazing guy named Michael Preston, who also had a small part in the movie and later became a Flying Karamazov Brother. One of the costume people was Susan Lyall, who was in Band of Susans, and the assistant property master was [filmmaker] Jem Cohen—that was fun, 'cause he was the only person I could talk about music with. So there were interesting little threads into the future in, at that point, unpredictable ways. Also the two bad guys: Kevin Tighe, who had been in [1970s TV series] *Emergency!*, that was very exciting for me, and then there was Gordon Clapp, who later was on *NYPD Blue* for a long time. He, his wife, and their two-year-old son were sort of my best friends when I lived out in Los Angeles, which was really nice. It was great seeing Kevin on *Lost*: he has a recurring part as one of the main characters' father, in flashbacks. He looks great and his acting is amazing. To me—in my memory, 'cause I haven't seen *Matewan* in twenty years—he looks exactly the same and is as vital and vibrant.

And then of course James Earl Jones being around was really cool. Watching him do his scenes and then watching dailies . . . He wasn't much of a social person, but watching him act was incredible.

Everybody who was present seemed integral, *everybody*. I felt that I got as much talking to Susan Lyall, assistant costumes, Jem Cohen in props, the first assistant director, my teacher/guardian, the preacher extra, Gordon Clapp—and it seemed there were half women, half men working on that thing.

Were you aware of who [*Matewan*'s cinematographer] Haskell Wexler was?

No, I wasn't. I may have seen *Who's Afraid of Virginia Woolf?*, and that's it. After the movie I think I found a copy of *Medium Cool*, which for some reason a local video store had.*

Matewan looks great. Wexler did a fantastic job. There are other aspects of *Matewan* that make it seem low-budget, which it was, but it's so beautifully photographed that you really don't think of it as a low-budget film.
Yeah, exactly. I think it's the cinematography, in combination with incredible locations, great production design, and great costumes. He's obviously a great cinematographer, but they gave him colors that looked amazing as well, and it's a beautiful part of the country. And he was a cool person; it was a joy to watch him work. Two or three years later, when I worked on this *Thousand Pieces of Gold* movie in Montana, the producer had been a line producer on *Matewan*, so she brought in a lot of the crew. Chris Cooper was also in *A Thousand Pieces of Gold*, so I was familiar with these people, and that was nice.

When I was shooting *Matewan*, Britt and Dave Pajo were talking to me about forming a band together, which ended up being Slint. Britt came and visited the set once. They were like, "You can play guitar and sing," and they sent me some demos. I listened to it and listened to it, and I was thinking, "I'm not a musician, I don't know what to do with any of this stuff." After three months

---

* A widely respected cinematographer, Wexler wrote, directed, and shot 1969's *Medium Cool*, which was largely filmed during the 1968 Democratic Convention.

they wrote to me, "We're gonna get Brian," and that was that. There was still the idea, maybe, that I would sing when they had their first show, before they were called Slint. I think they were called Beads: Tiny Matted Tufts of Hair—that might have been Britt, Ethan [Buckler], and Pajo. It was at a Unitarian church that Ethan's parents went to, during a Sunday service, and I sat on stage holding the kick drum in place, with the idea that one day my role would be greater, but it ended up not becoming that.

You started at Brown University in Providence, Rhode Island, in autumn 1988, but dropped out soon after—to continue acting? I was there for a semester, gone for a year, there for a semester, gone for a year, then did three semesters in a row. School was really pointless in a lot of ways, but maybe it functioned in the way it's supposed to, because I did meet people. But I thought you were supposed to get an education, you know.

[Freshman year] I came back here for Christmas break, and ran into this guy at Zena's [bar in Louisville], Steve Rankin, who had been in Actors Theatre for a long time and was out in LA doing some acting and some fight coordinating. He was like, "You should go to LA!" The next night, at dinner, I told my folks, "I think I'm gonna go to LA." I went there and there was some agency that immediately wanted to represent me, but then I ran into another actor from Louisville, Ken Jenkins, and he recommended his agent, so I signed with them. It felt very homey 'cause I went to high school with his kids, and I always admired him as an actor when I was a kid, so I felt really great to be there.

I was in LA for six months. I basically got two jobs: the first one was [TV movie] *Everybody's Baby: The Rescue of Jessica McClure*, and the second was *A Thousand Pieces of Gold*. I auditioned for *The Rescue of Jessica McClure* on a Friday, and I think we started shooting on a Monday, which I guess means somebody else fell through. It was shot in Bellflower, in southern LA. That was right after [Madonna's] *Like a Prayer* came out, so I had forty-five minutes to listen to *Like a Prayer* one way and Randy Travis's *Old 8 x 10* in the other direction.

I took *A Thousand Pieces of Gold* even though I had a callback for [TV sitcom] *Doogie Howser, M.D.*, and my agent was really angry, like, "You don't understand," and I was like, "No, I think *A Thousand Pieces of Gold* sounds a lot better." I went to Montana in the spring to shoot that, and that was when I was reacquainted with Chris Cooper and Mary Cybulski, who's a script supervisor, and met her son for the first time, Ray Tintori, who has now made some videos for MGMT, done some really weird animation work. *A Thousand Pieces of Gold* was a very valuable experience in many ways, the least of which was the acting part: meeting and interacting with everybody, being where we were, working with everybody even though my part wasn't very interesting or exciting. It made me think that acting was not where I could work, because this experience of making *A Thousand Pieces of Gold* was not normal; this was something that was rare and even looked down upon. [I] didn't want to be in that system, and now making records it's still a constant battle, swimming upstream. Maybe I just learned, eventually, that that's what a person has to do, but at that time I thought there's probably a life that's more natural, that I am suited for, and it's *not* this acting thing, obviously, because I've learned what the acting life is. There were a few hard lessons over the next couple of years, and the work that I put into music I could have directed towards acting. I just didn't realize a lot of it requires rewriting rules on a daily basis.

When it was time to renew the contract with the acting agency, I went to the office and told them, "I don't want to renew the contract. I don't want to do this work. This is not good work." That was a pretty wild day, 'cause it was ending something that I'd worked towards since I was nine years old. It definitely was a decision at the time that this isn't going to be my work; I don't know what *is* going to be my work, but shit, you know, this really isn't gonna be my work. There's lots of things that I didn't enjoy about acting in my teens, and I just thought it was because I was in my teens and that the next thing was going to be so much more interesting, and it was just worse, so much worse.

I think what directly led to it was, all the training, preparation, and performance throughout middle and high school, I always felt like it was in preparation for something that I had in mind that was related to things I got out of certain plays and movies, and that I think I'd experienced a little bit every once in a while—specifically that first time I did an improvisation performance with the older folks when I was ten—and sort of imagining that this future lay ahead. And then I went to Los Angeles, got the agent, went on numerous casting calls and numerous auditions, had numerous discussions with agents, did *Everybody's Baby* and saw how people that I admired—Ken

Jenkins and Gordon Clapp specifically, as actors that I knew
and/or worked with—saw how they were living and what the
issues at hand were, and what life in Los Angeles was like, and
what politics and processes most people were engaged in on a
day to day basis . . . and just thought, "I don't recognize what is
cool, I don't recognize what I was hoping for." It started to seem
like, "Wait, this actually has no relationship whatsoever to what
I thought I was preparing for. Uh oh."

2

LA VIE DANSANTE

ALAN LICHT: At one point you talked about wanting to have a cassette-recorder alarm clock to write down your dreams. Do dreams play a role in your work?

WILL OLDHAM: Making a record or touring feels like you are in a dream space, and you're interacting with other people who are also in a dream space. It really is like a dream where the rules don't really apply. It's a sense of logic you don't normally allow yourself to see; it's a totally different direction. You don't have a lot of opportunities to encounter it; you've gotta put yourself in the way of it. I feel like music is halfway between waking and dreaming. It's like, "Wait a second. At night I go to bed and I dream, and then I wake up. What's the difference between these two things? Why can't I just have one of these two existences?"

For me dreaming is a fully sensory reality and environment with events and interactions that to the protagonist feel as fully dimensional, or more, and surprising as anything that occurs during waking hours. The difference is that there's no real possibility of that reality being a shared one, although it's always interesting when people share a dream that you were present in. It's very polite, I believe, for someone to tell you of a dream experience they had with you, because it's going to affect their communication with you. So I feel like whenever possible, if you remember a dream that someone was in and if it's someone that you communicate with and care about, that it's important to share that experience with them, so that they know where you're coming from next time they see you [*laughs*].

I have never met anybody who shares this opinion with me, but even when I have a nightmare, I *love* it. Partly because I know when I wake up that it's, in many ways, hermetically sealed, and I can start to get perspective on it immediately. It's like going into a movie theater and having the opportunity to enter a completely different reality and see how prepared you are, in terms of your value system and your emotional strength, to deal with these surprise situations. On some level dreams are like training sessions, and I think that that's one of their functions—to put you through things to prepare you for reality's version of those situations. And if you have a recurring dream, perhaps it's because your subconscious is saying, "Go back to square one. You haven't built the stamina, you don't have the reaction time, you're not addressing the situation properly, you need to go through it again, and I'm not gonna stop giving you this dream until you've proven you can do it!"

It seems to parallel the reality of a song, in that there's no tangible evidence that any of the events or the relationships or emotions that are relayed through the course of the song exist *besides the song*. And yet it is fully real, especially for a singer who in the course of writing, recording, and performing it enters the song *countless* times. If there's any responsibility of conviction to the lyric, then those countless times can turn out to be pretty significant, and at times troublingly close to, or beyond, accepted reality.

In sleep you're protected by the fact that you're asleep and, for the most part, alone, no matter how close somebody else might be to you physically. For the most part you're asleep and alone, and it's all . . . up to you. And once a song has begun, it's kind of the same situation. You're there, and nothing is gonna stop the song from moving forward; nothing is gonna stop the narrative, if it's a narrative, or the emotional flow, if it's just an emotional flow, from going from one part to another part to another part to another part. A lot of it is predictable, because it's a song, 'cause it's written, but then a lot of it is unpredictable, either because there's a group of people that you're working with or a group of people in front of you who are affecting the energy and the emotion of the dynamic, or things have happened to change your feelings about the words and melodies that are coming out of your mouth. It's always unpredictable enough to keep it *alive*, but for that time you're navigating an alternate reality. It can be fantastic, in singing-time or in dreamtime, to be able to be alone or responsible for yourself and yet not have that be a barren environment or uneventful world to occupy for a time.

A lot of times the focal point of a dream is something that was in the background of your waking life; something that played a very minor role in your day somehow takes center stage in your sleep that night. And that can also happen in a song: someone can write about or name a song after something that might otherwise be inconsequential or commonplace, or use an everyday word or phrase that then takes on a new significance. Yeah, everything can have, at the most pedantic level, a symbolic equivalent, but one thing that also thrills me is we have an

understanding that the true equivalence is beyond our compre-
hension, now and for the foreseeable future. What a name is,
what a person is, what a gender is, what an action is, what a time
of day is—in poetic or lyrical or dream language they are *not*
what they are. We can start *there*, and we'll never know the end
of that sentence [*laughs*]. What are they, what is something in a
dream, what is something in a song? You can *try* to say, but . . .
For me, I think I'm wrong more often than not, if I try. I don't
know if I yield too frequently and too fully to the lack of responsibility that comes with claiming ignorance, but I do it a lot.

Have you had any interesting dreams lately?
I dreamt I was walking through an airport with Bruce Springsteen, and he said, "I've been riding a winning horse." I thought
that was kind of stupid, so I said, "I've been riding a winning
pig." Then he said, "Yeah, we're doing a show in Louisville, you
should come." I went, and he was like, "Would you sing 'Freebird' with us tonight?" Then I went to an abandoned hotel
downtown—the old Galt House, a haunted hotel—with him to
make a record. I was trying to get him to play like Guns N' Roses,
or something like that. He did a solo, and I told him, "Come *on*,
I know you can play this *stuff*," and he'd just be like, "Ah, I don't
know what you're talking about." He'd play something and I'd
be like, "All right. That was good." Then he said, "I think I know
what you mean now. Can we do it again?" And he did it again,
and laid down an awesome solo. I wanted to call a phone-sex
thing and record that, but then I couldn't figure out how to get
a quality telephone recording, so I just made monkey noises, if

I remember right [*laughs*]. Then I mixed it and put a live audience from a Sabah Fakhri show, who's a Syrian-born, classical Arabic singer, on it [*laughs*].

I had another dream where I was playing in the band for a guy named Black Elvis, who was a black Elvis impersonator—played in my underwear, with fake blood running out of it. We were on tour and had rented this crazy vehicle like an airport-rental-car shuttle bus. During a soundcheck, the sound man made an announcement asking Phil McKravis to come to the office. After the soundcheck was done, I went outside and it suddenly wasn't the club, it was a house, and Leonard Cohen was out front trimming the hedges. I went around back and Black Elvis was curled in a fetal position on a trampoline, and I was approaching him to console him and ended up stepping on a hornets' nest, and hornets attacked me. Then I woke up.

When you started playing open mics in Louisville with your brother Ned and various friends, under the name Palace Flophouse, was that when you made a decision to make music your work?

I realized I wasn't going to act. The music was a nice outlet, but it was kind of new; I didn't know what it *was*, it was something that was good to do. In general I just thought, "OK, it's time to give up on any thoughts or dreams and just do things one day at a time. I'm gonna go back to school 'cause it doesn't matter what you do with your life, so why not just go back to school? Nobody is telling me to do anything else. Everybody just says, 'That's what you do, you go to school.' " So

I thought, "Fine, I can go. I can take classes, it doesn't matter. I'll just do this and I guess one day I'll have to get a job, and that's what it's gonna be." I went through a whole school year, and the next summer moved in with Todd [Brashear] and Grant Barger in Indiana, where they were in an audio program [at Indiana University].* We'd been Palace Flophouse, and we decided to make songs and sing them as the Palace Brothers, 'cause we'd be trying to do close harmonies, like the Everly Brothers and the Louvin Brothers, that's what we were thinking. We did "For the Mekons et al." and "Drinking Woman" and this other song, "Two More Days," at the house on Grant's eight-track cassette, and then we did "Ohio River Boat Song" and the version of "Riding" that's on *Lost Blues* in the university studio.

I sent those to a couple of labels. I sent them to Drag City because Bob Nastanovich [of Pavement] moved here. I met Tanya Small through Nastanovich, and she said, "I want to give you a record I played on"—the Silver Jews' 7" *Dime Map of the Reef*. And that was the first Drag City thing I ever heard. I thought it was beautiful. I loved the music, I loved the way it looked, I loved the Drag City logo, I loved everything about it. Only later, in talking to Dan [Koretzky, Drag City label head], did we talk about where Drag City came from and how it started. But I'm sure we connected because we had a connection to a recent history . . .

* Brashear was the post–Ethan Buckler bassist in Slint, and currently runs Wild and Woolly Video in Louisville.

Like knowing what SST Records[*] was . . .

Yeah, exactly. Homestead, Touch and Go, SST. And we still talk about it a bit—we were talking about Blast First stuff a couple of days ago. Drag City had said they'd put out the 7" of "Ohio River Boat Song." Originally the first 7" was going to be "For the Mekons" and "Drinking Woman," and then Drag City heard the "Ohio River Boat Song" and asked if they could do that, in a classic record-label move.[†] The letters on the front [cover of the 7"] are all made out of a photograph that I took of Susie Honeyman's face, who was the violin player of the Mekons.

Then I went to one last semester of school, and I ended up taking—not for credit, but just because I was so desperate to find something to do there—ballroom dancing, waltz and cha-cha, and scuba diving, which were offered by the school, although I had to pay an additional $300 for each of these classes. I also took a country-and-bluegrass appreciation class. That was with Jeff Titon, who told us, "I just like to listen to country music, and I'm in the music department, so I'm teaching this class." It was very basic. I remember that was the first time I heard Don Williams, which was exciting, but otherwise it was mostly music that I knew.

At some point they [Drag City] asked me, "So when's the full-

---

[*] SST was started and run by the LA hardcore band Black Flag in 1978, and released seminal records by Hüsker Dü, the Minutemen, Dinosaur Jr., and the Meat Puppets, among others, throughout the 1980s.

[†] "For the Mekons et al." was ultimately released on the *Hey Drag City* compilation album in 1994.

length coming?" And I was like, "What?!" But I had been writing songs in the summertime, so I went to Jeff Titon and said, "Would you consider sponsoring an independent study class, 'cause I'm working on these songs, and most of them have some sort of trackable history to certain kinds of music, or certain songs, and I can meet with you every week and talk about these songs as I'm working on them?" And he said yes. All the songs were drawn from different kinds of old Scottish and Irish ballads, as well as some R&B, some gospel, and some blues things that I could sort of draw specific lines to. Later I found out that he's a leading ethnomusicologist; he has an article in the most recent edition of the *Journal of Ethnomusicology*.

I was living way, way off campus. I had all the songs that would be on *There Is No One What Will Take Care of You* pinned up to the wall and would just walk around the room every day working on the songs. I came back [to Louisville] for Christmas to record it. We recorded half of it on the first floor at Steve Driesler's house, which was a big double shotgun, and half of it in a house called Merciful that my folks co-owned with two other couples in the woods, about an hour and a half away from here, in Meade County, Kentucky, on a piece of land called Big Bend because it's where the Ohio River essentially does a full U-turn, with all of us sleeping on the floor. And to some extent I think the vocal qualities were affected by the wood-burning stove that we used to heat the room and the smoke. It made the air a little harsh. Eventually we went to Todd's house and mixed it in his bedroom. I remember [Silver Jews'] David Berman coming through town while we were making *There Is No*

One What Will Take Care of You, and coming by one day while we were recording at Driesler's house.

With the fleur-de-lis drawing on the "thank you" page of *There Is No One . . .*, was it consciously a Louisville record?[*]

I got this [fleur-de-lis] tattoo [on my forearm] when I was nineteen, knowing that I was going to be on the wander, and I didn't know if and when I would be back in Louisville, but I thought if I had a little home on my wrist . . . Jeff Mueller drew that fleur-de-lis on the "thank you" page. There remained, for a while, a strong feeling that we had something good going on in Louisville: a very strong and ever-fluctuating group of musicians, and a very supportive and very communicative community of people who didn't hesitate to educate and challenge each other, and then supported whatever fucked-up little direction people seemed to want to go in.

What was your sense of Louisville growing up? Were you aware of different celebrities having grown up there?

Just Muhammad Ali and a guy named Roger Davis, who was in some westerns or a western TV show. And Colonel Sanders. I think that was the extent of what I knew. I didn't feel like anybody else in the country or the world really knew anything about Louisville, Kentucky. It felt *great*; and it also felt like our own thing. It was cool going to other places, but they didn't give

[*] Fleur-de-lis is the Louisville city symbol, and also appears on the back cover of "Ohio River Boat Song."

a shit about us, and it didn't matter because it was an exciting place to be. I've learned as I've read comments on work that I've done or when I go to other parts of the country what people think of this part of the country, or parts further south more specifically, and I can't really relate to it. It seems as if they're saying, "Oh, you [can] write . . ." [*laughs*].

Even though you were an adult when it was made, listening to *There Is No One . . .* again now one gets the feeling of a child-hood picture, more so than with a lot of other debut albums I can think of.

The thing that was running through my head—that day I didn't renew the agency contract and for a good while afterwards—was that my life, effectively, had ended. This is what I had imagined death would be like, but now I don't know what to do—I'm still alive. So then it was like a new life starting from that point. I was nineteen or twenty. Then in making that record, again, I never had thought about making records, and it was very thrilling because I had all these tools that I'd accumulated over the years from listening to records, going to shows, going to band practices, watching people put records out, and doing all the theater productions, voice training, and line-reading rehears-als. So it made sense, like this is something I have an idea of how to do, but with no real teacher or anything at that point. So naive in so many ways, but so excited at the same time.

Where did all the switching instruments on the album come from?

It might have come from people just saying things, but I think one inspiration was probably the Bad Seeds records from the first one up until *Henry's Dream*; how even though the same musicians would be on each record, they wouldn't necessarily be playing the same instruments from one record to another, and just being excited with the idea of that, that you can just turn the music around by moving people around. Todd and I were talking about the record a whole lot, and Todd, then as now, is a very, very strong Rolling Stones fan. We talked about the Rolling Stones a lot, and were even gonna cover "Hand of Fate" for that record, and practiced it a few times, but didn't end up covering it. It's so great that they have credits on *Let It Bleed* and *Exile on Main St.* and *Black and Blue* that show who's playing what. It's like, this is a Rolling Stones song, *but* these two Rolling Stones weren't even there, didn't play on it, or Mick Jagger plays bass or whatever, you know? If you're gonna make a record where you attack each song with equal importance and equal energy, then each song takes a new approach, by definition. And then, as well, thinking about the musicians specifically that were there, and hearing stories from them about recording [Slint's] *Spiderland*. I think Britt [Walford] plays guitar on that record, and I tried to arrange "Long Before" like "Don, Aman," with Britt playing electric guitar. I sort of tried to match it up, except [Dave] Pajo was out of the country, so he wasn't part of this recording—he was studying in Norwich, England, at the time. And knowing that they each had a unique style of playing, Todd plays drums on that record, Brian [McMahan] plays drums, and Britt plays drums.

"(I Was Drunk at the) Pulpit" is a one-chord song.

In many of the records, and especially that one, there was just such a desperation about getting things performed and recorded that "(I Was Drunk at the) Pulpit" is an example of a song . . . I needed it to exist, I needed it to be recorded, so it's as simplified as possible, because if it got into complexities with a narrative that long I don't think we ever would have gotten out of there.

That's why you kept it to one chord?

I think so, yeah. It would have been long regardless, but if there were more chords then we would have had to attend to those chords, attend to the changes, make the changes beautiful, and make them functional. By having no changes it limited our responsibilities. Tying it to that one chord also allows for a lot of play in a live setting.

You've said that "King Me" was an attempt to write a Solomon Burke kind of song.

Yeah [*sighs*], rest in peace.* I think Todd gave me a Solomon Burke record when we were living in Bloomington together in the summer of '92. Either he gave me one or I found one at a thrift store, and I hadn't heard of him before. I think he was depicted in a painting on the front cover and maybe the exact same painting on the back. The record just looked so outlandish; I think that's why I would listen to it. But then when I listened to it, it reminded me of some of the deeper and more emotional songs that we heard at the 26th Street Tavern in Louisville, where we'd go and

---

* Burke died in October 2010.

see blues and R&B music, and seeing the musicians and seeing the audience have this relationship to this deep soul R&B music. The songs that cross over to a white audience aren't as deep and wild and powerful as most of the songs that haven't crossed over, and that Solomon Burke record was one of the first records that I owned that felt like it was a record of that kind of music. Basically, music that black people listened to that white people didn't listen to, that wasn't supermodern—because it wasn't hip-hop or it wasn't played on the radio, for example—but it wasn't out of date, because I had seen it played live a year before. I saw people out on a Saturday night between the ages of twenty-five and fifty-five having an intense relationship to this music.

Was that where "baby" came from, in the chorus? You rarely sing "baby," except also in "Without Work You Have Nothing" [from *Beware*].
Uh huh [*laughs*]. Maybe. I think it was just trying to make it into a love song. Maybe Solomon Burke's record was giving license to a more unabashed romanticism, and that's why it felt OK to say "baby." But it's nice, it's a great position to be in, to be in a relationship with a woman and be able to call her "baby" without her getting angry about it. It's a term of esteem and affection.

There's a monologue in "King Me" and in "Riding," and in "Happy Child"* there's a spoken intro.

* "Happy Child" is a track on the Tweaker album *The Attraction to All Things Uncertain* (2001), with lyrics written and sung by Will Oldham. Tweaker was a solo project of Nine Inch Nails drummer Chris Vrenna.

Oh yeah, yeah. I think the monologue in "King Me" is probably directly attributable to the Solomon Burke record, 'cause on that record he definitely talked a lot. In that version of "Riding" that has the spoken part [on *Lost Blues*], there was a sea shanty at the beginning of the song and then it goes into the body of the song, and to *me* there was a connection, but I didn't necessarily want to write the song to be the connection and I didn't want to leave the connection out, so I figured I'd just try to make a little spoken interlude to make the connection between the sea shanty at the beginning, the introduction of the character in the shanty, and then on to the body of the song. The form of the Tweaker song was defined by the instrumental track that Chris Vrenna sent, and that included this metallic, percussive, industrial intro with no melodic base to it. I wanted to take advantage of every second of the track, so that's why I used that semispoken part.

When the album came out and it became known that you had played the role of a boy preacher, Danny, in *Matewan*, did you feel that people were then dragging your character in the film into the voice they heard on that record?
I think they must have, yeah. In what people were writing about that record there were so many references to Appalachia, and it was very confusing, so it must be *that* [*laughs*]. From anybody's point of view that was working on the record, it was all rock and blues, gospel [*laughs*].

The press used to bring up religion, maybe because of titles like "Idle Hands Are the Devil's Playthings," "(I Was Drunk at

**the) Pulpit," and "O Lord Are You in Need?" but maybe as a
result of the *Matewan* role too.**

There's one song on the first record where religion is addressed
as such, but even that was sort of a beginning of learning to
avoid religion when dealing with . . . well, to misreference Danzig, to say that which should not be named.

From the music I heard while growing up it would be hard,
I think, for a lot of people to avoid religious themes in music
wherever you are. I don't know if they had a stronger effect, or
if it was just our household that experienced it. It just seems that
religion happens everywhere, but at some point there's a recognition that it's going on without incorporating anything from
your individual person. That's when it becomes as important as
anything concrete or abstract that just surrounds you. It's part
of the scenery, but at the same time, when you're in the kitchen
you don't need everything, but you do need some of it.

Our brains are so powerful and so is language, but language
is like the bricks, and religion and philosophy end up becoming
like the mortar that holds those bricks together. There are so
many gaps in the logic of this language and how it can explain
our plight, our existence, our successes, and that's where religion
seems to fit in. Language is too incomplete and religion fills in.
Why do I feel bad when this happens? Well, religion comes in
and says you don't have to think about it. You can go to work the
next day or do whatever, you don't have to think about it. It fills
in the cracks of what we can't speak about, what we can't say.

What is normally called religion is what I would tend to
call music—participating in music, listening to music, making

records, and singing. I think records and music are more appropriate and more respectful of the human soul than the churches
are. And more respectful of the needs of humans to communicate with the aspects of themselves that are neglected by language. I don't think people think about God so much as they
think about themselves and how they're going to get through life.

The comments [about *There Is No One*] I thought were the
coolest were from those people who said they weren't sure
whether or not they should laugh. I remember listening to that
first album and smiling and laughing a lot just because of the
way we were able to fit together things that didn't necessarily
belong together.

Which is something that happens on a lot of your records.
Yeah, there's a lot of stuff that's supposed to be, in a good way,
funny throughout the records. I've always tried to make the
records as funny as possible. "You Don't Love Me" [on *Beware*],
that is kind of a comedy song. There are very few songs that are,
from beginning to end, intentional comedy.

Some folks that get into music really wish that they were
getting into the comedy racket, and that is certainly the case
with me. I've had comedians tell me that all comedians wish
they were musicians. I'm not sure if it's true or not. I think
something that singles me out from a lot of people involved
with music is that I would prefer to be a Marx Brother rather
than Mick Jagger if I had my choice. I know that on some level,
when you're experiencing say the Marx Brothers or Abbott and
Costello or the Little Rascals, or the stand-up comedy of Steve

Martin or Richard Pryor, the impression is they're living on the correct plane of existence. Living moment to moment, and very quick with their brains, quick with their voices, or in the case of Harpo Marx, quick with their actions. And also using that speed of thought to turn dark situations into light situations. So they're the ultrawizards of society, because they can conquer the most complex and devastating of issues and turn them into something that's nothing but laughter, really just release the power of those things.

We were together somewhere once and a Bugs Bunny cartoon came on, and you said it had always been a big influence.
Just the comic timing that Bugs Bunny had, and Porky Pig and Foghorn Leghorn. They had such great timing and this confident way of not letting anything get to them. The default was absurdity, in a Marx Brothers way. When things get tough, the tough go crazy, you know, the tough become absurd, and nothing is tough anymore. Oftentimes, when things get to where I wouldn't know what else to say, rather than feel at a loss it's more exciting to look for what would Groucho say at this moment, or what would Chico say or what would Speedy Gonzales say. They were good role models, in that way, although it might be better sometimes to actually find the right words.

Have you ever tried doing comedy?
I did comedy with Zach Galifianakis at Largo, in LA. I went one night and sang a couple of punch lines; there was an extended moment where he was sitting at the piano and I was sitting

next to him, and it was my job to try and disarm him and make him laugh during his own routine. Dan [Koretzky] and Rian [Murphy, also of Drag City] promoted a full season of comedy nights at a small venue in Chicago, bringing comedians from Chicago and all over the country. So Dan asked if I would do stand-up, and I ended up doing a night with Galifianakis and two or three local comedians, but as I got closer I began to realize, "I can't do ten or fifteen minutes' worth of material." So I worked it out that I would be the emcee of the night and did it like a classic late-night talk-show host, where I did a couple of routines, but primarily my job was to introduce people, with a comic flair. I treated it like a course in heckling and made big cue cards for hecklers, giving them ideas that they could use to heckle the comedians with that night. And then when I would introduce the comedians, I asked them to give me a joke from their routine, and then I would introduce them by saying "This is an example of the kind of humor that they are going to be showing you tonight," and I would read their joke [*laughs*].

I like heckling, and it's unfortunate, because of a growing reputation or being recognized, I can't really heckle anymore because people just think I'm being a cocksucker because I can be. Whether it's good-natured heckling or totally destructive heckling or totally positive heckling, I think that it's good.

When did Palace Brothers start playing live?
We'd finished the record, mixed it, turned it in, mastered it, done the artwork, all that. There was somehow an offer: Big Star were reuniting; it was the first Big Star show, in Colum-

bia, Missouri. They offered us something *crazy*, $5,000 or some-
thing like that. And it was just, like, "Do you guys want to put
a set together and go play this thing? If we have a seven-piece
band, we can still make six, seven hundred dollars apiece." I
can't remember if Paul [Greenlaw] came or not, but otherwise
I think it was everybody who was on that record—Todd, Britt,
Brian, Grant, and me. We only did two shows like that.* We also
did a cover of [Leonard Cohen's] "The Butcher" during that
time, which I remember as being really fun. We played at one
in the afternoon, Big Star probably played around 6 p.m. Dan
came to the show, and when we got offstage, he said, "I'll put
your records out as long as you want to make records" [*smiles*].
That was amazing.

**The next release after the album was the "Come In" / "Trudy
Dies" single.**
With [Royal Trux's] Neil [Hagerty] and Jennifer [Herrema]
producing as "Adam and Eve." That was the first time [for me]
there was a collaboration with anybody else on Drag City; that
was also the first time I met and played with Liam Hayes, who
plays Mellotron on those songs and then started putting out
records on Drag City [as Plush].

I happened to hear about Royal Trux about six months
before I heard about Drag City. I remember before I met or
saw them being in Chicago, and maybe even staying at [David]
Grubbs's apartment, and he was playing some music on a cas-

---

* The other show was a Kentucky Derby house party soon after.

sette player. "I've got to listen to this. It's this band Royal Trux
and I'm supposed to play keyboards with them at Lounge Ax."
"Bad Blood" was the song, and I asked him, "Wow, what's up
with Royal Trux?" and he was like, "I think they want to be the
Black Crowes" [*laughs*].

**He's a few years ahead of the game there: that wasn't until
Thank You [*laughs*].**
[*laughs*] Yeah, yeah. But he's often been ahead of the game.
After the "Ohio River Boat Song" single was turned in, but
maybe before it came out, I was living in Providence, and Royal
Trux came through town, with [Rian] Murphy playing drums,
and stayed at our house, and it was very exciting. Meeting Neil
and Jennifer, and realizing that there's a lot of people in music
who are into the whole scene, or something like that, as much
or more than they're into what they're doing, and Neil and Jennifer weren't, you know . . . they were into what they were doing,
and that's it. And that was something that I understood from
meeting them. It made it so much more interesting, and inspiring, to be making music when I was getting daily, or at least
weekly, reports on what Neil and Jennifer were up to, and how
they were approaching things, especially through the eyes of
Koretzky. 'Cause he was such a fan of theirs; he was completely
psyched about every decision that they were making, and so I
would get to hear all of them, and it was *so* exciting.

**You've said that your records, for a while, were almost an
answer to Royal Trux's.**

The 7"s, mostly—they set the bar, yeah. A year later, we did the "West Palm Beach" / "Gulf Shores" single with Kramer, and that's because Neil and Jennifer did "Back to School" and "Cleveland" with Kramer. Absolutely. And just the thrill of each Royal Trux 7" that came out or recording session that I would hear was so exciting. It was just like, "You can *do* that, you can make each thing sort of different."

I think we were supposed to do a tour, opening for Royal Trux, that was supposed to culminate in that show [Drag City Invitational in Chicago, 1993], *maybe*, and I had to cancel it. I was starting to realize that this was a new thing, and I didn't understand, nor necessarily desire, any part of it. And it was difficult. That's one thing I didn't understand about the artist thing: what does it matter, you know? I just want to make this music and be able to listen to it and have other people listen to it. How can I reconcile my experience of listening to music with the process of making music? Why play shows when I just want to listen to the records, you know, and have people listen to the records? Why would they want to see a show? You can't drive a car when you're seeing a show, you can't make love to your partner while you're seeing a show, or cook breakfast or go to sleep; you have to stand in a club. Why would you do that? That's not listening. And Drag City, Domino [Records, Oldham's label in the UK], they're always talking about shows and promotion and all this stuff.

You're bound to the music and you're bound to the stage for a period of time, so you have to find your joy in that time, which is a really unpleasant time. I don't like being on stage in front of people, but knowing that that's a restriction, well, I'm one who says, "This is your lot—deal with it." So now you're onstage, there's a bunch of people standing there, or three people or however many people standing there, and the only way to make it into a great thing is to disappear into the song as much as possible.

On Drag City's roster at this time there were several artists who were very reluctant to tour and to give interviews. I'm thinking of Bill Callahan [Smog], in particular, as someone who was resistant to touring and didn't really take to the interview process in a way that seemed to satisfy either journalists or maybe himself either; Jim O'Rourke would never really do a tour after a record of his own; and Silver Jews would never play live at all, up until recently. I think this was all a bit frustrating for Dan Koretzky.

Especially touring, which he was always riding me about. It was something that I really didn't want to do. At the same time, he would always ride me half in jest and half seriously, I could tell, and I figured, mostly out of respect for him and our relationship, I would try to do it, sometimes. And then doing interviews or press: it's probably because it just feels so wrong most of the time; it's just a waste of time, because it doesn't have anything to do with anything, and it demands a lot of time *and* a lot of thought, and the thought has nothing to do with anything, unless you want to get better at giving interviews, and I *don't* want to get better.

It's just interesting that up to a certain point bands on the label shared not just certain musical sensibilities but an aversion

**to promotion; that most of the people Drag City gravitated
towards then were hesitant about even an indie-rock version
of standard record-industry publicity.**

Yeah—and then, beautifully, there was Neil and Jennifer, who
had their own way of dealing with those things. They understood something about promotion and publicity, but they
seemed to be the aggressors and sort of do things the way they
wanted to do them. It helped to show how it could be a positive
process, at least just the idea of doing posters or publicity photographs, or things like that. It was like, "Oh, these can be all
about construction, propaganda, and actually relate to the process of making the record in that way. They can be an aesthetic
extension." But usually the interviews wouldn't be, and it's just
like, "Well, why muddy the waters?" What you're trying to do is
make something that's a piece of work; why would you then do
something that's not related to that? But with some of the things
you *could*; the Trux were the only ones who seemed to actively
engage with any aspect of promotion or publicity, although it
was still from this very guarded, very shielded position.

And they were actively touring.

Yeah. They dealt with tours as almost a workshopping way of
approaching music—not workshopping songs, workshopping
whole things, ideas about playing a song or a set.

**I don't know if they always did this, but I remember one gig
at the Cooler where they showed up with their gear and everything *right* before they were supposed to start playing.**

There was a period of time when there were drugs and stuff involved where that might have been more a symptom of what was going on rather than a decision; but there was also definitely a period where they worked into the set what they called their soundcheck song, and the first song would be that. They'd get up there, play it, and say, "We need more of this." The set had begun, but they'd be calling out things to the sound person about their monitors and things like that.

But it was also like, "We're not wasting our whole day making it to the afternoon soundcheck and then figuring out how to kill time or watching the opening band."
Which is really smart. There's good things about the other ways of approaching it, but if you want to be sure that you can concentrate on your set, the best way is to show up when it's time to play and then play. [On an in-store tour] if the in-store starts at 4, I get there at 4, so that I can just walk in and start playing right away and there's no chance for anyone to say, "Oh, you know we met a long time ago?" or "I know your cousin," or anything like that, because you don't want to be there; you want to be fully "Boom!" right into the song. You don't want to remember anything about an accepted reality, you don't wanna share an accepted reality with anyone until after the show, because then the shows become part of the accepted reality and you can pretend that that's when life began—an hour ago [*laughs*].

Sometimes I've missed an opening band just because I can't get my mind around watching, and then that feels bad. You feel unhappy that you can't walk fuckin' thirty feet out into the club to watch the group because you feel like it will make the set that people paid money to see less focused and less good. It's not a good feeling. And then you see people afterwards and you're like, "I wish I could have watched your set." But also, half the time, it's a club where the only way of watching it is to stand in the audience, and then people want to talk to you so you can't watch the band anyway, and then other people can't watch the band also, so you're just kind of screwed [*laughs*].

What are your recollections of the first European tour, with Rian, Pajo, Paul [Oldham, younger brother], and Henrique Prince, who was someone you found playing violin on the streets of New York?

It was a month-long trip, all around Europe. I remember the Peel session, which was very exciting, partly for the different Peel sessions that I'd heard: the Specials and the Fall . . . Also, at that point, Pavement had done a Peel session, which Dan had given me a copy of. I liked their *Perfect Sound Forever* ten-inch, and that was kind of *it*, but then I liked their Peel sessions a lot. They did what became a Silver Jews song, I think, or was a Silver Jews song ["Secret Knowledge of Backroads"]. That was great. I just thought of the Peel sessions as this opportunity of great potential for recording, so I was determined to bring four new songs to the first session [two of which later came out as the "Little Blue Eyes" / "The Spider's Dude Is Often Here" 7"].

I remember one night, maybe in Hamburg, where we all switched instruments and played the set that way, just 'cause at that point the grueling road life was not very satisfying; you know, just going to these fucking clubs and bars and playing, and then traveling the next day.

At a festival [Hardly Strictly Bluegrass, October 2010] a guy came over to talk to someone I was talking to. He introduced himself very briefly, and went on to turn to this other guy and just kept talking to him. I just kept staring at him, and I couldn't tell if he was putting me on or not that he didn't recognize me. After a minute I was like, "Henrique, we toured together, do you remember?" And all of a sudden his face exploded and he was like, "Will Oldham!" It was Henrique Prince, whom I hadn't seen since '93, who's in the Ebony Hillbillies and who played this festival.

The Lollapalooza tour in 1994, playing first on the second stage, was a better experience?
It was amazing. We* could play, to almost nobody, and every day still have the rest of the day ahead of us to do other things, including playing other shows if we wanted to. It was just great to get to play shows for money, and have no audience, because that's my dream: to get paid and not have an audience, that *is* my fantasy.

When you first started touring, did it remind you of being on a movie set, in terms of a group of people coming together?
No. I mean, touring was absolute agony for the first four or five

* WO: "With what I don't think had yet been called the Anomoanon, but it was Ned, Jack Carneal, Aram Stith, and Jason Stith."

years, it wasn't really pleasant or fun at all. But making records *was* like that. It's having a script, it's being in one place . . .

It's more precisely analogous to it.
Yeah. And touring became that, eventually, but it's still not quite the same, 'cause you're in a new place every day, dealing with a pool of material . . . It doesn't feel like you're building something from scratch every day.

I feel like I probably haven't slept in the same bed, say, for three months running since I was eighteen. I've just kept going from the time I graduated high school to the present day, pretty much [*laughs*]. Which might not be unusual, but I think it *is*, a little bit. I think that it's a natural inclination that I have, so I had to find a way to make a living that supported that natural inclination. Most things about my existence have to do with multiple places, because my audience does not live in one place. My audience is all different things, all different people, constantly changing, and at any given moment can be such a wide variety of people and places. It's because of, and results in, the fact that I go to so many places, not just to perform for people but also to meet people or see what's the air like here, what's the color like here, what's on the radio here, what are these record stores like, what are these restaurants like, how tall are the trees here, can you see the Northern Lights here, what's the swimming like here, how much development is going on in the outskirts of this city, how beautiful is this drive? All of those things, and then: what is it like to sing this music in this other place, what is it like to listen to music in this other place or with a different set of people all of the time?

I'm not of the group of people who make music or other kinds of art who feel like they have inherently within them something that needs to come out or is worth coming out. I feel like everything informs and helps add value to anything that does come out. For me it's by pursuing, absorbing, or just complacently being bombarded by things from all over or that have value to me but are discovered in different times, locations, etc. So that is what I would say is gained, but it's only because inherently I don't have the ability to sit still. I would have to do this anyway, and thank God I can get something out of it.

So the traveling part of touring wasn't a problem, except there wasn't enough time in each place?
Right. I remember hearing from Dave [Grubbs] and Clark [Johnson] how well they [Bastro] were treated over in Europe and just thinking, "Oh, that sounds so *great*." But then the first time touring, starting to understand that going to Berlin is not going to Berlin, going to Stockholm is not going to Stockholm, going to Madrid is not going to Madrid. You're not going to these places; the tour is its own destination. You go on tour, and *that's* like going some place, and the other stuff, that does not equate to what other people think when they say, "Oh you've been here, here, and here?" No, not really. I haven't really been to those places. Every once in a while, yes, if you get two or three days or it's been a specifically unique and powerful experience, but for the most part I haven't been to the places that I've

toured. It took a few years to start to make tours that were geographically oriented, so that we might do two or three weeks in California, Washington, Oregon, and then I could say, "Yes, I've been to California, Washington, and Oregon. That's where I went, that's where I just was playing shows." 'Cause we did it, you know, we traveled two hours and played a show. So you could meet people, see them night after night if they went to multiple shows or you played small places two or three nights running— that's when touring started to become great. Or touring Italy for two weeks.

You've consistently used tour managers, but they're not necessarily road-warrior, professional tour managers.
Essentially it's a job that has to be done. I have an idea of how it can and should be done. I feel like it's vital for anything you do to be its own thing, and the problem with road-warrior tour managers, God bless them, is that a road-warrior tour manager likes things to be the same as on another tour. You're out exploring the world and playing places and playing with musicians and it's all novel, so you can't have someone there who's treating it like it's a workaday, this-is-how-we-do-it, exact same thing, 'cause then it's no fun. So it's having someone there who, if nothing else, is eyes and ears while we're on stage but also appreciates the novelty of what everyone's going through on a daily basis.

And it's often a new experience for them too.
It should be a new experience. Sometimes it's great working with people who really know their shit, but really only if you

know at that time that you're going to be showing them something that you know is going to be new to them. We did two weeks last spring with Ben Corrigan: great guy, British, really great tour manager. We played some places that in some ways I didn't feel like he necessarily experiences all the time, so it was fun to be able to be like, "How about that?" "Yeah, how about that!" And also because it was a logistically challenging tour, in that instance it was helpful to have somebody for whom overcoming obstacles is second nature. Especially over there [Europe], where having an inexperienced tour manager and getting into difficult situations is not always rewarding [*laughs*].

I wanted to ask about Robert Duvall's film *Angelo My Love* **(1983) and the notion of travel. Were you familiar with the Gypsy lifestyle when you first saw the film in Louisville in the early 1980s?**
No, not when I saw that movie. My dad would take us to strange movies at that movie theater [the Vogue], like *Angelo My Love* or *Walkabout* or *Pumping Iron*. He wouldn't say, "We're going to see this movie about *this*"; he'd say, "Hey, come on, the movie starts in five minutes, let's get out of here." *Angelo My Love* was like going to see Samhain or Big Black, because you're seeing a movie and it feels as powerful as any other movie, but it also feels real and accessible. Your experience with it feels kind of private also, 'cause I could tell, even when I was watching it and loving it, that I wasn't going to be able to talk about it with anybody, 'cause none of my friends were gonna go see that movie and none of my dad's friends were gonna go see it. It was this

thing that we did, and then that was it, end of story, but it was huge and full.

We had actually done a summer trip once where we had driven into Quebec and gone to the Church of Sainte Anne de Beaupré. It's a location in the movie, when there's a big festival there and the crazy, evil uncle and his wife, who are also kind of lovable, show up a day late at the church. And I had *been* there, so it was like, whoa, you know . . . It was a special place, I remember, because there's a relic that's a forearm bone of Saint Anne, who was Mary's mother, and there are all these crutches and wheelchairs when you walk into the church, from people who were able to leave their affliction behind after they'd been to the church and touched the relic or drank the holy waters, put the holy water on 'em. So it was like, "I exist in the same world as Angelo," and we were the same age, and I was like, "Huh, that kid's like me."

He's so self-possessed in that movie; he's walking around and in his mind he's just another adult in his Gypsy community. And whenever something comes into conflict with that, like in the scene early on when he's in the school and he's kind of a fish out of water, he can't take it and has to get out. Did that leave an impression?

I would imagine that it left an impression because he seemed like a real person that did what he wanted to do, except that, I think helpfully, to an impressionable mind like mine, there was no conclusive end. So it was something to take in, but not to feel like, "Oh, if I act like that, I'm gonna end up in a good way." In the end you don't *know* how he ends up. So it was exciting to see, but I didn't walk away thinking I want to *be* like him, because I didn't necessarily think that he had it better than me. On some level I thought, "School is fine. I'd just as soon go there as sit around the house, you know?" I didn't live in New York City, I lived in St. Matthews [a Louisville neighborhood].

I watched it again recently, not that long after reading a biography of surfer Miki Dora, and it occurred to me that surfing is another lifestyle that involves moving around a lot.

Reading, extracurricularly, when I was fifteen or sixteen, *On the Road*, and being caught up in his confidence—and linguistic style as well—was more distractingly inspiring, like you were talking about maybe Angelo was. I was just reading the scroll version of that book now, and I see aimlessness, and it's not a happy story. As a kid it seemed like a strong story, making it seem as if there's a lot of things out there that you could become a part of, but now it doesn't at all . . . It's misleading, that book.

3

DAZED AND AWAKE

ALAN LICHT: Over the years, there have been changes in how much information is given about each of your records: the credits, or lack of them, and the lyrics. Then there's all the name variations in the Palace series.

WILL OLDHAM: There are different reasons behind all those different things. Using different names for different records was intended as a "buyer beware." Printing the lyrics has more to do with foreign-language audiences, thinking that it gives the music a better chance of finding a foreign-language audience if they can sit and figure out what's being said. And it's easier to do one layout for the world rather than do one for Europe and one for the US. Plus, who knows, maybe some Mexicans would buy the record.

And printing credits: I think for those of us who make records, it's our business how we put it together. Same with a book; in a book you basically have the name of the publisher and the name of the writer, and you're led to believe that those are the two things that created the book. That's not the case—there's an army of people involved with the production of each book, most essentially the editor or editors who work closely with the writer on shaping, forming, and developing a piece of work, plus the writer's agent, blah blah blah. Somehow it doesn't matter to us that any of that information is never publicly, readily available, yet we want that on records. Look at all these endless, bullshit lists of credits at the end of movies; I guess it works

as a résumé for the best boys and the key grips and everybody
else, but I'd think that would be something that you could tell a
prospective boss, like, "I was the assistant costume designer on
Forrest Gump." You could check their references; you don't have
to watch a two-and-a-half-hour movie about a mildly retarded
guy to prove that so-and-so was the assistant costume designer.

**Palace's reception was really positive from the get-go. It
seemed like people knew about it immediately, and even
within a month or two of you handing me the first 7", I opened
an issue of *Tower Pulse* and there was a picture of you in there.**
That's amazing, right? Then, it was neat; and now, it seems
improbable. Like I say, I was kind of just born, and I didn't have
any idea of how the world worked, so it made sense, on some
level, because I felt like we were putting a lot of good, honest
work, energy, and enthusiasm into doing these things, so whenever there was some sort of feature about it somewhere, it was
just like, "Thank goodness." It probably did more so then, but
I still feel like there's a pretty dubious relationship between
press and record sales. Some of those things were neat because
I would pick up *Tower Pulse* when I would go into Tower Records
and flip through it.

**Press can also reflect a buzz that's going on, and even that
first show that I saw in New York, at Threadwaxing Space in
1994, was a relatively big one. So the interest was always there.
It was there by word of mouth or whatever it was; it wasn't manufactured by the press or some promotional maneuvering.**

I think it's probably safe to say that on some level—for some of the records more than others—it got heard and recognized and talked about by a certain group of people because, even though I was pretty naive at the time, there's no avoiding the fact that the music was informed in a certain way and shared, definitely. All of us who were involved with playing and making it had a history of knowing music. We weren't necessarily trying to make a certain kind of music, but we *did* know what we liked and what we didn't like, and that we didn't want to make music that we didn't like. In general, there's probably more people that *don't* make music like that than do, that people just make music related to their tastes, and this wasn't specifically like that; it was trying to make a new music that respected all the music that came before, but that was also new and had its own right to exist. Because if we would play something that sounded like Naked Raygun, then we woulda been like, "Huh, I guess that sounds like Naked Raygun." Or like the Mekons or like Slint or like Johnny Cash or anything that you could say, then we wouldn't have made it. So, there was that kind of informed-ness going into it, and it probably felt good, for some people, to hear music like that. That you couldn't be like, "Ah yeah, sounds like this, blah blah blah"; that the exploration that was going on was either subconsciously or consciously apparent. Each recording session, each song being written, and each song being recorded was like, "Wow! And we can do *this*, and we can do *this*, and we can do *this*. Whoa, did you *hear* that?" Without any cynicism . . . so at that point, a lot of people who were more or less peers and who had also grown up hearing, or had at least caught up with, the incredible period of underground music in the 1980s were listening to something that was related to that stuff; not that *sounded* like it, but that took that stuff into account as being good music. And some of those people were now writing for magazines, so they were the first to hear it and they had the opportunity, then, to write something about it.

Especially when the first Palace Brothers records came out, which was at the height of "grunge" and the mainstream's interest in what was going on in the independent-music world, did you ever consider going with a major label?

When bands like Hüsker Dü or the Replacements went from independent to major labels and failed in such a depressing way [in the 1980s], that was very significant to me. Doing things the mainstream way seems to mean doing things somebody else's way. This will almost always end in failure. The movie *One Flew Over the Cuckoo's Nest*, along with the [children's] book *Harriet the Spy* and the Tim Conway movie *They Went That-a-Way and That-a-Way*, formulated my fear of overarching decisions made by others.

A long time ago there were a couple of offers. I've had meetings with major-label people; I would think about the possibility, but in the course of the interaction the impossibility became more and more obvious with each passing moment. It didn't seem like they were relationships that could be trusted, and it turns out that they couldn't have been. Those labels just don't exist anymore, while Drag City and Domino are still there and still open for business. The people there are still approachable and still accountable. I thought of it like this: if you were sitting down at supper and you had a nice plate of food in front of you and you were enjoying it, and someone came along and said they wanted to serve you dinner in another place, or even another room, why would you leave? Why would you go eat dinner somewhere else if you already had a great dinner in front of you? It's not that the major labels are evil; it's just that it would be stupid not to be thankful for what you have in front of you. A tour bus or a wall-size ad at Virgin Megastore is not only *not that great*, but it's not really missing from my life. A tour bus would make touring like an office job, and anything is better than that.

Days in the Wake, the second album, was originally self-titled [*Palace Brothers*] or untitled. Where did the title *Days in the Wake* come from?

I don't remember. It was like that [self-/untitled] for the first six months, or nine months, or a year—I don't remember. Dan [Koretzky] and I would talk about the gravity of a self-titled record, and at that point I just wanted to make a record and was still being frustrated by the necessity of titling anything or having an artist name. At first it seemed funny, or weighted, to have the title be *Palace Brothers* and have it be a solitary voice for the most part. It seemed like that would say something in and of itself, but then I was like, "Yeah, but who cares about that kind of statement?" So I thought I'd give it a title.

Also, there were things about finishing that [first] record: it was like coming back to Louisville and focusing on a project for the first time with these old friends, and there were things

that happened that made it obvious that these were not working relationships that could be sustained; with Britt [Walford]
and Brian [McMahan] specifically, but in some ways with Todd
[Brashear] and Paul Greenlaw, 'cause Todd had a trajectory
towards stability and family, and Greenlaw kind of had the
opposite—at the time, at least—and it seemed like the different ways of approaching music that Britt and Brian had were
coming more strongly to the fore at that time. And I was living here, paying rent here. I had a mailing address for the first
time since I graduated high school four or five years before, so
it felt like I was learning about the not-being-able-to-go-home-
again concept and recognizing that whatever we had had, as a
group energy force throughout the teenage years and beyond,
this new life as adults was going to be different. So I *think* that's
where the title came from.

In other words, days in the wake of that realization.
Yeah.

**When that record came out, a lot of people drew comparisons
between its cover and the covers of Jandek records.***
Right, which I hadn't seen. I asked Dan about it, and he was
like, "You haven't heard of Jandek?" And I said, "I don't know if

---

* Jandek (generally perceived to be an individual but, according to a "label
representative," technically a group name) has self-recorded/self-released
sixty albums (and counting) on the Corwood label since 1978. They uniformly
feature a blurry photo with no text on the front cover and song titles, the
album name, and the Corwood address on the back. He/they have also only
granted two interviews, and until 2004 had never performed in concert.

I've heard of him," or hadn't seen his records. Dan had a bunch and showed them to me, and I was like, "Yup, that's exactly what it looks like" [*laughs*]. The cover was from a roll of film from a trip that I'd taken where I was traveling, for a while, with three other guys. The photo was on my camera, but I don't know if it's a picture of me or if it's of one of the other guys that I was traveling with. I really don't know, but I like the picture. It's definitely a picture from a pub in Ireland, and it's either me or this other guy with a pint of stout raised to the mouth.

This is another example of people jumping to conclusions, because the record is solo singing and guitar, which so many of those Jandek records are too, so people think it's inspired by Jandek.

Yeah, that afternoon Dan played me a song here or a song there, but I think I've probably spent a total of about nine minutes listening to Jandek in my life.

Where was the album recorded?

Houses here in Louisville and in Birmingham [Alabama]. There was a couple of ways I tried to record *Days in the Wake*, and one of them was with Grant [Barger], who had recorded the first record. He had moved to Chicago. We went to his place, and by that time we had made "Come In" / "Trudy Dies," so I'd met Liam [Hayes], and we went to try and record on Grant's eight-track. There was a snowstorm; we recorded a couple of songs and then abandoned the session. I also contacted [Nashville producer] Bob Johnston, to see if he would make that record. He said, "You have a nice voice. Sounds like a guy I worked with a long time ago named Loudon Wainwright." We talked on the phone a few times and ended up meeting in the parking lot of the Great Escape record store in Nashville. We talked, and I was like, "This guy is a *freak*"—*and* he was too expensive. I think he wanted $1,250 a day or something like that. And I wound up making the record for forty bucks [*laughs*].

I remember hearing "Blood in My Eyes," the Bob Dylan song that's on *World Gone Wrong*, on the radio over in Moscow, and remembering that I'd heard *Good as I Been to You* once or twice and thinking that was a better record. When the first PJ Harvey album came out, there was a limited-edition release of demos, just her and her guitar, and it was *really* good. So I listened to those two records a bunch, just thinking that I *like* listening to these two records, and if I'm gonna try to pull off a record that's a person by himself it would be good to listen to other records that are a person by him- or herself that were recently made as well.

Days is mostly just you, with brief appearances from your brothers Ned and Paul . . .
Paul is on two songs, and Ned is just on "Come a Little Dog." I think my sister-in-law Jennie might be on that song too, playing some flute or some percussion.

Was "Pushkin" inspired by a trip to Russia?
Yeah, by the statue of Pushkin. One day, on the set of *A Thousand Pieces of Gold*, this guy comes up and starts insulting me and making fun of me for being an actor. It was the third electrician, Bryan Rich. We became pretty close; it was kind of a

small group of people. In the fall of '89, I called Bryan because he'd said, "You should come up to New York and just live with us." There was a loft on Plymouth Street in DUMBO [neighborhood in Brooklyn], and there were four other guys there. That was when I was learning to play the guitar, and Bryan was also making me write songs. Then Bryan was living in Moscow, and I just continued from the end of a tour and went and stayed with him for a while there, and we wrote a couple of the songs together—"(Thou Without) Partner" and "You Will Miss Me When I Burn." He used to be constantly telling me stories about one thing or another—literature, history, and his own life—that were huge embellishments on the truth. I think he had told me a bunch of stuff about Pushkin that probably wasn't true, mixed with things that *were* true and that were really exciting.

I think there's a Leonard Cohen quote and a Phil Ochs quote in the lyrics on that record, and that one song is named after *The Wanderer* by Henri Alain-Fournier ["Meaulnes"; the book's original title is *Le Grand Meaulnes*]. I found that book at my parents' house, and it compelled me because the edition we had had an Edward Gorey cover. Even as a kid, [illustrator] Edward Gorey was attractive to certain minds, and he certainly was to mine.

"All Is Grace" is also the last line of [Robert Bresson's 1951 film] *Diary of a Country Priest*.
They're his dying words. I remember taking an *invaluable* class [at Brown University] with a guy named Michael Silverman.

It was a senior seminar about the films of Bresson. I'd never heard of him, but I was just looking in the catalog and thought it looked interesting. Went in, and Silverman was like, "What year are you?" This was when I came back, a year later, for my second semester, so I was a freshman but a sophomore's age, and there was just six other people, and he said, "Well, you can stick around." He was like, "We're gonna watch these movies, and the reason I want to teach this class is, I don't really understand the way they make me feel. So we're just gonna watch 'em and talk about 'em." And that was great, that class was *so good.* He screened every Bresson film except for *The Trial of Joan of Arc,* which he couldn't find a copy of, and *Les Dames du Bois de Bologne,* an early one. He would also choose a companion movie: the only one I remember was a movie called *The Lacemaker* with Isabelle Huppert, which he showed with *Une femme douce.* He always chose another movie so that we would have something to talk about whenever he was at a loss. I think he was a mentor kind of guy to Todd Haynes and is in *Poison* as the father, when the kid does the flying out the window.

"I Am a Cinematographer" was after reading Bresson's *Notes on the Cinematographer.* I had no inclination towards cinematography, but I was excited that that book made sense to me and was inspiring. I thought, "I like these ideas, even though I'm never gonna make a movie, but it helps me to understand ways of looking at the world through eyes that are then gonna retranslate it into something else." That song more than any other was about a melody and words that rhymed. There was a joy in writing that song because it was a total mystery.

It's interesting that that song—and the album—ends on the word "Louisville." It's a slight connection to the first album (even though *Days* is such a departure from it) in that Louisville is referenced visually on that first record and then referenced again here verbally. Thereafter it's not referenced at all.

Right. "No more Kentucky, no more Louisville."

I've noticed the first lines of the opening songs on your records remind me of the opening lines of a play or a movie, and a lot of the ways your albums end remind me more of the ending of a movie or a play than they might of the way another record would end. Do you pay extra attention to the opening lines or endings of movies or plays?

Maybe subconsciously. When I'm given the opportunity to make a decision, I feel that it's also a responsibility, so fortunately or unfortunately I can't be passive about what the opening line is going to be, even though I might not, on another person's record, pay attention to what the opening line is. Every time I'm putting a record together, I think "OK, this is the thing that's gonna identify the beginning of the record, so any time they put it on this is the note or the tone or the lyric that's going to signal to them that this is the beginning. What's it gonna be? Is this gonna work? Is this preparing someone in a positive way for listening to the whole record?" I think of it in terms of other records that do that for me, but I don't know if other people made that decision when they sequenced or wrote a record.

It really does feel like the curtain has gone up when one of your records starts.

The way each song is related to the other songs and the last song is an arc of some sort, which might be identifiable. I don't know what it is, I know it feels . . . right. One thing either washes something else away or builds upon it.

Also, on many of your records the last thing you hear is not the chorus of the last song played ad infinitum. They often end on a verse, and sometimes not even on a rhyme. I've gotten the same sensation from plays or movies that don't have a "big finish," where it's more like, "Oh, that's the ending."

Yeah, definitely. More so than the beginning, I think of the ends of records as more like the ends of plays or movies.

A conclusion.

Yeah, concluding but trying to ensure that there's a post-listening experience. Like when you walk out of a movie theater or a theater, it isn't over; you're encouraged to bring it with you as you move on to the next thing that you do.

Is it a problem when people put an album of yours on iPod shuffle, or something like that? Of course, when you play a concert, you mix the songs up too.

Yeah, that's one of the different listening experiences that you imagine as a possibility. I remember reading once the Rolling Stones' idea that each song could be a single, but obviously their records don't function like that throughout the 1970s. Sometimes I feel like the identity of the record is pretty ambiguous and not very successful, but each song is the beginning of a whole new experience and approach that on the better records is related to the other songs. Like, with *There Is No One What Will Take Care of You* everyone would switch instruments, thinking about the Rolling Stones, and still thinking that the ideal is that the songs can each have their own existence.

Each song can be its own world, and then a record can be another whole world.
One thing that makes me listen to music again and again and again is that sometimes I just wish I could live in the world of that song. There's been a few times in my life where that has become a crazy part of reality, at least for a moment, where I just got to live in this world that normally we don't have access to. We'll never go to Mordor, but it's that kind of feeling, where all of a sudden it's like a dream, just like you can dream yourself into the greatest places and then all of a sudden wake up. You're like, "Wait a second, I can play this record again and again and again, and reenter this world."

It's something I enjoy about films too: they become their own environment.
Yeah, like these are the rules for the next 111 minutes.

Jacques Tati's *Play Time* is one example of that. Even just the way it's colored, you wouldn't mistake it for any other film.
Yeah. Then there are the extreme examples, which I ultimately think are failures, things like *Popeye* or *Dick Tracy* or *One from the Heart*, which set out to do that but maybe spend too much time

creating a new set of rules. They didn't actually get a chance to live those rules or live that world.

The *Hope* EP followed *Days in the Wake*, recorded in London and Chicago.

At Acme Studios in Chicago. That was the first full session with Liam. London was with Sean O'Hagan and Rob Allum [both of the High Llamas], recorded in the studio called The Stone Room, which I realized, after we'd gotten there, was where *Curse of the Mekons* was recorded, which was a pretty big record for me, so it was exciting to be there. I had wanted Heather Nova to sing on those sessions. She grew up in Bermuda with Cynthia [Kirkwood, Bryan Rich's then wife], which I thought was a funny coincidence. That's why I wanted her, but then she couldn't do it. Laurence [Bell, head of Domino Records] then found Briana Corrigan, who had been in a band called the Beautiful South and was beginning to embark on a solo career.

That was the first time I started to get a footing, and part of it was because it was an EP. It's not as tense as making a full-length record, and yet you can stretch out a little more than on a 7". Working with O'Hagan was great, working with somebody with such facility and confidence.

How did he get involved?

I don't think they [Stereolab / High Llamas] had anything to do with Drag City yet, so I might have asked Laurence to set up a session to record a couple of songs. Maybe they ended up being piano-based songs because of O'Hagan, in terms of the arrangements, and then the Chicago songs were piano-based because of Liam, so I thought, "This is a good six songs that go together." I played a little bass on the Chicago sessions, which was exciting; might have been the only time I played a bass on any record. And working with Rian [Murphy] and Liam was so much fun. After having done a few different recording sessions with different lineups and different arrangements, doing these sessions was the first time I felt like the work was starting to pay off and could be a little more relaxed, but still getting some music that I thought was good out of it. The joy of making those songs was part of the reason for calling it *Hope*, as well as "hope" being a big Rhode Island thing, a Providence thing.

With "Winter Lady" and "Christmastime in the Mountains" was there any idea of making a winter record?
I can't remember what time of year it was. "Christmastime in the Mountains" was another Bryan Rich song, Bryan and a guy named Steve Baker. I'd actually recorded him singing that on videotape once, when I was visiting him when he lived in Vermont, and learned it off the video. I just loved it whenever Bryan would send me songs. "Stable Will" was written by Bryan, with two words changed by myself. "Winter Lady" was just 'cause while I like Leonard Cohen's music, at the same time I feel like he's relatively uncoverable. Even with all the covers that people have done of his songs, I find they're, for the most part, meaningless, mainly because they're in the guise of songs, but they're not *really* songs. They seem to be something else. There

seem to be one or two that are like songs, and that's one of them. It's sort of like a country song—it's like, "Help me make it through the night, let's hang out tonight," you know—and it's just a couple of chords, and I thought that would be fun to do.

When I interviewed Vito Acconci, I asked him, as a music enthusiast and someone who started off as a poet and moved into performance-art activities, if he was a fan of Leonard Cohen, and he said he loved him, because when Cohen used the word "I" it never seemed to be the same "I" from song to song. He said he felt like there were "a thousand 'I's'" with Leonard Cohen.

Yeah, and I never feel like he's singing about himself, even though he probably says "I" and "me" in almost every song. Just understanding that using the word "I" is a signifier and not a self-reflexive thing; to use the word "I" to represent a relationship to self and to identify a force that's moving through this song, and that's it.

I remember reading one review of *Hope* that said "All Gone, All Gone" was a rewriting of a Leonard Cohen song called "If It Be Your Will," on *Various Positions*, which was compelling and upsetting because he was deriding it ["All Gone"]. I was trying to figure out why he would *think* that, because that's one of the records that I know better than most other records in the world, 'cause I'd had it since I was fifteen and probably listened to it more consistently than any other record. I realized that from the first chord to the second chord, at least, was the same progression and both songs begin with the word "if," and then after that I couldn't figure out how the two were related. On some level it was upsetting because I thought, "Is that right?" Then I thought, "It isn't right, and why do people write things that they can't back up?" And it's something that I've encountered again and again, and I'm sure you've encountered again and again, where a writer writes a sentence that could never be backed up, and it's accepted. It's mind-blowing. I remember one review of *There Is No One What Will Take Care of You*, calling it "fiddle-drenched."

And there's no fiddle on there.
No. It's *ridiculous*. Music writing can just be so *ridiculous*. And they publish it, trying to steer people towards or away from a record with lies. Positive or negative.

You've done so many 7"s and EPs. What are the factors in deciding when a group of songs is an album or when two songs are going to comprise a 7" or four to six songs are going to make an EP?
I think of the six-song model created by the first three Big Black EPs as six-songs-are-an-EP. I was surprised when I started making records and people were like, "No, no, *four* songs are an EP." And *eight* songs, Drag City has a term for that—a "mini-LP," which is a different price when they sell it to distributors.

Has there been a case when you've had five or six songs and decided to keep going because you felt that it was the basis of an album and not an EP in and of itself?

It's usually the other way around. The songs usually take from four to fourteen months, so by, like, ten months in I wouldn't begin a group of new songs. By that point, I know that it's becoming a full-length record. Except for the last two, during every other record there's always been a moment in the recording session where I've thought that we're only gonna get an EP out of this session [*laughs*]. I'd think, "Well, there *are* six songs that are salvageable from this session." But then I'd stick it through to the end. It goes record by record, but it's pretty straightforward in that here's a song or two songs that I can't imagine fitting with other songs, but then here's a group of songs that are sort of growing together; and then there's one that might sort of fall away as the others create a bond with each other, and then that song might end up, somehow, becoming half of a single 'cause it's been worked on, but all of a sudden I've found that it's disparate from all the other songs.

Most of the singles I think have much more of a definable atmosphere to them than many of the records, and that's because it was allowable to do that with just two songs. Experimentations with a single can be broader. It's committing one song to this experiment rather than committing ten. I'd written that "West Palm Beach" / "Gulf Shores" 7″ as an attempt to try to use the Jimmy Buffett formula to make a hit record, by singing songs about the beach, trying to tap into people's collective memories, and fantasies, of what it was like getting away from wherever they lived and going to the beach. Positive and negative, but *all* nostalgic.

Were you into Jimmy Buffett back then?

I was only fascinated by him. It was one of those things where I saw how many people loved him, and how much they loved him, and I thought, "I don't wanna have disdain for these people, I wanna figure out what it is." So I listened to his records, read books about him, read books by him, just thinking, "I gotta learn this." His records, for the most part, were not good. I was thinking I was gonna listen to them and think, "Oh, there's actually a good record in there," and there *isn't*. There's great songs, spread out among all of his records, and he's very interesting—like, I didn't realize that he was also part of the [Thomas] McGuane / Jerry Jeff Walker / Hunter Thompson Key West scene. And that he worked at *Billboard* before he made records. I believe that his success is built on the fact that he saw how the industry worked, and then made records to fit the industry, not because he wanted to make records necessarily.

That's like Neil Sedaka writing "Oh Carol" because he looked at the *Billboard* charts for every country, tracked down every single that was number one, listened to all of them, then sat down and tried to write a song that had elements of each of them—and he had a hit with the song.
Amazing. Or like the British band [the KLF] that wrote the book, *The Manual (How to Have a Number One the Easy Way)*, and then had a hit record and burned a million pounds.

Over the course of your career has having a hit ever seemed attainable? And how would you deal with it if it actually happened?

I'm sure I still am in ways that I have yet to discover, but I was very naive when I started making records, which is exemplified by whom I sent the first recordings to to see if they wanted to put a 7" out: Ken Katkin [Trash Flow / Homestead], Gerard Cosloy [Matador], Drag City, and Interscope. I sent them all the same two songs and said, "Would you be interested in putting out a 7"?" I didn't see . . . it was just four record companies. Gradually I learned, hearing stories, whether they're true or not, that the Offspring became a hit because Epitaph did things like buying new computers for a promo company, or things like that. What the entertainment business is built on, and what the music business is built on, is people working together, and when you're a music listener you don't understand that. I used to assume that it's a record company, it's radio stations, it's listeners, it's musicians, it's songs, and then I learned that no, hits are a different business. Publicists, booking agents, talent agencies or managers, record companies—*they* make hits. With each other and for each other. I've never run in those circles, and neither has Drag City. I'm not working with people who make hits. Again, there's probably an exception here or there, but basically any hit you've ever heard is in that system.

That's certainly true over the last thirty or forty years . . .
And it's super exciting to listen to records from pre-1970 and understand that there is a relationship between the way that we make records and put them out. It's not insane to see a relationship between those records and the records that I witnessed being made, or that I love but that most people in the

country will never hear. The process, at least, is closer to the way records that everybody accepts as great records were made in the 1940s, 1950s, 1960s than to any other time since then. But it *is* insane to see a relationship between the records that I have any sort of potential for direct contact with and any big records from 1970 on. The country as a whole might accept Aerosmith, Led Zeppelin, or Carole King, or whatever, as making the great records of the 1970s, and whatever else in the 1980s . . . all the David Geffen California stuff. It's very misleading to think that we know those records because they were the best musicians around at the time, and that they're just great records and they rose to the top because they're great records, and not understanding that we know them because of politics and money and isolation and fooling the artists themselves into thinking what they were doing was correct and good, and inflating egos and overspending, and all this stuff. I think that's a shame, but it's part of the way things work now. Except it's less a part of the way things work now because those distributors have to share power with peer-to-peer [online] music communities.

I love the story, which could be apocryphal or not, of how they did it at Chess sometimes, which was to have a loudspeaker outside of their storefront office, and when people would walk by and dance to the new songs they'd just recorded, they'd be like, "All right, that one's gonna be a hit." Beautiful. Or the ability to cut a song, make an acetate, send it to a DJ that night, find out if people call in and request it after it gets played once— amazing, you know? Went into the studio that morning . . . on the radio that night! Went into the studio, and the musicians learning a song sometimes.

"Like a Rolling Stone" is a great example of that: even on the released take they're still learning the song. Al Kooper doesn't even know how to play the organ, and he's playing the organ part.

I saw him open for Jimmy Webb at the Bottom Line, sometime in the 1990s. He did a solo set playing keyboards, but he was talking about the irony of it.

4

HAPPY ACCIDENTS

ALAN LICHT: You use different musicians on every record, and then the musicians who tour with you don't necessarily reflect who played on the most recent record—or on any record.

WILL OLDHAM: I didn't start making records until I was twenty-two or twenty-three, and everything I knew up until then had to do with acting and theater and movies. You don't use the same people in every single play or every single movie. So I just learned it that way. Reading about the movie business, or even being in it, you see that every film is different and its particular character will be shaped by whether a director works with a different cinematographer or a different set of actors, but in music it's much rarer for people to actively seek that out. The focus always tends to be on the latest record by a particular artist, rather than treating each record as its own thing. My dream is also that each [record] has its own unique audience; that there might be some crossover, but that each record might serve a purpose to individuals that another record might not.

I know you try to maintain a difference between who plays on the records and who plays on the subsequent tours.

I don't know if I try to maintain a difference as much as it *happens* that way, 'cause they are different things. I can sort of understand it now, but it never occurred to me that a tour had anything to do with the record, that they were related whatsoever, you know? For years people would say, "I saw you on the *Arise Therefore* tour,

I saw you on the *I See a Darkness* tour," and I'd be like, "What does that *mean*?" I don't have any idea what they're talking about.

It seems completely inappropriate to tie your fate to the fate of a bunch of other people inextricably to the point where you'd be like, "We're gonna have breakfast, lunch, and dinner together *most* of the time for the next decade." There's only one person in your *life* whom you should do that with. It just sounded nightmarish. Also, at any point on a tour or in a recording session you can always fall back on knowing that you're learning something from somebody, but if you're always playing music with somebody and spending all your time with them, then they're not going to surprise you, they're not going to teach you anything and you're not going to teach them anything. Also, it's nice to play with people who have lives that are constantly refreshing and reenergizing themselves, and to meet up for a while and then spread out again and come back together.

On some level it doesn't matter, with a record, how well you know you can get along with someone or how well you know somebody travels. A record is going to be a lot more specific and urgent. Think about the classic difference between a Nashville session musician and a Nashville touring musician: that kind of delineation doesn't necessarily exist in the independent underground-music world, but it doesn't mean it *can't* exist, that you can't superimpose that idea. And it could even be for one person, like Jim White: you can think of him as a certain kind of recording drummer and a certain kind of touring drummer, and think of them as two different skills, even though for him it might be a continuum. He might be approaching a song the same way in those two situations, but you can imagine that they're almost two different people. Like, "Would this be a great record for Jim White the studio musician, or would this be a great tour for Jim White the touring drummer, the live drummer?"

That's like an actor who is skilled in the theater, and sometimes they make the jump to film or TV acting, and vice versa. Right. TV to film, or even character to lead. Brad Pitt's a really good character actor. I love watching him play characters . . . and don't like watching him play lead roles [*laughs*]. Or Eric Bana, who is so unbelievable in *Chopper*, and since then is one of the most absent forces in movies of anybody I can think of. You watch a scene and you're like, "Where is he? I don't see him. Where's the character? I don't see the character, I don't see anything happening here." How can this happen with this guy that pulled something off so incredibly well? But yeah, it's the same. And then [on] each record, each set of songs being a different set of songs, how will the musicians complement each other? In a recording, it doesn't matter as much if there's a personality complementarity as much as it does if there's a musical one, whereas in a tour it has to be both.

As with the road managers, there are a lot of musicians you've taken on tour for whom it's been their only touring experience—they hadn't toured before or since. Yeah. Andrew [Hunter, drummer on a 1995 tour] has been in Afghanistan for two or three years now, as a chef, cooking food

for contractors. Howard Greynolds said he wanted to play guitar and tour-manage [on another 1995 tour], but I can't remember how many sets he played on or how many songs he played
on each set, because he played so quietly that none of us could
hear him [*laughs*]. I think the plan was that he would not play
on the first or the last song of the set, so he could go set up the
merch and then play the rest of the set. But again, he played
so quietly, I would be like, "Make it louder, make it louder!"
Probably sounded interesting, but I could never hear it at all.
He was just too shy, too timid. Traveling with Bryan [Rich, in
1998] was just so great, because he's probably a B-grade guitar
player, and then *live* he was F minus minus minus. Everywhere
that I spend time with Bryan, he's this brash, infallible, confident kind of guy whom I love, and in this instance he was just,
like, destroyed every night. He wanted to enter into it with confidence, but it was something that he had no confidence in, in
any way [*laughs*]. People after the shows would be like, "It was
like you were in different rooms." One girl came up and said,
"I saw the show and I have one question for you: *Why?*" [*laughs*]

**I remember saying to you, when we toured together in 1995,
that one night the band would seem to be pretty together,
pretty tight, and then the next night it would seem like—**
They never met before? [*laughs*]

**I think what I said was that it was like they were in different
solar systems, and you said, "Yeah, but that's cool." Which I
was really struck by—that you were open to both characterizations and were getting energized by that.**

Yeah, I mean, still, to some extent, touring seems like a necessary evil for making records, and the best you can get out of it is to have a challenging and stimulating experience onstage every night.

And a somewhat unpredictable one . . .
Well, that's what makes things challenging.

There can be other challenges, technical things like the monitors feeding back. One of the things I most remember about the 1995 tour was the show at Oberlin College, where Andrew Hunter, who was a bear of a guy but very sweet-tempered, was getting so much feedback in his monitors that after the first couple of songs he threw down his drumsticks and shouted at the sound man, who was a kind of Ronnie James Dio lookalike, a very short, long-haired metal guy, wearing all black, "What are you trying to do to me, you fuckin' sack of shit!" and tore offstage charging after this guy, really looking like he was gonna kill him. You guys went offstage for twenty minutes, and somehow the situation was defused—you went back on and finished the show.
But that's, like, a headache. The challenge that's worth it is the challenge of collaboration. The other challenges aren't worth it.

The inherent challenges as opposed to the logistical challenges that are unforeseen?
Right. And you're not necessarily going to play a better set if your monitors are fucking up. That night or the next night.

Then it becomes an obstacle.

Unless you learn to play without monitors, which is still better sometimes than playing with them, depending on the venue. Playing in old theaters and such, it's sometimes better to play without a monitor because the acoustics are so good; it can be a thousand-capacity theater or 1,500 capacity or 2,000 capacity, and you can still hear stuff off the back of the room—your amplified voice, for sure, but sometimes your own voice, during quieter moments. It's like, "I could sing off-mic . . ." but that's not fair to the audience, 'cause they're hearing everything else through the PA.

Have you ever taken a sound person on tour?

On two different European tours, and I never again thought that it was worth having a sound person traveling with you. One of the things I like about a tour, almost all of the time, is meeting the new sound guy or sound woman and working with them.

And for the most part you've found them to be competent and sympathetic to what you're doing?

For the most part they're competent, because they know their room better than any sound guy you're going to bring with you, period. They know their room and they know their system— and one of the fun parts would be, when they *weren't* sympathetic, to see if we could *make* them sympathetic by the end of the night. The most rewarding nights would be when the sound guy who was an asshole at soundcheck would then at the end of the night say, "Really dug your set, man." That's so amazing [*laughs*]. Very rarely, like one in thirty, would it be a bad experience overall.

In some venues I feel like the sound person has a set idea about what it's supposed to sound like, and there's even a "sound" that they want to be uniform to the venue, which can compromise what a band is trying to do up onstage.
Yeah, another thing that's kind of thrilling for us is the idea that every show will be different because of the aesthetic of the sound person, and that people might come away with absolutely different opinions of the way a show sounded, based on what city they went to, because of the sound person, and that's really exciting [*laughs*]. In the studio there's a sound, of course, in the end that's unknown at the beginning, but as all the elements reveal themselves the sound reveals itself, reveals how it's supposed to be. But on tour it seems like if you begin to try to think that you have control over the sound, you'd never get any sleep. When would you stop thinking about that? When would you stop being obsessed or upset by that? Never. With every different room, every different sound system, every different temperature, time of day, or whatever affects the sound, it seems to be more advantageous to think of the room, and the technicians, as part of the novelty of the experience. They're extra factors, if not members of the ensemble. They're not *quite* that, but they're factors in what makes one show different from another.

And because the personnel on every tour of yours is different, it's not like it's a set band that has a set sound that they're

looking for a sound engineer to recreate for every audience, no matter what the venue.
Yeah, that's right.

This also reinforces the fact that there's really no relationship between your live shows and the records. It's funny to read what bands who made albums that have become very highly regarded have to say about the album, how disappointed they often are as far as how it represents the way they actually sounded or how their songs sounded live. Maureen Tucker told the guys who ran *What Goes On*, **the old Velvet Underground fanzine, "All this devotion is based on the records? That's sad." 'Cause she felt the records didn't sound anything like what the band sounded live.**
I like that kind of story, especially because I like records. So hearing how musicians react to the way a record sounds is always very interesting, because Moe Tucker might think, "That's weird, I don't put a lot of stock in that because that's not what we sounded like live," where *I* would think, "I don't care what you sounded like live, because this is how the record sounds. I don't care if it was different, I don't care if it was better, *I don't really care.* For me, you were rehearsing and preparing for *this*, whether or not you feel like you understand your participation in it." That's not what the record is about. It's not about the intentions of any individual; it's about how forces work together to make this thing. There's misgivings in any recording session, and it's exciting to know that you're not supposed to feel confident about every step of the process. You're supposed to

have moments where you're like, "I don't know what's going on here," or "I brought a song into the session, and now it's a different song," and to understand that that's OK, there are probably a hundred songs that you love that went through the same transformation.

I think also there are happy accidents, and that's something that happens a lot on film sets too. In *Visions of Light*, a documentary about cinematographers, they show a clip from *In Cold Blood*, where Robert Blake is delivering a monologue. He's sitting by a window and it's raining outside, and the shadows of the rain hitting against the window are reflecting onto his face and it looks like he's crying. It's very effective, but apparently this was a fluke. It was something that wasn't in the script or planned; it just happened in the way they jerry-rigged the lighting and the rain effects for this particular scene. And this sort of thing also happens in recording sessions.

Yeah, it does, and some of them are happy accidents and immediately recognizable as such, and some of them are accidents that you have to accept that in retrospect become happy, [because] you realistically don't have time to do another take on something, or a great take was recorded over, or there was distortion there that you couldn't get rid of, and you're just like, "Well, let's move on, this is what we have." And then you realize that it affected how you mixed it and how you relate to the song in the future, and all of a sudden it's an invaluable part of the recording, something that you weren't even *happy* with. It was an *accident* and then you just grew to love it.

This relates to something that [film director] Nicholas Ray wrote that I wanted to read to you, since you've said that you think of songs as "little scripts" that you give to players on records:

The script provides a foundation for improvisation. The script allows me to know and have on paper what I want so I can communicate it with facility to the other people with whom I'm working. Sometimes I feel lazy and would like to have it all there in front of me, but the tightest scripts I've worked on have not turned into my best films . . . And new ideas come up all the time. Actors bring you ideas. Who are you working with, after all? You are working with people. You have to find out who they are so you can use them, the materials within them, their experiences, so you don't have somebody up there just saying lines.*

Yep [*laughs*]. I love Nicholas Ray, and I think I love his movies because I see a beautiful relationship between structure and expression, where one couldn't exist without the other. Writing a song is like coming up with the skeleton for working with people. Playing a solo show is such a mockery, for me, because it's like doing a staged reading of a screenplay. I don't see the value. That's *not* what the songs are for, that's not why they exist, so they have no value to me in that situation, unless I'm getting paid like $5,000, and then I think, "Well, I could probably make a record off of this show, and maybe I'll learn something about

---

* Nicholas Ray, "I Hate a Script," in *I Was Interrupted: Nicholas Ray on Making Movies*, ed. Susan Ray (Berkeley/Los Angeles: University of California Press, 1993), pp. 189–90.

playing or singing over the course of it." But otherwise it's just agony. This is not the way these songs are supposed to be; they are so that people can get together and mess around and discover things about making music and making records.

It's a group experience.
And experiment. It's my excuse for getting to be a part of somebody else's process. I want to know how and why somebody can play or approach music in a certain way, and the best way of doing that is to bring raw material and watch it happen. I came at this thing not as a creator but as an audience member. Before I made things, I was an audience member, and a lot of what I'm doing when creating things is wanting to evolve as a member of the audience. If I, say, create a record and ask Valgeir [Sigurðsson], Dawn [McCarthy], Emmett [Kelly], Paul [Oldham], and Jim [White] to collaborate, it is because I, the audience, want to hear them work together with these lyrics and chord progressions and melodies. I try to ensure that I am allowed the position of audience member so that I can agree that records like *Arise Therefore* are good records, because I am in such admiration and awe of everybody's work. When I listen to *Arise*, it seems like this is the kind of song I wanted to hear; a song where the chords that David Grubbs is playing on the piano occur in reaction to this vocal melody, or something like that. "Master and Everyone" was a song that I felt like I could stand behind as an audience member as well, because the lyrics are sort of found lyrics, from an old Italian folk song, so when I sing that song I can be like, "Ah, these lyrics are awesome."

Early on you recognize your role as a member of the audience. Any member of the audience can only be so strong. Everything is a translation of that—wanting to be with the audience, wanting to realize the feeling of community that was imagined when you were alone. Being a solitary member of the audience is not a healthy or natural state. It is something that you have to communicate; you have to be with other people, you have to do things for other people as much as you can. As soon as you respect another's distance, something automatically becomes better about your own life. As soon as you smile with someone or share with someone, things just get better. The only thing that I know how to give is music. I want to sing, I want to display emotional dynamics, I want to be in the audience, I want to take people for a ride like people have done for me so many times.

In December 1994 came the recording of *Viva Last Blues*, in Hueytown, Alabama. You were listening to Stevie Wonder's *Music of My Mind* and Sly Stone before the recording for inspiration . . .

And Cat Stevens. We found this amazing studio, the Bates Brothers' studio. It was a fairly modern studio. They recorded mostly MIDI and sequenced gospel music, and they also had a vintage-keyboard collection. They had a functioning, tuned-up Mellotron, a great Hammond [organ], and a great Rhodes [electric piano]. Hueytown was about twenty-five minutes from Birmingham. There was a really good barbecue place called Let's Eat Smoked Meat, and their slogan was, "You don't need no teeth to eat our meat." That's the only thing I remember about Hueytown, really. We were in a sort of outlying industrial area, very nonpicturesque.

Viva **had a great lineup of Liam Hayes, Bryan Rich, Jason Loewenstein, and Ned.**
And [Steve] Albini, because in making a record everyone comes at the same time, so I feel like the engineer is a part of the lineup. His method of recording is one that I find very valuable: to record things with a lot of fidelity to the sounds that are being produced and to be willing to, to be eager to experiment. I remember calling Paul and asking for recommendations about drummers, and he recommended that I call Loewenstein. So I did, and to my surprise he came. But I'd known him for a number of years, meeting him when Sebadoh would come to Louisville. I guess at that point I knew Lou [Barlow, also of Sebadoh] from seeing Dinosaur Jr. play.*

With "Blues" in this album's title and in some of the song titles, like "No More Workhorse Blues" or "Cat's Blues," and often being in song titles on the other records, I was curious as to what your relationship to the blues is. Is the word meant to signify something in these titles?
Probably just that it was identifying it as some sort of created lamentation. If you just had the title, like "No More Work-

* Sebadoh had also covered "Riding" in a May 1994 Peel session. Barlow was the original bassist in Dinosaur Jr.

horse," it might make the song feel and sound more desperate and pathetic, whereas I wanted there to be an understanding that I *know* it sounds bad. It's not a cry for help, it's a song-form, and the song-form is something that has to do with desperation or solitude or forlornness. But that it's OK, because you can make a song out of it. Whatever the source may be, just the idea of making it into a song is a glorious achievement, and a rising above whatever sentiment is in there.

This is probably the most rollicking record up until this point. Everyone's just having a good time. It was one of the many records where, after a couple of days, I'm sure I called Dan [Koretzky] and said, "Yeah, I don't know what's going on, it's just not happening. Maybe it'll be an EP." But for the most part it was fun. All the individuals were so positive all the time; it was just [my] anxiety about making a record.

How did the cover drawing, by Dianne Bellino, get chosen? When a group of songs starts getting toward when it's time to record them, usually by then I also like to have some sort of secure idea of what the cover is going to be. Dianne had drawn that pencil drawing of a cheetah standing on its hind legs, but in a natural position, not a personified position. It's standing up, which you don't imagine that cheetahs would do, and it has these obvious feline qualities that endear most big cats to children. And the way it was drawn just seemed to fit; it seemed expressive of some of the things that are in the songs. It was sitting on a shelf in our apartment in Birmingham, and as I was working on the songs I was looking at it and thinking that it would be the cover. It was a good sort of totem, 'cause that's what they usually are: they're like good little totems for keeping the music focused. Just in calling people and making studio arrangements and working on the songs, it was a serene thing that I could look at and think, "This is the picture of what we're going to be doing."

Part of why I wanted to discuss the cover art of your records is to emphasize the thought that's put into it, and that the packaging is not an advertisement for the record, it's actually an organic part of it. Even before downloading, with CDs record packaging was minimized, which maybe accounts for some of the decrease in CD sales, because it's not an object that has any aesthetic value; it's just a plastic thing that has music on it that comes in a plastic container. So, with downloading, if you can get the music without the plastic thing and the *other* plastic thing, it's not going to make too much difference. But even the period when people were putting a lot of work into record packaging is a relatively short one: the idea of a color wraparound sleeve only came in the mid-1960s, and then only lasted twenty years, just twenty years of record covers being (potentially) a major statement. And they were not always taken that way: I certainly knew people over the years that were buying tons of records and would be like, "Who cares about the cover?"

Viva Last Blues was an expensive process finding the right paper stock for the covers, 'cause we used a different kind of paper than the regular one. Six months ago I was informed by Drag City that that stock is no longer available, so we had to go through it again and search paper stocks to find out what the new *Viva Last Blues* cover was going to be in relation to the old one. For *Lie Down in the Light* I think we mixed a custom-color CD jewel-case tray, which I don't know if anyone cares about [*laughs*]. Part of the joy of letting a record go is knowing that you sent it out to sea in as seaworthy a vessel as you could, and that it's appropriate to the record. Doing the *Wai Notes* thing with Dawn [McCarthy], we have a photo that looks and feels like a photo and is pasted to the package. The front is one of Magnus [Johnstone]'s drawings letterpressed, and then the CD is held on one of those single circle things, so the whole thing is fragile and sort of matches the cassette that I got in the mail from Dawn with the music on.

When Albini gave me my copy of *Lungs*, so long ago, I took it home and was thrilled to find the photograph in there: a photograph that had written on it "Me," with an arrow, and "My brother," also with an arrow. I thought, "This is cool, he accidentally slipped this photograph in the record." And then later, reading about it and talking to people, I realized there was like a Cracker Jack prize with every different copy of *Lungs*. All kinds of stuff—photographs, bird feathers . . . there was a relic in every copy. Pretty neat. Or with Glenn [Danzig], there were 800 copies of [the Misfits'] "Horror Business" 7" on yellow vinyl and twenty on black vinyl. It's so cool because the music is still great, and it doesn't matter. It's just these little things that make the object special in addition to being good.

***Arise Therefore* was recorded a year after *Viva*, in December 1995, with David Grubbs, Ned, and Albini. You've said in**

interviews that all three of them were heroes, and that made this record really exciting to do. Can you elaborate on why you consider them heroes, and what constitutes a hero in your mind?

People who do things that are inspiring and somehow straddle the line between being extremely generous and self-serving at the same time. With Dave or Ned or Steve, they're people with whom I have personal experience of them being open and generous; and then, with people whom I've never met and they don't know who *I* am, they're laying it out for people, they're not keeping things to themselves too much. They're working very hard and are very focused, but it doesn't seem to have value unless it's available to other people.

I never would have heard Phil Ochs or Leonard Cohen, both very important artists or musicians to me, if it wasn't for Grubbs, for example, and countless other things as far as the ways in which he was instrumental in bringing Louisville music to other places, whether it's just through his record collection or through communications or through actually creating relationships with bands and helping to make people feel like coming to Louisville was a good idea.

And getting records *out* too.

Yeah. And honestly, I wasn't ever that big a Squirrel Bait fan. I was a fan, more, of Bastro and Gastr del Sol, up to that point. Which was even more exciting: that this person that I liked a lot and was endlessly influenced and impressed by was getting better and better, musically, as the years went on. That's one of the biggest gifts you can get, that you put your money on the right guy [*laughs*], or that you were watching somebody who turned out to be worth watching [*laughs*].

Ned, since I was little, was always making essential contributions to my knowledge of music and books. Eventually, he became absolutely essential to me making music at all, because he invited me to live with him in Madison, Virginia, at a time when I didn't really understand if I had any place to go in the world. And then, once there, he was just like, "Why don't you write music? Here's a four-track, and here's how it works." And he was in the first part of Palace Flophouse and was completely supportive and contributive.

Everything or most of what Steve does is fairly open to anybody, to participate in or observe. If you don't understand the process, you can ask him, and he'll answer you. And to continually be involved in, and to create for himself, projects that were important to me, to some of us, whether it's the recording of somebody else, or the way that Shellac [his band with Bob Weston and Todd Trainer] works, or the building of what's now Electrical [Albini's studio in Chicago], as well as the way that it's run . . . He's aggressively hands-off in terms of the music, and I think he's that way all the time with the music that he records. If you could see a thought balloon, his would read, "I'm doing my job, you do your job."

The drum machine is really integral to this record because of the neutrality of its sound; it's a constant, like a statue standing there no matter what the weather is.

That was neat, and it was the first time that I went into the recording studio with anybody where there was a known element. When I was writing the songs, I was talking to Britt [Walford], and he was apparently excited about the idea of making a record together. Then, as it got closer, he called and said, "I don't think I have anything to contribute," or something like that. And I was just like, "I can only disagree with you up to a point, because I can't keep fighting you." *Viva Last Blues* and *Arise Therefore* were both records that I talked to Britt about playing drums on, both of which he agreed to and then backed out of. Then I was trying to think of another drummer, couldn't, and once again turned to my younger brother for help, 'cause I knew he had this drum machine [Maya Tone]. I asked him if I could borrow it. But then I was like, "Well, if I'm gonna use this, I don't want to be sitting in the studio figuring out what sounds good, what beats sound good at what tempo." So that forced me to find a beat and a tempo for all of the songs, and whatever other variations there were on the Maya Tone, and then I recorded the songs like that and sent them to Ned and Dave. So we all knew what the chords, lyrics, and basic melodies would be, and we all knew exactly what the drums were gonna be like. But we didn't know what each of the three of *us* were gonna be doing in relation to each other and to that. But it was cool; we went into the studio and that's exactly what it was, the Maya Tone didn't change—she was amazing, completely consistent with her parts. And Steve had respect for her, and I knew if he ever wanted to raise an objection that I could say, "Dude, I learned it from you!" But he didn't; he liked it.

I wanted to work in that studio at Cannon Falls, Minnesota [Pachyderm Studios], 'cause Steve had made the Nirvana record [*In Utero*] and the PJ Harvey record [*Rid of Me*] there, and working with the drum machine with Steve, I felt like I was tapping into some of his collective history. He had used a drum machine, but at that point he was also known for having a discerning taste for drummers and drum sounds, more so than he had in 1987 when Big Black ended. In the time between, part of what he did was play with great drummers and create great drum sounds. On some level it was asking him to put that away.

A lot of the statements in that record are about the quality of being transient or being in transit: in "The Sun Highlights the Lack in Each" there's the line, "Condition is uncertain and unlikely to go," which resonates with the album's first line, "How could one ever think anything's permanent?" (in "Stablemate"). And then there's "She won't come, I'll be gone" in "You Have Cum in Your Hair and Your Dick Is Hanging Out," and "I am not fit and I am not willing to go on / I am here and I am not going to be there" in "The Weaker Soldier." In light of all this, it becomes even more interesting, even though it wasn't preconceived, that you used the drum box, which is a musical instrument that has no transient qualities at all. It's a fixed thing—if you turn it off and back on, it's going to be *exactly* the same—and the record seems to be about the impossibility of that elsewhere in life. Even having the finished record come out as satisfying as it did is a sort of a paradox,

**having made a fixed statement—a record—about the way that
things can never really be in stasis.**

That first line of "The Sun Highlights" came from a collection
of poetry; it might have been a Frank Stanford collection, actually, called *Things Uncertain and Likely to Pass Away* or something
like that [*Conditions Uncertain and Likely to Pass Away*, a posthu-
mous collection of short fiction published in 1991]. It's funny
'cause I remember Koretzky seeing some band in Chicago, and
I asked, "How was the show?" And he said, "It was pretty good,
but every song sounded like a rip-off of 'The Sun Highlights the
Lack in Each.'" And then a couple of years after that, maybe
when we were recording the Tortoise record,* I realized the
[song's] chord progression must have been an unconscious rip-
off of the Minutemen. It is very similar to the "It's Expected I'm
Gone" chord progression, so much so that sometimes when we
play that song now, we'll play it with D. Boon's guitar rhythm.

**A couple of the songs on *Hope* also take place in transit—
"Winter Lady" and "All Gone All Gone"—but it seems a little
lighter on *Hope*; on *Arise Therefore* you're exploring the impli-
cations of what that means in a much more serious way.**

Not only lighter, but in "All Gone" the implication is that things
are impermanent, but if you're willing to join the battle for,
against, and with impermanence, to join the singer, then *do*

---

* *The Brave and the Bold*, the 2006 album of covers BPB made in collaboration with Tortoise, contains a version of the Minutemen's "It's Expected
I'm Gone."

it, you know? Make a battalion out of us. Whereas the voice on *Arise Therefore* is recognizing an individuality about the trek through transient existence. It isn't necessarily something done with a constant companion.

It reminds me of that line I like in *Two-Lane Blacktop*, spoken by Warren Oates's character to the hippie wanderer played by Laurie Bird: "If I don't get grounded soon, I'm going to go into orbit."*
Yeah, yeah. And then it's like, "Well, maybe orbit's where we belong!" [*laughs*]

The title *Arise Therefore* came from some translation I had of the *Bhagavad Gita*. It was where the guy's about to go into battle and he starts praying and complaining to God, "I don't wanna kill people, I don't wanna go into battle." And God is like, "What's your problem? You think killing people is wrong or something? Just go do it. Go forward with your existence, go forward with your action, let me worry about judgment. Yours is the path of combat." I guess the idea being it's not really our freedom to choose our roles, in this life at least.

Is "The Weaker Soldier" related to this too?

* *Two-Lane Blacktop* is a laconic 1971 feature directed by Monte Hellman about a cross-country car race between a pair of nomadic young hot-rodders, played by James Taylor and Dennis Wilson, and an aging, equally itinerant muscle-car freak, played by Oates. A cult classic, WO and AL recorded a track for a tribute album to the film, *You Can Never Go Fast Enough*, released on the Plain label in 2003.

Sure. It was probably a state of mind that was open to martial concepts at that time.

Listening to "You Have Cum in Your Hair" again, the word "soft" in the line "It's so soft now underfoot" in the first verse stood out to me, just because you use the word "hard" so much in your songs [*laughs*].
"Hard" is a nice word to sing. Also, "You Have Cum in Your Hair" is one of those songs where the first verse and the chorus was written by Bryan Rich, and I wrote the second verse.

Was the title his or yours?
I asked him, "What's the song called?" And he was like, "I don't know. It doesn't have a title." When we were recording the song, Albini told a joke about the piano player in a restaurant who goes off and masturbates, and his boss screams at him, "Get the hell back out there, you got a job to do!" So he rushes back out, and someone comes up to him and says, "You know, you have cum in your hair and your dick is hanging out." And he says, "No, no, but if you hum a few bars I'm sure I could pick it up." So in the course of that joke there's a title without a song, and we had a song without a title. I just figured we'd put 'em together.

The cover is a drawing by Gene Booth.
Gene's drawing was done just for *Arise Therefore*. I asked him because [during the October/November 1995 tour he played on] he would draw very intense, detailed flyers for every show. He made them on the day of the show. He would make ten cop-

ies and put them up right before the show, but each one was so spectacularly different it was hard to believe that they could come day by day from the same pad.

You've also said that *Arise Therefore* was the start of a new cycle of making music.

Mm-hmm, 'cause that was the first time that it was like, "OK, the education period is kind of over now. Now it's *make songs and make records*." At that point, there had been enough shit thrown at the wall, and now was the time to see what stuck. It seemed like up to that point it was all, "What if we did this? And what if we did this?" Or, "Can a song work like this?" Or, "Can I play with these people or record in this situation or tour like this?" I always thought of those Palace recordings as like going to school, learning what all this stuff was, from the process of making a song to interacting with press, record companies, and audiences. That was the university I went to. Every step was full of fear and anxiety. Knowing I had to get by somehow was what got me through it. The alternative was much worse—doing nothing, rotting.

All of a sudden the lyrics started to actively mean more. Whereas with a song like "Blokbuster" where everything it meant to me is in code, all of a sudden the songs were in a different kind of code. I couldn't escape from it. With the *Arise* songs, every lyric meant something specific, so that was a weird position. When I listened to the record, it felt like a haunted kind of record. I didn't know what to think of it, except that I liked it. I also felt that the songs had value because they made me feel so uneasy.

According to Billions Corporation, via the Royal Stable website, the final Palace show was on December 29, 1995, at the 400 Club in Minneapolis.
That might have been a solo show.

So what was the final Palace show? Who knows?
I never cared, honestly, in terms of calling something something. I would decide when it was time to lay out the artwork, and I would find out when we got to the venues what the band was called. Whatever they put up on the flyer, that's what the band was called. So I never paid any attention to that. At that point, if it was booked as that and it was after *Arise Therefore* came out, then that's just because I'd rather go play a show than make an issue out of what the act is called. The Palace name was something for records, but it didn't make very much sense to transfer it to the live situation in the first place. Appearing under a moniker implies certain things that are not going to be realized.

Is this also the period when the lost album was recorded?
It would be. It was after *Arise Therefore*. Laurence [Bell] had introduced me to Mick Turner in London, at a pub, and we'd talked for a long time, and then talked about making a record of the Dirty Three* and me. We decided to do it. I think I moved to Louisville for a little while, sublet an apartment, and worked on songs. I had the songs ready but started to get nervous about

* Instrumental trio of Warren Ellis (violin), Mick Turner (guitar), and Jim White (drums) formed in Australia in 1992.

playing with guys I'd never played any music with. With each record, I would try to repeat the things that worked on the record before, usually with no success whatsoever. In this case, we were gonna make it with Albini at this Cotati, California, studio called Prairie Sun, and I was like, "Well, I'll ask Ned and Grubbs to come and play the session also. At least that way I'll be coming in with more confidence,"—'cause I'd never met [Dirty Three members] Jim [White] or Warren [Ellis], only Mick.

Had you heard their music?
Mm-hmm, through my brother Paul. He followed them from the *Sad and Dangerous* record on. Then a week before they were supposed to come, Warren's passport got lost or stolen—in Holland, I think—and he said, "I won't be there for the beginning of the session at least. I might not make it for the whole session." So then I thought, "Oh shit"—I couldn't reschedule the session at that point. But Colin [Gagon, keyboardist] was living in Marshall, California, and I thought maybe he could come in and somehow substitute the aural space that I'd somehow been imagining—Warren and the violin—with an accordion. And then I asked Tiffany White to come out also. I met her on a tour—she jumped in our van after we played in Memphis. She was wasted and had a cast, but Pooh [Johnston, guitarist on the November 1994 tour] always had a nylon-string guitar with him, so he started playing music and she started singing. It was really good. We recorded, and then Warren got there in time for the mix and was able to overdub a couple of parts. Because of all that I felt sort of disjointed and unfocused, but we mixed it, sequenced it, took it to

Chicago, and played it for Dan [Koretzky] and Rian [Murphy]. Dan was very enthusiastic about it, but by the time we finished listening to the record I started to have very strong reservations. Dan O. [Osborn, Drag City art director] and I started working on the artwork, and then after another week I was just feeling like, "This record is not a good record." So I bought it back from Drag City, who paid for the recording.

Did it have a working title?
Yep, *Guarapero.* Two songs came out on a Spanish EP [*Western Music*], two songs came out on a 7" on Howard [Greynolds]'s label [All City], but that was under the name Bonnie Prince Billy ["Black Dissimulation" / "No Such as What I Want"], two songs came out on [singles etc. compilation] *Guarapero / Lost Blues 2* ["Sugarcane Juice Drinker," "Call Me a Liar"], and the rest of the songs got rewritten for *Joya.* But that was a pretty depressing year, having spent a long time preparing for a session and then not having a record to show for it. I still wanted to put one out, and that's when we put *Lost Blues* [singles etc. compilation] out.

I was interested in the cover design of *Lost Blues*—the black block on the cover and the elephants in the gatefold.
One of my two songs on the Box of Chocolates album* was

---

* WO: "After I left [the DUMBO loft], Mike Howe's grandmother died and left him some thousands of dollars inheritance, and he decided to make a record. He wanted to make the record of his songs, Bryan's songs, and my songs, and that was Box of Chocolates." [*Fearful Symmetry* LP, released 1990]

called "The Ephant" and was based on . . . My mom and I, when we went to New Delhi, we went to an Indian astrologer, who read our charts and told us what we were in our past lives. In my past life, he said, I'd been an elephant, and the life before *that* I was a bug who lived on a rock, and if I was *good* in this life, I would be a woman born into a wealthy Western family, and if I was *bad* I would be an elephant again! And my mom's mom went traveling at some point and brought back a batik thing that had these elephants on it. For a while, when I was traveling, I kept that with me to wrap around me when- ever I was sleeping on the couch or on someone's floor. That's what that was, a close-up of that sheet. And also, to sort of hark back to the "Ohio River Boat Song" artwork, it used the same color scheme and there was a Paul Greenlaw elephant drawing on that. So these elephants were going back to that. That record is, in part, dedicated to Paul Greenlaw, but it just says "P.G."—which someone told me they thought was Pussy Galore, but it wasn't.*

The font [on the front cover] was the same as on Madon- na's *Bedtime Stories,* and the block was supposed to be sort of Rothko-esque.

It sort of reflects the listing of the contributors on the back, where "writers/players/recorders" is presented as a block of names rather than sorting out who did what where.

---

* Greenlaw also did the cover art for, and played banjo on, *There Is No One What Will Take Care of You.*

Still, at that point, because every endeavor was such a commu-
nal effort in so many ways, I didn't like the idea of saying, "Jason
Stith played bass." Jason Stith played bass, but also, if he weren't
there, the whole thing would sound different. Not just because
of the music, but because the music was created by everybody
who was around doing things, and the confidence or lack of
confidence or the aesthetic or lack of aesthetic that people gave
each other . . . all those things.

You were trying to credit presence as much as anything else.
Yeah. And I didn't like how the public would always call them
"engineer" or "producer." It's not the case; the producer kind
of *is* that group thing. People would think of the engineer as
being different from the musicians, but at all these sessions the
engineer *wasn't* different; he was an equal part of the whole
thing. I can see where it would make sense, because oftentimes
an engineer is an engineer, but on *these* records an engineer
wasn't an engineer and a musician wasn't a musician.

What is the writing of a song? Well, at the end of the day, the
writing of a song is a formality that has to do with the music
business, and there are mechanical royalties and all that shit.
It's just this *political formality*—that people are record producers,
and they get this title, "record producer," even though it is all
different things. But that's why everyone was grouped together
that way, 'cause at the time I was still trying to wrap my head
around, *How do people decide how to credit records?* I guess I think
of making records as like making movies, and if that's the case,
then the producer is like the movie producer, who I feel in some

ways is like the real author of most movies—as opposed to the director, like many people say. And in that way, I would have to take credit for being the producer of these records, because I make them up and bring them to life, or whatever.

Tell me about *Joya*, the only full-length album, up until that time [1997], credited to Will Oldham.
For some reason, I had the chance to house-sit my older brother's house [in Birmingham, Alabama]. I asked Dave [Pajo] to come down. We were gonna make this record, and we made a valiant attempt, but after a couple of days I said, "This is going nowhere, it's not gonna work." I called Dan: "This isn't working. I think that's it, I don't know how to move forward with making records or making music or anything like that. Let's say the day is done, that's it." He was like, "*Really?*" I was very happy, just felt such relief thinking I never had to make music again. But then he was like, "What would it take, blah blah blah," and I said, "If there was somebody else, like an old-school producer, somebody, to be a guiding hand . . . I could imagine doing it. But I just don't have the energy to think about everything." So then we hatched the plan that Dan and Rian would produce the record, in Chicago. We'd record at CRC. Steve [Albini] used to work there, and *Spiderland* was recorded there by Brian Paulson. So I thought that that could be an interesting way to work. Dan got the Fourth of July weekend and was able to bargain down for rates. We reserved for five days, and I called Bob [Arellano] and Colin, asking them if they wanted to come to Chicago and make a record. [When

I was at Brown University in 1988] I met Bob and Colin right away, lived on the same hall with them. Bob was a year ahead of me and he was the counselor on our hallway. Then he graduated from Brown, went to graduate school at Brown, and became an adjunct professor there, working under [novelist] Robert Coover, who was the senior in his department, one of his principal colleagues.

Were Bob and Colin playing music when you knew them at Brown?
Yep. They might have played a little bit together. I think there was actually a month or so when we played music together. We were called Robert and the Country Priests, and it was all covers. It was Colin on accordion, Bob on guitar, and me just singing. I think we played on the street a couple of times, or in our apartment; didn't have a show or anything.

So, at the *Joya* session, I would be in the vocal booth, Dave playing drums, Colin playing bass, Bob playing guitar. Everybody had song sheets, some of which had chords on 'em, but most didn't, and I would be in the vocal booth, saying, "OK, here's the next song. It goes like this: these chords, these chords, then it repeats, this bridge, and then it's over. All right, everybody got that?"

"Uh, I guess so."

"OK, record."

We'd record, and if we made it all the way through the song, then I would say, "OK, next song. This is how it goes!" Nobody had ever heard any of the songs before. When there was a mistake, I would get my Roland XP-50 keyboard out. I found a string pad, and if there was a really glaring mistake that somebody made I would just hit that chord, as a kind of Band-Aid. So there's two or three points on the record where there's a string part that comes in for three or four seconds that's not on any other part of the song. We tracked for two days and mixed the third day. And then we'd only used three of the five days, so Dan had to fight with them again about not paying for the fourth and fifth days.

Was the title *Joya* a sort of play on the Minutemen's *Joy* EP?
Yeah, but it wasn't an EP, it was a full-length, so I added a letter, and a lot of the songs are in A, so it was the letter "a." Right after that, Bob and I went to Mexico; he'd gone down there a couple of times and done ceremonial peyote eating in a town outside of a town called Real de Catorce. We flew into Monterrey, and as soon as we got there we found there was a popular Mexican soft drink called Joya. So we went to the Joya factory and got key chains and T-shirts and things like that, which was pretty exciting.

The cover of that record is a picture of a goat named Chevre who had been Bryan Rich's pet in Burundi. He'd sent me that picture, and when I was in Burundi we ate the goat. Bryan had the man who guarded his house and made his food slaughter the goat. It was a gold-colored CD because I was a big fan of the Smithsonian Folkways Indonesian series, and the first few were made on these gold-colored CDs. I asked Drag City to find out who manufactured those, and we did that for the *Joya* CDs.

The first song on the album is "O Let It Be," and then there was the Madonna song, "Let It Will Be."
Which came later, much later. It's just a funny coincidence, 'cause I had taken one of her songs, "Open Your Heart," or just the title, took a couple of lyrics. And on that *Joya* record there's the song "O Let It Be," and then she made the song "Let It Will Be," in which she also says, [Madonna lyrics excised here due to copyright] to the same chord progression of "O Let It Be."

"The Gator," "Rider," and "Apocalypse No!" are probably your most opaque songs.
Huh. For singing, I find them extremely vivid, visual. That's interesting [*laughs*].

I don't mean opaque literally, but narratively they seem the most abstract.
I think of "The Gator" as being very much like Maurice Sendak's *In the Night Kitchen*. It's a picture book, sort of a large-format picture book, about a guy, if I remember right, who gets rolled up in bread dough or cookie dough. He makes a suit and then a plane out of the dough, and flies it into a night kitchen. The kitchen is occupied by three men who all look like Oliver Hardy, but they're wearing chef's outfits, and like the Wild Things in [Sendak's book] *Where the Wild Things Are* they seem to be sort of strangely positive/negative, semiadult, crazy forces in the story. The Gator was like a Peter Pan to a Wendy, or a Tinker Bell to a Peter Pan; it's a fierce animal that is the animal soul of the boy described in the song, which allows the demon

of the protagonist to fly through the world at night and trumpet others' trumpets or trumpet on his hollowed bone.

"Apocalypse No!" began as a single line that [Silver Jews'] David Berman had written on the wall of our house in Charlottesville, when we were supposed to be making a Silver Palace record. I carried it on from there, imagining it—which I still do, every time I'm singing it—as the narrative of a complex male friendship, and a specific moment in that friendship that seems like it's potentially cataclysmic but in the end isn't. It's either something that was just another event in the course of the relationship or an event that helps the characters recognize the strength of their bond.

And "Rider" is almost like a two-and-a-half-minute version of the King Kong record *The Big Bang* [1995], which is a concept record that's supposed to be about outer space, but at the end you realize it's about sperm being ejaculated and finding its way to its destination. "Rider"'s sort of like the reverse, somewhere between *2001* and *Deep Throat*. Someone once made a really beautiful poster that incorporated all the lyrics to that song, and when we played with the Picket Line,* it was a song that Oscar [Parsons] particularly was very firm about wanting to play. Seems like people have found a connection to it, and I don't know if it's the science-fiction aspect or the sensual aspect of it, or the combination, or just that it's got two parts in three minutes . . . but I love it.

---

* Louisville-based band that BPB has performed with both live and on record (*Funtown Comedown*, 2009).

Being able to make a song under three minutes, or even under two minutes, and still have it really go somewhere is pretty exciting. In the music of the Minutemen, there was something so empowering about the short songs they had engaged in up to *Project Mersh* and *3-Way Tie (for Last)*, and then they started to stretch the songs out. But I know as a listener sometimes you like a longer song, you know? When a song is really, really great, sometimes you feel, "I need it to be longer. I need it to be four minutes, I need it to be six minutes, I need it to be twelve minutes. Yes, yes, this is where I need to be right now." It was only when we used to make mix cassettes that the value of a great short song had practical value as well, because you could always put it at the end of one side of the tape.

Of course, in the age of AM radio everything had to be under three minutes, or two minutes thirty seconds, so people were writing everything to be that length. It's something I still think about if I'm listening to a song and the vocal doesn't come in until after a minute has already elapsed; I'll think about all the songs that are halfway over at that point, whereas this one has barely even started.

Right, yeah. Or thinking that those format prohibitions and the limitations of side lengths on 78s etc. probably distorted the views of so many budding songwriters into thinking that the natural length of a song was three minutes or under, when even the performers who were recording on 78s were probably doing four-minute, seven-minute versions of the songs that we hear as these three-minute versions.

That's something that happened with Indian ragas: in their natural form they usually last about seventy-five to ninety minutes, and we're used to them being twenty-minute album sides, which is a condensed version of what they would ordinarily be. Or the songs of Oum Kalsoum, who was Egypt's most popular singer for most of the twentieth century. Her early recordings, from the 1920s and 1930s especially, were all five, six, seven minutes, and those were all songs that live would run between thirty and fifty minutes.

5

THE ALTER EGO

ALAN LICHT: Given your involvement with film and with song-writing, are there movies that you feel made good use of songs?

WILL OLDHAM: There was one year where I didn't watch any movies that I hadn't seen before, with a couple of exceptions: if I was on a plane, and also if it was gonna be my only opportunity to see, you know, whatever Scorsese movie, whatever Bertolucci movie came out that year on the big screen. I remember after that year was up—it was a New Year's resolution—the first movie I went to see was *Proof of Life*, with Meg Ryan and Russell Crowe, and it had a score that was really exciting, which I loved (the fact that it *had* a score, not the score itself). It was sort of an action-adventure espionage movie, but it didn't seem to have a music supervisor; it seemed like they hired someone to write a score for the movie, and I was really psyched to not be listening to all these songs. The end credits had a Van Morrison song called "I'll Be Your Lover Too," and I thought, "That's cool." The director, Taylor Hackford, I think that was his choice. I think he's a music guy, but it was neat because there were *no* songs with words, and then *one* song with words. It felt like this song was here for a reason, and the reason could be traced back; you could probably ask somebody why, and they could say it's here because of *this*, and I liked that.

Was it *There's Something about Mary* that had nothing but Jonathan Richman songs in it? I like him a lot, and while those weren't my favorite Jonathan Richman songs, I liked that whole idea of

132 OLDHAM ON BONNIE "PRINCE" BILLY

lacing one voice throughout the whole movie and having it be a conscious decision made somewhere during writing and prepro-duction, and not during postproduction. "This is the voice that we wanna have, and this is how we want songs to work with this movie." That's all I ask for, that a little bit of time and respect be given to the musical part of filmmaking. Someone wrote to me and said, "We wanna use your songs in our movie, and we've already got this artist, this artist, this artist, this artist." And I was thinking, "Well, that makes for no integrity to your movie. All these different voices combined with the actors', writer's, direc-tor's, and director of photography's voices. That sounds like the worst place to be. That sounds like a music festival."

You generally haven't allowed your songs to be licensed for films.

I've never been into the idea of taking a song that belongs in one place and putting it into a totally foreign, totally different context. People are constantly contacting me saying, "I've been editing my movie, and I've been using your song in the editing process. What would it take to license the song?" And for me it's like, "Regardless of what you've been doing, my song doesn't belong in your movie." That's where the conversation should end. Music should be made for movies. My rule was that no songs were available for license, unless they were used diegeti-cally. Some French movie [*Quelque chose d'organique*] wanted to use "Blokbuster," and they said, "Well, this is [diegetic]. You're gonna see them put the record on, and they're gonna be listening to it during this scene, and then we'll put it on the soundtrack." And I told them, "No, you can't put it on the soundtrack, it's on a record already. What's the point of that?" So then I wrote a song for the soundtrack ["What's Wrong with a Zoo?"] that's not in the movie, which I've never seen.

David Gordon Green contacted me and wanted to use "Careless Love" from *Ease Down the Road* in an opening sequence [of *All the Real Girls* (2003)]. I said, "The song's not available for license; if you're interested, I could submit a song"; I was trying to send him something that I felt was tonally related to the song that he wanted to use. I submitted "All These Vicious Dogs," and he was really psyched; he said it fit really well, even certain lyrics fit what he had in the picture. For *Wendy and Lucy* [2008], Michelle [Williams, actress] said that Kelly [Reichardt, director] told her she had to hum and whistle some stuff, and she asked if I would give her melodies. I was working on the *Lie Down in the Light* songs, so I sent her melodies I was working on for the song "Lie Down in the Light." Then Kelly asked if I would make a somewhat non-organic-sounding rendition of that melody for the end credits. I liked it, and hearing that music come in was one of my favorite parts of the movie, because it reminded me of an educational film that you'd watch in middle school that always had an emotional impact even though it felt very sterile. I felt like that was accomplished with that piece of music. It made me proud.

Kelly Reichardt had previously asked you to do an instrumental score for her short film, *Ode* [1999], inspired by the song "Ode to Billie Joe" and shot on Super 8.

Working with a boss, with Kelly, was nice, and a nice experience of making a record with my brother Paul, just he and I.
There wasn't a lot to be talked about. Kelly would say, "Here's
this scene, here's the set music I used for it and why I used that,"
and then I figured she knew why she was asking me to do it. We
both knew time and money were issues, in terms of the lack of
both. There was no miscommunication—it was a good job. It
was liberating, because you always imagine other sides of the
argument when you're making a record, and in this case the
imagination didn't have to be used as much, because the other
side of the argument was right there speaking to you. And that's
good because instead of thinking, "Either this is wrong with
the song, this is wrong with the song, or this is wrong with the
song," you have the song and the person sitting right there, and
they say, "*This* is wrong with the song." And it's good because
you can concentrate and move through it quicker as well. It's
more focused.

**When you released the soundtrack as *Ode Music* [in 2000] you
called it "silent music."**
Which came from either reading or watching a documentary
about Oum Kalsoum, in which it's declared that instrumental
music in the Arabic tradition is called silent music.

I got a lot of requests from people over the years to use *Ode
Music* in their movie, and I'd just go . . . [*rolls eyes*]. This guy
[Jason Massot] made a documentary [*Seafarers*] following these
four different merchant-marine guys from four different coun-
tries who were all in the port of Rotterdam, which is one of the

biggest commercial seaports in the world. He wanted to use *Ode Music*, and I said, "I really can't, but would you have the time or the inclination to let me try to make music for this instead?" So I recorded that right after recording *Master and Everyone*, with Paul and Dave Bird.*

It sounds similar to *Ode Music*.

Yeah, and again, he knew what he wanted, and I didn't want to be like, "No, that's wrong." I wanted to give him something that was related to what he wanted, and I loved making the *Ode Music* record with Paul, so this was trying to do it in the same way, with some new elements.

You've said it's influenced by Mick Turner.

Yeah, we did those records like Mick Turner performances. We used loops that were created at the beginning of the song and made during the course of the making of the song. A nice thing about using the Boomerang [looping pedal] is also that you can overdub onto it.

Along with Mick and Jim White, you were part of the Boxhead Ensemble for the 1997 *Dutch Harbor* tour. Was that tour about making a live soundtrack to the film [*Dutch Harbor*, a documentary about the titular Alaskan port by Braden King and Laura Moya]?

---

* Bird was a founding member of the 1990s Louisville band Out, and later played guitar in Speed to Roam with Paul Oldham.

It was different on different nights, depending on the restrictions of the venue. Sometimes it would be done as a live soundtrack to the movie; sometimes it would be done before the movie and then they'd show the movie, or vice versa; sometimes they would show some footage from the movie over the music but then also show the movie afterwards or before—every night was different all around. That was one of the most, if not *the* most, relaxed and free and fun musical experiences and/or tours I'd had up until that point. [David] Grubbs was on it for a while, Rick Rizzo was on it for a day or two, and Mick and Jim [White] were on it the whole time I was on it.[*] It was great being with Mick and Jim; they were the first people, not counting Drag City people, I'd met since starting to make records that I felt were real friends. I met a lot of people that I loved and worked with and liked, but mostly I hadn't met anybody that I felt a connection to like I did before I started to make records. Mick and I would stay up all night in the room talking. I don't know if you ever engage with Jim in musical discussion, but he's fun to talk to about song and show structure. There are very few people I could talk about music with in the way I enjoy talking about it with Jim. And also [in the *Dutch Harbor* tour] it was nice to play music and feel a *part* of something, instead of feeling *responsible* for something. That was really a wonderful, wonderful experience.

---

[*] Guitarist Rizzo formed Eleventh Dream Day in mid-1980s Chicago with drummer Janet Beveridge Bean (a Louisville native). Since then, the band has revolved around a core trio of Rizzo, Bean, and bassist Doug McCombs (also a founding member of Tortoise).

It was pretty improvisational. Michael Krassner was the musical director, so the first night he might say, "OK, Fred Lonberg-Holm, Jim White, and Scott Tuma, you go up and do three pieces, and on the third piece I would like you, Grubbs, to go up."* He would do the whole thing like that, and the next night he might get more specific and say, "OK, remember in that second piece, that part where you all did it like this? Do *that* again, but this time I want this *other* person to join you and be part of that." And that was how it was organized.

One of the things I was fascinated by in the solo shows you did on the tour with Run On [in 1997] was the attention you gave to each individual show. You were playing with a backing tape, and it was the same set every night. The first show of the tour was at Lounge Ax, where you were wearing a black T-shirt, not playing guitar . . .
I think I played guitar for most of the set except the last song, "Stable Will," and then I took off the guitar and danced around.

I felt like that was more true as the tour went on, although I could be remembering it wrong . . .
[*laughs*] Me too, me too.

. . . but I really remember there being no guitar, and then the guitar being used more and more as the tour went on. And

---

* Lonberg-Holm is a Chicago-based cellist; Tuma is the leader of shadowy Chicago band Souled American.

then it became less physical, too, and there was a different outfit for every night. In Lexington you were wearing an engineer's cap, pulled way down, and in Louisville you were wearing a white dress shirt. Were there other tours where you took such a specific approach to each show?

I feel like on most tours that's the idea, that each place is gonna be a different thing. It's more essential in playing alone, and there's more leeway, but the place is always part of the show. If there are less people onstage, then it's a bigger proportion of the show. I like being able to have a memory of a show based, always, on why that show was not like the show before or the show after. And usually it's down to everything—the audience and the sound, and who else is playing on the bill.

In retrospect, it seems like with the Palace records there was a reluctance to commit to a single name because an identity was still being formed. On *Arise Therefore* there was no artist credit, and the following record was credited to Will Oldham, which both implied a transitional stage. But once the credit settled on "Bonnie Prince Billy" it seemed like the singing voice had stabilized as well.

Those two records were beginning to show, to myself and whoever was listening, that an identity was a default way of thinking, both for the singer and for the audience, but that they were different and that was problematic, it was an unexpected dilemma. It was like, "Well, I still wanna make records, but I don't know how to deal with this thing."

With *Viva Last Blues*, at the time that seemed like a supreme achievement. It took so much work to get the different kinds of people there, and it was such an incredible group of people. From then on it was imagining that the records were going to be experiments too. The 7"s were experiments, but I tried to be more confident about the records—like, "I like all this Palace music so I don't want to tarnish it. I wanna leave it to be what it is and I'll make other things. If I fuck up with the other things I don't want people to be [like], 'Oh, that's that shit' " [*laughs*]. So yeah, made a record with no name, and then with the next one I thought, "Still wanna make a record, don't know what to name it." But it's the music business—you make a record to put in the store that people can buy, and stores need classifications. They need an artist name, they need a record title. And I wanna make records. I liked that we were able to make *Arise Therefore* with no name on there, but I figured that there would be limitations in asking the system to go along with you and understand. You don't want it to be a task for someone to sell your record; ideally it's inspiring. So maybe it's not 100 percent straightforward, but at the end of the day you want them to make money, 'cause you want them to want to have your record listened to by people. You don't want them to be like, "You know what, I don't want to deal with this shit. Fuck it." So then it's, "OK, rather than come up with another stupid name I'll just use my own stupid name." And then a year later it's, "Ah, you know there's a way of dealing with this problem and making it productive and not a handicap." From then on it was exciting to understand that it was OK, that the lyric-writing could be like each individual movie or song world, but they could be interrelated as well;

that you were always entering a place where the rules and the reality were in flux. And there *was* a thread, in that I was a common factor, but it didn't have to be an "I" that I knew; it could be an "I" that was changing. Or that wasn't changing, that I was learning more about.

It sort of gave a name to that situation, which was one that you had maybe wanted all along.
No. All along I *didn't* want it. All along I was resisting 'cause I was thinking about records like movies, and I wanted people to approach each record as if it were its own world and *not* have to deal with an artist's name. "I like this record that's called this, and these are the songs in it, and this is what happens."

That someone would have to go back and figure out that this is the same person that made all the records, like you would with a series of movies?
Yeah, that you might *eventually* do with a series of movies. Or not—have it not be important. Like right now we could probably come up with a movie and say, "Oh yeah, who *was* that actor? I don't know. I loved that movie, I watched it six times. I know some of the dialogue in it. I didn't realize that actor was in other movies." But again, that doesn't go with selling records. An undercurrent of all of it is coming to the gradual understanding that almost everybody whose work we know and love in music and in movies was participant in the process of buying and selling. That's kind of exciting, that every piece of media that we absorb with affection and love and adoration is related

to the survival of the people who made it. And it's a fun system to participate in, because you can let the weird rules that you create within the world of a record bleed out into the process of making and selling it as well, which is really exciting. But it means that you have to accept that that system is there, and that you participate in it.

But not too many people take advantage of that possibility.
Not too many people take advantage of it because one of the sometimes stated and sometimes understood goals of the system of making records and movies is making the process, or some aspects of the process, invisible. Even when I get joy out of watching a movie, and out of seeing how it's made, I'm still pretending that there weren't executive producers. I'm watching everybody in production; I'm not watching executive producers on the movie, I'm not watching the distributors and the theater-owners and the advertising and marketing department—that's supposed to be invisible. As the audience, especially as kids, we assume that none of that even exists. And if it *does* exist, that it is always a force that is in conflict with the product, with the end thing . . . Never imagining that it's a positive or cooperative or collaborative or *good* symbiotic relationship; you just assume that they're different things, and realizing that they aren't necessarily or don't have to be different is fun.

Making records is commerce, and it's about fooling yourself as a writer and a performer and fooling the audience into not thinking about it and accepting it. It's like when you walk down the street and say, "Look at that girl's ass, it's so great." You're ignoring also the fact that she farts shit out of that ass. It's the same kind of thing.

The "Bonnie Prince Billy" name was conceived on the flight home from a January 1998 Australian tour you did with Liam Hayes, Mick, and Jim. You've said that name is like Nat King Cole or Bonnie Prince Charlie . . . and even driving around in Louisville, I keep seeing "Bonny" this and that.
Yeah, there's a neighborhood called Bonnycastle, there's Bonneville, things like that . . . At the time, that's what I thought of. The obvious thing, which I know that I knew, didn't even occur to me, which is that Billy Bonney was Billy the Kid.

Your publishing company is Royal Stable, so "Prince" . . .
Yeah, it fit. It was a very practical thing. I was overjoyed because it sounded nice and also had a relationship to what had come before. Bonnie Prince Billy is such a ridiculous name. It had no preconceptions to it; nobody could say what the music was going to be like on hearing the name. But it turned the music into an individual, which seemed to be what everyone—the audience, or at least the people that I was forced to talk to about the music—was seeking. They were seeking some sort of individual responsible for things, and I was just like, "OK. We'll make one up. One who doesn't really exist, and therefore I can continue to feel confident that there *is* no individual responsible for things, but *you* can think that there *is* one!" [*laughs*] The alter ego is somebody that has no background, has no childhood,

has no real existence. Will Oldham has a private life, and Bonnie Prince Billy doesn't. Bonnie doesn't have bodily functions that leave stains. There are different kinds of tours and different kinds of performances, but for the most part, since Bonnie came around, the idea is that they're reentering the same basic character space of somebody who is also aging and maturing but in a nonhuman way. Once you get in a groove on a tour that works, it's like, "OK, gotta fill the van up with gas, make sure everyone has eaten, check into the motel"; once you've done that a few days in a row, it becomes second nature and you can just be the imaginary person.

The thing about Bonnie Prince Billy is I wanted to perform with other people and play to people, but if I do a Palace Music show or whatever there's gonna be a scene, or expectations, and that means our freedom to experiment during the course of the set is gonna be limited. So I think the first actual Bonnie Prince Billy sets were with Britt [Walford], and they were at some Lower East Side bar that might have just existed for six months or a year. We played improvisational sets, doing keyboards and vocal loops, and it was billed as Bonnie Prince Billy and the Sheik; he was the Sheik. I was thinking, "We could play as Bonnie Prince Billy, and no one will come, 'cause he doesn't exist yet." Also, if I wanted to play a hundred shows a year and I wanted to sing the same song at every show . . . a hundred times a year, singing the same song, how else can I honestly occupy the song, unless there's some other way, some other interface that can honestly occupy the song at every performance? Because there's no way an individual can, without remaining static in their development and their emotions. And that definitely shouldn't be part of the equation.

In general, with all due respect to all the stuff that happened before, from the beginning of the Bonnie Prince Billy "moment" I think everything got a little more interesting and better. All the recording, the touring, the singing, the songwriting—*everything* got better from then on. *I* think [*laughs*].

The March 1998 tour of Italy with Bryan Rich, was that under the Bonnie Prince Billy name?

First tour under that name. I was Bonnie Prince Billy and he was "Toro D'Oro." And it was amazing because I'd studied Italian and my mom's side had Italian heritage and I'd been to Italy, but I could never get a show there. I ran through a number of European booking agents over the first decade of playing shows; everyone would say, "You can't get a show in Italy. The Italians can't be depended upon, there's no venues, there's no organization, blah blah blah." Then Giovanna and Agostino from Uzeda* contacted me and said, "Why don't you come and play a tour in Italy? We could put together fourteen shows." And then I threw them the curve ball and said they had to be Bonnie Prince Billy shows, and they said, "No problem." And just crisscrossing the country, going to all these places that we haven't been able to get a show at since . . . We might play a tiny town with a room as big as these two rooms [in his house], and it's slam packed with

---

* Sicilian "math rock" band in existence since 1987, with several albums to their credit on Touch and Go.

a hundred people, or we might play a slightly larger town, in a room with 600 capacity, and there might be twelve people there. Every day we had no idea who we were going to be playing to or what kind of places we were going to play—big city or small town. Now, when we go overseas, Italy is the place that I feel most at home, because of the quality of the people that we work with over there, as people and promoters, and as musicians.

And the next year was Lucky Prince Bonnie's Summer Tour, with Bob Arellano, Colin Gagon, Mike Fellows, and Joe Propatier.

That was kind of the first Bonnie Prince Billy tour really. I feel like it was the first tour of the tours that I do now, where I was just starting to realize that we could make all the rules we wanted to make and tour how we wanted to tour. It just meant that every step of the way we were doing what we wanted to do. No more having to tour the way other people tour, or attempting to pretend to do that. The beginning of the tour was with Quix*o*tic; the end had the Anomoanon. Bob made a great short movie, *Bonnie vs. Boredoms*, about that, five or ten minutes long. He shot it all with a Bolex, black and white, without sound, and he put sound over it. At one point we played the This Ain't No Picnic festival, and the Boredoms were there. Bob tries to build this pretend narrative that it's Bonnie versus Boredoms, but it's him coming from experimental film.

In the US, essentially I like playing from Florida, across the south and up to Oregon. There's the odd place, like Missoula or Charlottesville, that I like playing, but otherwise I don't like playing the rest of the US, and that was the beginning of under-standing that that's what I liked. The first tour with rainYwood [2002], that was the full evolution of this great new style of tour-ing. rainYwood has sort of morphed into Brightblack Morning Light; it was Naybob and Raybob and P-bob, and Jody Jean Marsten, who is now Bob Arellano's wife. P-bob now has his own music project, and Naybob and Raybob have Brightblack Morn-ing Light. I think they suggested that we do a tour together, an intensive West Coast tour. We played so many great places. It was like that Italy tour except with a great band. We did a normal-length tour of three or four weeks, but hit three states. And we did that by playing all over the place in those three states, which was really cool. We camped out after the shows instead of getting hotels or motels, easily three out of four nights, and we had two or three surfboards in our van because Rob [Kieswetter]'s* a great surfer, Sara [DeVincentis, actress/singer] is a surfer, Aram [Stith, guitarist] is a surfer, and I like to surf, so we'd try to camp near the water as much as possible. I know we did a Sade song and a Dolly Parton song—

An Aretha Franklin song . . .
Oh yeah—"Sunshine," which is a song that was written by King Curtis that Cynthia Kirkwood had given me on a mix tape.

The Mountains and Deserts tour was our second annual trip like that. We'd done the West Coast, and we basically moved

---

* Kieswetter (aka Bobby Birdman) is a solo artist and member of the Cali-fornia band Little Wings.

one set of states over for this one. And then the next one [Pebbles & Ripples], instead of moving another set of states over into the dreaded Midwest, we went to the Southeast. Each time we picked up exactly where we left off the time before: we ended the West Coast tour the year before in Solana Beach; we began this one in San Diego, which is the next city down. [On the 2002 tour] we had to return the van and the equipment; Rob Kieswetter was from Nevada City, and he and Colin and I went to return the equipment, while everyone else flew home at the end of the tour. And Rob was like, "Why don't we play a show in Nevada City?" So Colin, Rob, and I played a show in Nevada City, and Joanna [Newsom] was there and gave him [Rob] her demo, her early recordings, to give to me. At the beginning of that tour I heard Faun Fables for the first time too. We played in Seattle and were staying in this guy's backyard, and before bed we were hanging out in his living room, and he put this music on. So on the Mountains and Deserts tour, Dawn [McCarthy, of Faun Fables] and Joanna played a bunch of shows with us, which was very exciting. Joanna played her shows solo, but Noah [Georgeson, her then boyfriend] was with her, and they traveled in another vehicle. Dawn played her shows solo and traveled in our van with us. Another part of a tour is whom you're traveling with, 'cause in the end you come away with having spent all this time with these other musicians and having seen their set every night—it's inextricable. Once I realized that, it was like, "OK, I just have to plan for that and always be traveling with people that I want to be around twenty-four hours a day, for better or for worse, for that period of time."

I bought uniforms for everybody on these tours, so everybody had black overalls for this one, tan overalls for the first one, and striped railroad overalls for the third one. And everyone wore 'em religiously. I just bought them as a gift, at the beginning of the tour, but everyone put 'em on before every show.

Did you go camping as a kid?
We had a neighbor who lived behind us, and his parents found out about this camp in Indiana, and they were like, "Chris is gonna go. Do you wanna go?" I'd been to a couple of camps and hated them, but this one sounded interesting and I liked Chris. The first half of the summer was boys' session, the second half was girls'. And the middle of it was a coed session, a ten-day trip where you showed up at camp, hung out for a day and night, and then the next night everyone would pile into this bus called the Big Brown Turd and go somewhere on a hiking and rafting trip, boys and girls. It was another nice mix of people, half campers, half counselors—all crazy Hoosier teens. The third year I went it was an epic journey to Colorado, and we hiked in the San Juan Mountains. I learned about the Grateful Dead and Neil Young and John Cougar, which were things that nobody I knew listened to, but they would sing "Cortez the Killer" around the campfire and play "Casey Jones" and things like that on the epic bus rides. And Violent Femmes. So that was the first time I'd heard any of that stuff. I mean, I'd heard John Cougar on the radio, but *they* knew every song on every record up to that point, which was *Uh-Huh*. And we listened to [Neil Young's] *Live Rust* a lot. It was the first time I started to understand that other people *lived* outside of Louisville and had well-rounded existences!

After *Matewan*, it was decided that my mom and I would go on a trip, and I wanted to go to India. My mom and I traveled around Delhi, then we went to Kashmir, and then I hooked up with a group of people to go on a trekking trip in Ladakh. So I was by myself, with a group of ten Americans, hiking through the Himalayas for a couple of weeks, camping out, going to monasteries and villages—all on foot, no roads or anything—eating food prepared by Sherpas; mostly vegetarian stuff, but if we wandered by some people's house that had a goat, we might buy it, the guys would slaughter it, and we'd eat it.

Being in India for twenty-four hours sort of rewired me forever. I was very excited to go there—because of music, mostly. My little teenage brain was not prepared for what it meant to be there, and it was like sink or swim. I had kind of a meltdown in the first thirty-six hours where I just couldn't function. It was sort of like being razed, having my consciousness destroyed, but then being like, "Oh, wait, here's a piece of it, here's a piece of it," over the course of the next day. "OK, we can do this. It's different, but we can *do* this." And then coming back here [to Louisville], and realizing how that rebuilding had affected my brain and that all of a sudden this became a place among many places. Eventually I grew back to learning that it was home, but it was also very foreign to me for a long time.

I See a Darkness was the first Bonnie full-length, recorded by your brother Paul, played by Bob, Colin, Paul, and Pete Townsend. Did it seem at all like a second debut album?

With *I See a Darkness* and the singles that were recorded then ["I Am Drinking Again," "One with the Birds"] we were mapping Bonnie's genetic code. Once that was done he could live, like a monster . . . a second birth—or the nurture side of the identity argument. That was also the time when we decided to split off from Drag City and form an independent record company, Palace Records. We had already done Palace records and 7"s by other people. The [Anomoanon's] *Mother Goose* record was probably on Palace through Drag City.

It was pretty much written and recorded at this farmhouse out in Shelbyville [Kentucky] that my dad had. It was right at a time when I felt like I needed some place to live, so I thought, "Oh, that's great, I'm gonna move there." And Paul finished engineering school right then, and he was like, "I need somewhere to live too," so we lived there together that year and recorded it there.

On this record and *Ease Down the Road* you use the word "fuck" less in talking about sex, or otherwise, which was an interesting development, because "fuck" was really striking in the earlier material and then it disappeared, sort of in conjunction with the other ways in which the overall work was developing. Was that a conscious shift?

There was a conscious shift in terms of understanding that there was now Bonnie to sing through, and there was a conscious shift to try to write songs with bridges in them, embracing the bridge and the chorus instead of avoiding them; and in terms of understanding that I could be free to write in the first person by becoming disembodied and writing from this other first person that *did* exist, but only in the abstract. So maybe if there was still any sort of violence or anger in it, the tone of it shifted into something that was a little more playful. Making a record was not like making a record before, so in making songs there was no need to be violent to the audience or to say "fuck" or anything like that. I guess at that point there was a shift where I was like, "Why should this have to be *hard*? This is *making records*, this is making music. If this really is hard and painful and difficult, then this is the wrong thing to be doing." Saying that to myself, and then myself saying back to me, "Prove it, *prove* that it should be fun."

I wonder if there's any footage of wolves rolling on their back and laughing when they've just been chomped on by an elephant? Death figures quite a bit in *I See a Darkness*, but in positive, empowering ways. It's not desired or looked forward to. I was hoping to make the songs bleak enough that with some perspective it appears almost ridiculous: ridiculous like at the end of a certain day the only thing on your mind is how you can hang yourself, and that if you're standing ten feet away looking at yourself you might break down with laughter at how stupid you look and how vain your attitude is at that moment. That's sort of what I was hoping would be part of it: that the bleakness is totally there, totally obvious, and totally valid, but at the same time that it shouldn't be taken to mean that the obvious way to end bleakness and depression is to do something drastic like take your life or drink for eight days straight.

If it's fatalistic, supposedly *bleak* content, it's being denied by the medium itself. It always takes energy to turn an idea into music and keep it from being just an idea. The goal is that, inherent in the effort to make the music, there is an optimism, whether or not there is some kind of superficial bleakness or darkness. And the idea behind *that* is to be encouraging to anybody who shares some of those ideas. Because at the end of the day sometimes you just feel like God put another anvil on your back and that the best thing to do would be to fall forward and let it crush your ribs, just give in right there. But as long as there is some sort of harmony going on with another being, if another being is creating some music or conversation, even if it's harmony about this momentary or permanent bleak existence, it can give color and nuance and vitality to something that seems like it would inherently be the opposite. Like, there is no way you could make darkness fun. But there *is*. You can.

Even before the Johnny Cash version, "I See a Darkness" struck me as a classic in the making. It's a very moving song.
I had a friend who was in a somewhat confusing point in his life, wrestling with ideas of creativity as well as addiction. The voice of the singer imposes upon that person—the object of the song—a kind of hope or an assumption that that person will rise and keep rising. It's an entreaty or prayer that as that person rises, he or she will have the strength in hindsight to carry the singer up with him or her.

In the CD's lyric booklet, the second and fourth lines of the song are in parentheses. Was that something that you had thought of as being parenthetical, or was it just when you were writing it out that it seemed parenthetical?

Yeah, it seemed parenthetical, and the way we do it live now is
how I imagined it. I will sing the first line and Emmett [Kelly]
will sing the second line, and then I'll sing the third line and
he'll sing the fourth line. And from then on I sing the lyric, but
for some reason, even though the point of view doesn't change,
I've always thought of it as an answer line.

**In "Death to Everyone" you say "buddy," which you also say
in "I See a Darkness." Was that meant to reflect back to that
song, or was one written before the other and there was an
implied connection?**
All of those songs were worked on all at once. I think for that
record and *Ease Down the Road* I had a ninety-minute cassette for
each song, and I would sit and go through each cassette every
day and try to mix up the order, so that the songs were interrelated and had a different significance every day. I think it was
just using the same language: especially for that record, I was
trying to come up with Bonnie Prince Billy and his whole universe, and the universe had to have a spoken language, so I was
trying to be consistent from song to song with this language.

**The song "Black" seems like it's related to an idea of struggle
that's also in the song "I See a Darkness"; that it's sort of an
elaboration on that, but more of a solitary rumination.**
Yeah, yeah.

**Is that partly why you chose to do that one solo, just voice and
acoustic guitar?**

No, it was done solo acoustic because I had worked hard on the song and I really liked it. We did another arrangement that's very much like the "Death to Everyone" arrangement, and kept working and working on it and just could never get satisfied with it. And by the time I realized that it wasn't really working, all the different musicians had come and gone. Rather than giving up on the song, I said, "Let me just try to put a workable version on here"—so the song could still be on the record, but it was sort of a last resort to do it alone. Some people seem to have an appreciation for that song, or are drawn to the song maybe *because* it's a solo performance and they might not have listened to it, liked it, thought much about it if it was the full band thing, which is interesting. I haven't fully wrapped my head around that idea, but I feel it's a similar thing to [Bob Dylan's 1984 album] *Empire Burlesque*, the record that has "Dark Eyes" on it, about which you think, "Oh, that record is kind of crap, except it has this one amazing song." And I really think that the songs are probably all equal, and that's not even that great a song, but people do seem to like a person by him- or herself [*laughs*], singing songs. I can't say I share that appreciation. It mystifies me, but I feel like people like that song more than it merits for its performance.

It could be because "Black" is sequenced so close to the end of the record: a listener might be going through the record and hearing all these full band arrangements, and then when something is finally solo acoustic it tends to stand out a bit more. If it's placed earlier in the record it becomes more of

a break, but maybe it carries more weight if it's put near the end. That might be true of "We All Three" and "Old Jerusalem" on *Viva Last Blues* too: since they're the last two tracks on that record it gives them an identity that they might not have if they were integrated into the rest of the songs in a different way. Were those also songs where a full band arrangement was attempted, or were they always meant to be solo acoustic?

I don't think that we tried either of those full-band. I can't remember why they were like that. I may have hit a wall at some point in terms of my ability to communicate verbally to everybody; it could have been that I just didn't know what else to *say*, because I was realizing the limitations of my ability to express musical direction in the course of making that record. So that could have been why they're like that. And then it's nice to have them at the end so that you don't have to fuck with the volume knob if you're listening to it and turn it way down again if you turned it up because it was a quiet song [*laughs*].

You use horns on "Today I Was an Evil One," which you don't use very much, although they're also on "So Everyone" [from *Lie Down*] and a little on *Beware*.

On "Today I Was an Evil One" I'm sure they're synth horns. I think it was inspired by Colin's piano part, mostly. It had sort of a barrelhouse, drunken-bar sound to it, and in that environment, when you want to raise the energy, how do you do it? Well, you raise it with a horn section.

Had you used Sammy Harkham's drawings before?

First time. He'd interviewed me for a fanzine when he was in high school, in Sydney, and then we'd started a correspondence. And then I asked him if he would consider illustrating the lyric book.

A lot of firsts. It was the first time doing it in this way, which was: Paul, Pete [Townsend], and I recorded all the songs, for the most part; then Paul put away his instrument and Pete left; then Bob came and recorded his parts and left; then Colin came and recorded his parts and left. It took a month, to make this record, and that was the first time a record took more than a week, and the time was used in a way that I really like a lot.

You've said that everything from *I See a Darkness* onward is related.

I think so, yeah.

In terms of . . . everything?

Everything . . . yeah.

Describe your experience with Johnny Cash recording "I See a Darkness." How did he come to hear the song?

The first thing I heard was a couple of years before the recording, when Drag City called and said, "Rick Rubin wants all the lyrics to *Viva Last Blues* to show to Johnny Cash so he could record a song from it." So I typed up the lyrics and sent them off, and didn't hear anything for a year or so. Then somebody told [Matt]

Sweeney* that they'd been at Rick Rubin's and my records were all over the place. I have heard—and I don't know if it's true or not—that Rick had originally presented the song "Death to Everyone" as an appropriate song for Johnny Cash, and somehow "I See a Darkness" rose above that in Cash's eyes and ears. Sweeney saw Rick at a show, introduced himself, and said that he was playing with me. And then Sweeney called me and said that Johnny Cash had just recorded "I See a Darkness." We had a Bowery Ballroom show a week or two later, and he invited Rick Rubin to the show. He came, sat on the side of the stage during the whole show, and asked if I wanted to play piano on the song.

Which you agreed to do, despite not knowing how to play piano.
Yes. I was thinking, "I don't know how to play the piano, but I don't know how else I'm gonna get to participate in this recording." He called ten days later and I had to admit, "I can't play the piano, but if there is any possible way that I could meet Johnny Cash and June Carter Cash in any way, that would be something really important to me." Rick said, "Well, we're going to have a session out here in Los Angeles, and Johnny will be there and June should be there, if you want to come out and meet them." I bought my plane ticket, got there on a Sunday morning and kept calling, but no one was answering. Finally we talked, at about one in the afternoon, and Rick said, "Yeah, we're about to get started,"

---

* Sweeney was a member of the indie-rock bands Skunk and Chavez, performed with BPB regularly from 1999 to 2001 and 2005 to 2007, and is currently a session guitarist.

so I went over. I was sitting in the office at Rick's house, and then Rick comes in and we go downstairs, and he said, "Johnny, this is Will Oldham, he wrote that song 'I See a Darkness.'" We shook hands, and Johnny Cash said, "All right, let's work on that song now." So they pulled that song out and we just did it for the next four hours. I remember it was as if I was a Colorform or paper doll that had just been pasted into the situation.

You wound up coaching Johnny, because he was having a hard time finding the rhythm of it.

Actually conducting him. Yeah, he said it had to do with the entry into the lines, that the vocal lines started on a different beat than he's accustomed to, which I still don't understand. And he *had* done a vocal, and they played it for me, and I remember being just blown away by it. He wasn't happy with it for some reason, and I don't remember what the difference is between what he had recorded and what we ended up with. So we get this idea where I would do a guide vocal, and did that. They pulled up his old vocal and my vocal, and everybody says, "Oh, the voices sound great together." So we decided that I'm going to do the chorus harmonies. He's still having problems with the timing, so they get this idea where I'll sit there in the vocal booth and conduct his singing. It was pretty exciting, because as he was singing the song, he's looking to *me* as the authority. He'd look at the words and the microphone and sing, and then he looked at me between lines. After a couple of hours June came in and said, "Oh, I love that song. We were at our house in Jamaica, and the first time I heard it, I told Johnny, 'You have *got* to record that song.'" That, of course, gave me goosebumps.

A very memorable day for you in the studio. Was he talking a lot about music?

Yeah, *only* about music: about singing different songs and where he heard different songs. And watching them do, from scratch, "That Lucky Old Sun," that was really good, to watch them do three takes of that song.

How was he approaching the vocals in each take?

That was a song he'd known forever, so he could make one take kind of a subdued recitation of the song and one would be more dynamic and emotional, and then just see how it worked with the musicians. It was also nice, after he left late that afternoon, to go upstairs into Rick's little den / listening room with Benmont Tench and some of the Heartbreakers guys that were playing on that session. Rick played the original "I See a Darkness" and a couple of other songs for them, and hearing them compliment the sound of the recording, which was Paul, and Pete's drumming was really exciting. I remember when we were recording [*Ease Down the Road*] I got the unmastered Johnny Cash record [*American III: Solitary Man*], and I realized, "Oh, that really happened"—'cause until then I really didn't believe it.

A few years later you also got to watch George Jones in the studio, when you sang on "Knoxville Girl" by Charlie Louvin.

That was amazing. I did it probably a month after my dad died; it was the first music-related thing I did after he died. [Engineer] Mark Nevers is a great guy, and he'd been talking about this record [*Charlie Louvin*] for a while, and just said, "If you want to come down, actually a really good day to come down would be *this* day, because Charlie's gonna be there, George Jones is gonna be there." So I went to Mark's house, still all fragile and shaken, and spent the day with Charlie Louvin. Bobby Bare Sr. was there as well, so it was a pretty neat day. And then I witnessed George Jones doing his parts for that record—unbelievable. I called Todd [Brashear] when Jones walked in, just kept my cell phone on the whole time he did his takes so that Todd could listen in on the session, 'cause he's a *huge* George Jones fan. There's a photo at the Wild and Woolly cash register of me talking to George Jones at Mark's house.

How would the takes differ? Was he working out phrasing and stuff like that?

Working out phrasing and slight melodic changes. The thing that it reminded me of most was watching James Earl Jones do multiple takes of the same scene during *Matewan*, where you'd just think, "How did he do that? How did he do a completely different interpretation, using the same lines, with the same actor, the same angle and everything, but giving the director and the editor two or three fully realized performances?" And George Jones would just say, "Let me try that again." And he'd do another one, and you'd just think, "*Unbelievable.*"

It's fifty years of recording experience.

It's *understandable* that he should be able to do it . . . but *witnessing* it is another thing.

6

FREEDOM TRIP

ALAN LICHT: **I wanted to talk about the idea of community, which I think a lot of the songs reference or celebrate. The recording sessions of *Ease Down the Road* and *Beware* in particular, and maybe some of the others, seem like a kind of short-term community, and the records feel like an expression of that.**

WILL OLDHAM: That's a central thing. To go a little psycho-analytical—and this is something that I started to think about as I got older—through a strange and random series of circumstances and events, I went to a preschool and then my folks switched me to a different school for kindergarten because they thought maybe I'd have more friends there or something—I don't know exactly why. First grade I went to another school because it was our local public school, and then I got in an accelerated-learning program, but our public school that had that was full, so they sent me to another school that was way out in another part of town that I still haven't been to since second grade. The next year there was room in my local public school, so I went there. The next year I got bussed—got bussed two years in a row—to downtown, along with students from all over the city, and then from sixth to twelfth grade I went to another public school downtown that also was made up of students from all over the city, which was supposed to be half black, half white, half girl, half boy. So, during those times, when I probably should have learned, or come to accept, ideas of community, I think I was observing them, but always like an anthropologist, because I wasn't part of any of those communities, ever. They were all nice people, and they seemed to have communities, but I think it's similar to how some people end up in the arts: you trace it back and they had a childhood illness—something that made them shut off during a crucial developmental period. I didn't have *that*, but instead I had this weird thing which made me turn to movies and books and records to find a community in there.

I feel like that's one of the main jobs of making the records: creating, but also identifying and maintaining, these abstract communities that nourished me growing up. By making a record and putting it out there, you can find someone who's in your community, who lives in Manitoba or wherever, because they hear the record. And eventually you can work with some of these people, you know? In the making of *Matewan* and *A Thousand Pieces of Gold* there were these very, very strong, interesting, vital communities that were just assembled for the making of something but that would continue to have repercussions in each person's life for a long time. And that seemed amazing, 'cause that was something I could relate to: getting together briefly, having a purpose, and then taking it somewhere else.

Ease Down the Road and *Greatest Palace Music* are the most specifically about a personal community, 'cause they each gather people from all over the place whom I've worked with or know. And *Beware* is, somewhat, but that's sort of a focus on the Chicago music community, people that I knew and *didn't* know—people that other people who played on the record knew. So it was more professional.

I was reacting more to the spirit of that record. There are more backup vocals than on some of the other ones; it seemed like more of a documentary of a group endeavor.

Right, and it kind of was because it was the one and potentially only time where a band was assembled, toured, and then recorded. Not having toured *those* songs, but played together, so we had gotten accustomed to singing together.

One of the things that keeps me going—one of the most exciting, inspiring, just most *fun* things—in relation to this community idea is the discovery of—and you never know where it's gonna come from—interrelations. I think I first listened to Half Japanese,* with any time or interest, at the [King] Kong house, when Darren [Rappa] and Ethan [Buckler] lived together in this apartment. When I went to audition for *Matewan*, my whole family went to see Penn and Teller and loved it. I don't remember, at least in that first off-Broadway show, if Penn Jillette made any musical comments or references or anything; it may have been straight magical comedy, like the Marx Brothers mixed with Doug Henning. But then later, finding out there was a connection between Penn Jillette and Half Japanese, understanding that there was 50 Skidillion Watts [record label that Penn Jillette was involved with that released records by Half Japanese] . . .

I know I first heard Kramer's name in relation to Half Japanese, and then when we recorded "West Palm Beach" and "Gulf Shores," Kramer said, "Let me set up these mixes now. Why don't

* Long-running, and seminal, joyful-noise indie-rock band started by brothers Jad and David Fair in 1975.

you watch this movie? Have you ever heard of it?" It was *The World's Greatest Sinner,* and so that's the first place I heard of the film and got into Timothy Carey. Once I saw him, I was like, "This guy is so familiar and I love him for some reason, I really have an affection for him, and I can't think why." And it turns out it was because he was in *East of Eden.* And then what Timothy Carey leads you into is great: a nuanced, different, and deeper relationship to Kubrick and Cassavetes and Hollywood in general.*

***Ease Down the Road* was again recorded by your brother Paul at the farm, with Todd Brashear, Mike Fellows, Paul Greenlaw, your other brother Ned, Dave Pajo, Bryan Rich, Matt Sweeney, Jon Theodore, [multi-instrumentalist] Matt Everett, [director] Harmony Korine, and Cathy Irwin all playing on it. This, to me, is a "community" record, not only in the actual recording but because it's people not only from different time periods but different locations; people that you knew from different places you had been living too, with the whole idea of community not only being one geographic location but also that it can be spread out . . .**

. . . in time and place. We were gonna structure the session like *I See a Darkness,* where we do the basic tracking and then have everyone go away and have other people come. I played a show [during the final concerts at Lounge Ax in January 2000] with Ryan Hem-

---

* Carey acted in the Stanley Kubrick films *The Killing* (1956) and *Paths of Glory* (1957), and the John Cassavetes films *Minnie and Moskowitz* (1971) and *The Killing of a Chinese Bookie* (1976).

bry, a bass player, and it went well, and I asked him if he wanted to play bass on this record. He apparently broke his wrist, and he said, "Yeah, yeah, but I'm working on it every day, rehab, it's gonna be fine." I was like, "OK, just keep me posted," and then maybe forty-eight hours before the session was gonna start he called and said he couldn't do it. And I said, "Man, that ain't right." But then I called Fellows and asked him, "What are you doing?"

"Nothing."

"Come to Kentucky and make a record."

Mostly I knew him through the Trux [whom he played with under the name "Mighty Flashlight"].* And I knew Jon Theodore from Baltimore, 'cause he and Babyleg [Brian DeRan] used to be roommates, and I'd seen him play [drums] with Golden and hung out with him a bunch of times. This was pre-heavy involvement in Zwan for Sweeney; it was the tail end of the first segment of playing with Matt, 'cause then there was two years or so when he was MIA, during the Zwan time. My mom likes to tell the story of going to the grocery and running into Cathy Irwin's mom. Maybe they sort of knew each other but they were reacquainting themselves, and Cathy's mom said, "Oh, right, your son is in Languid and Flaccid, my daughter's in the Dickbrains."†

* Fellows had also played bass in DC punk bands Rites of Spring and Government Issue.

† Languid and Flaccid was an early band of Ned's; the Dickbrains were a short-lived punk band from c. 1980. Irwin has a long-running country duo with Janet Beveridge Bean called Freakwater.

Had you known Harmony for a while?

Yeah. I still haven't talked to him about it, and I suppose I should, but my suspicion is that I first encountered him when I lived in Birmingham. I think he started to call me, but using another name—Jared. Later I found out that his best friend in college was this guy Jared, so it could have been him and Jared calling, or it could have been just him. When I got to know him, it was like, "I know that voice." We talked on the phone, and he presented this long, sort of movie-treatment idea and asked if I was interested in acting in it. It felt like he was making it up on the spot, and included things like the Ritz Brothers and blackface and cruise ships, and all this stuff that later I understood were part of his lexicon. Maybe he was trying to shock me or fuck with me with the blackface and trying to make the story more outlandish as it went along, thinking that at a certain point I'd say, "Who is this? What the fuck?" And I was more like, "That sounds amazing!" I think he liked my music and had a respect for me, but was also trying to sort of make fun of me. But I didn't know that at the time, 'cause everything he said sounded exciting to me, and I was like, "Yeah, that sounds great, let's do that." And he said, "Really?" Then I got a two-page letter of apology, saying that the money had fallen through, and the money was supposed to come from Martin Ritt, but it was nice talking to you on the phone, blah blah blah.

Then, when *Gummo* was being made, he and his production people called. We were living in Iowa, and he says, "Would you want to be in *Gummo*?" I said, "I don't know." Then they sent the script and said, "This part." And I said, "Sure." And then they went, "OK, you can come out for an audition." And I said, "What? I don't really want to be in it that bad. I'm making music, I live with my girlfriend, and I don't really need to come out to New York for *any* reason, much less to audition for somebody. And that's with all due respect. I know that's how that system works. I'm just saying I don't do that sort of thing." At that point I think I was talking to the producer's assistant, and she said, "That's ridiculous, even Tom Cruise would have to audition." And I was like, "Well, call Tom Cruise, because he's a professional actor and I'm not." And so that was the end of that.

In "A King at Night" there's the line "You fuck and what's to do," and then—
It's someone else saying, "You fuck" [in the background], and that's Harmony doing that.

It's something you also do in "A Sucker's Evening" [from *Arise Therefore*], turning "fuck" from a verb to a noun—"Fuck him with the something / the fuck he deserves it."
Yeah, yeah, yeah. It's a significant journey from the darkness of "A Sucker's Evening" to the light of *Ease Down the Road*, making it actively humorous. Although with "A Sucker's Evening," you're supposed to be able to laugh at how retardedly brutal the song purports to be.

I liked the title "A King at Night," since the lyrics are about the king starting his *day*.

The obvious title of that would have been "Another Day in My Kingdom," or something like that, but I was in Maine, and some friends have this little cottage, and on the bookshelf there was a book—I think it was a tale of chivalry, written in the early twentieth century—called *A Prince by Night* or *A King at Night*, something like that [*A King by Night* (1926) by Edgar Wallace]. I just thought, "That's nice," because the spine was really beautiful and the evocation of a sort of style and chivalry made me feel like the writer's aspirations were Arthurian, and that's what mine are, and maybe if we intersect at a certain place, we will intersect at this Round Table edition, even if neither of us would have gotten there on our own.

I love that song. When we play live, sometimes I can't get into the pocket with it, and that's frustrating. I feel like that's where it is right now. It's been over a year since I've felt like I could put it across, for some reason. I've played it so many times where it feels *so wonderful* to play.

The synth at the end of "Grand Dark Feeling of Emptiness" reminded me of "Popcorn."*

The first time I heard "Popcorn" was in 2006. Shary Boyle, the visual artist, used it as part of her performance, and I was with Dan [Koretzky] in Los Angeles, and I was like, "What was that music?" And Dan was like, "That was 'Popcorn,' you don't know that?!" I'd never heard it before. That was supposed to be more

* An instrumental hit for Hot Butter in 1972, originally recorded by Gershon Kingsley in 1969.

like a punch line, just 'cause the song . . . part of the objective, with Bonnie Prince Billy, was to fill the light into the songs, sort of in an Addams Family kind of way, or Misfits/Samhain where there's all this very apparent morbidity and darkness and unpleasantness and power and all that, but it's being brought to you by people who get a fair amount of joy out of it.

They're having fun.
They do it because it feels good, not because it feels bad. You don't write a harrowing song because you want to be harrowing all the time but because it feels good.

On "May It Always Be" I noticed there were three "stay with me's" and three "we'll play bride's" and three "won't we be's," which is I think the only instance where you do something like that in a song.
I don't know why I repeated those lines three times. I just figured after I did it once I should just keep going with it. For a long time when writing songs I would try to avoid repetition, try to avoid choruses. I'm not sure if I've ever recorded a song that has a repeated verse in it.

A bunch of the songs on *Days in the Wake* have repeated lines.
They have repeated *lines*, but not like a verse and then a refrain. On *Hope* and *Days in the Wake* having those repeated lines was sort of experimenting with the mantra experience, figuring that there can be too many words at times, or too many ideas to get across, not only for the listener but for the singer. It can be

rewarding to pull the same syllables through your mouth three times in a row to make the idea last longer—and I think that song is about trying to make things last longer.

I feel like when I was working on "May It Always Be" I was thinking, "Oh, this is a song that Johnny Cash would sing," 'cause that was very soon after going to Los Angeles for that Johnny Cash session. Also that the bridge part was like a throwback. It kind of reminds me of the song that was on the Box of Chocolates album, "The Ephant," both thematically and the [chord] progression as well. I'm pretty sure Todd sings on that bridge, so it was a nice feeling having that voice in there recording that lyric. I had to go pick somebody up at the airport while Sweeney worked on that guitar solo, and when I got back there it was. That was pretty exciting. I've always thought it seems strange the way that guitar solo sounds transparent. It feels like it's written on glass or something. It's powerful but not dense; you can hear all the other elements of the song behind it, even as it's screaming out at you.

"Careless Love" reminds me of Scottish music.
There's an old song that was definitely the springboard for that song: [*sings*] "Oh love, oh love, oh careless love / look what love has done to me." The version I've heard has the verse about apron strings, which is in a bunch of songs: "Cut the apron strings off"—you know, that they don't tie in the back anymore because she's pregnant. It was a song I heard from Bob Arellano's then girlfriend, a woman named Carolyn Cooley, and it might have been in a film that Dianne [Bel-

lino] made called *Lucy Jane*, which she made in 1993 in Rhode Island.

"A Minor Place" [from *I See a Darkness*] and "A Sucker's Evening" also have a Scottish feel to them. Even though it might not be especially evident at first, there's a musical basis there. Yeah, there's probably a lot of Scottish elements in a bunch of songs. "Careless Love" is one we did on tour in Scandinavia [in 2003] with Aram Stith and Chris Freeland. We'd do it every night, but the challenge would be to come up with a new arrangement every night, which was really fun.

What were some of the arrangements like? I remember there was a Bo Diddley rhythm—you know, someone would come up with kind of a groove and then we'd try to work up changes around it. But we'd do it at soundcheck and then play it. That kept us interested in the tour, what was going to happen with "Careless Love."

There's also the dissonance of it: the melody is against the drone at first and then it turns a corner and is in tune with it. There are some other songs that are sort of dissonant, like "Cat's Blues" [from *Viva*], "A Group of Women" [from *Arise Therefore*], "Sheep" [from *Ease*] and "The Seedling" [from *The Letting Go*]. Is writing those songs different to writing ones that are more normally consonant? For "Cat's Blues" I was listening to a lot of Oum Kalsoum recordings from the 1920s and '30s and just trying to put an interval in from the music I was listening to. I didn't want it to feel like a homage, and I didn't want it to feel stylistic; I just wanted to see if there was anything I could take from the music I was listening to, because I couldn't take the language, obviously. "Cat's Blues" started off more slow and open. We recorded it a couple of times like that, and I was about to just throw it out, and then we just played it through, like it is on the record. That was exciting.

"A Group of Women": I think I was living in Iowa and reading Miles Davis's autobiography, and again just trying to think about how to set a melody against a chordal backing that was unfamiliar to me, to see if it could open up possibilities and ideas. "Sheep" was more like a little bit of flamenco noises and a little bit of the Fall, specifically the *Slates* EP, and then "The Seedling" just ended up sounding that way [*laughs*]. It was written on a tenor guitar that I had tuned in a certain way; *Ode Music* was also from that guitar. And I ended up not bringing that guitar to Iceland; I think I used a loop pedal, one of those Boss Loop Stations, with my big fat National electric guitar. We've played it far more dissonantly since the recording, and that's one of the songs where we used both Ryder [McNair] and Nico [Muhly]'s string arrangements. They were both fairly different from each other but seemed to latch onto an inherent or imagined dissonance of the song. The strings make it seem far more dissonant than it would have seemed without them; it would have just been a heavy minor groove without the strings.

In "Ease Down the Road" and "Mrs. William" there are references to adultery, which I don't think comes up much in other songs.

Yeah. "Mrs. William" is more from a distance, and then "Ease" is right up close to it. In a way it was a proposition. It's strange that "Ease," both in its title and its execution, does make certain things sound easy that probably most people would agree are not easy. In that way, it could be the most inherently evil song in the canon. But it was a fun song to record. I don't know how much what a song is about makes it easier or more difficult to play at different times, but that's another song that I've gotten so much joy out of playing, and for some reason in the past year or so I haven't been able to get into it.

Do you think going to a live show is sort of like cheating on your record collection [*laughs*]? We were talking about Mission of Burma reuniting, and I said people who hadn't seen them the first time around might want to go to a concert just to stand up and be counted as a fan of their records, and you said something like, "If they really liked their old records, then they wouldn't go see them live, out of respect for the records." And I remember about twenty years ago I went to some show, and between bands they played the entire *Blank Generation* [1977] album by Richard Hell, and that was a record that I had only listened to by myself, at home, as a teenager. For years I don't think I knew anyone else who owned that album, and it was weird for me to hear that record being played over the sound system in the middle of this show. In that case, it seemed like the record was cheating on *me*—I go out to a show and all of a sudden the record is there too, when I thought it was my own private thing . . . even though I realized I wasn't the only person in the world who knew this record.

Yeah, it would almost be like going to a strip club and seeing your girlfriend dancing there, and you'd be like, "Ohhh," and it doesn't feel good at all. My experience of *Blank Generation* was Ned and I listening to it in Virginia when we were living in the woods together, and for me it also seems like a very complex, and fantastic, solitary-experience record. And it's confusing for many of us listeners, more so probably since records started to become art forms in and of themselves. You never know when you listen to a record if the people who were making it were making something that was supposed to be its own thing; if you're listening to a piece of art or if you're listening to a well-made recording. I'm very drawn to this Willie Nelson record, *Yesterday's Wine*, one of the more powerful and satisfying records that I own, and yet at the time [1971] he was making record after record after record after record—just like he is now, I guess—so it's hard to know if he thought about it ahead of time. It has a magic to it, and the experience of a world, but did he ever try to do anything with that world live? There's interesting little mixing things on there, where on one song there's heavy reverb on the vocal, and then the song goes right into the next song, with no break, and the vocal's super dry, super upfront. And was Willie Nelson even there when it was mixed? Was it him? Was it maybe the engineer? Is the person responsible the engineer or the producer, and not Willie Nelson at all? Was Willie Nelson just a color on the palette of the engineer or producer? So is it a piece of art, or is it its own thing?

Most of us don't know either, when we go out and play live. Some people replicate the record, and I feel more of a responsibility toward replicating the intentions behind going in and making a record. You go in to make a record and you have ten, twelve, fourteen songs, and playing live it's almost like, "Let's pretend we're making a record and we have this many songs to choose from, but we only have one time to play them. But at the same time, it has to be the same thing, we have to make something within these limitations that is as unpredictable and as merited as a recording session and the resulting record can be." But it's very confusing, because people don't come, necessarily, to hear things like that, and you don't know at what point a record turns into a piece unto itself and not just a representation of what an artist is doing. The Richard Hell thing feels so powerful, and magic, and the tension and interplay between the different players feels like it's specific to that record. And if you saw it live . . . maybe some of the live shows would have been like that, I don't know.

When I was playing with Arthur Lee I felt like I owed it to the audience to try to play the songs note for note, as much as possible—
—like they were on the record . . .

Yeah, because I thought if someone was coming to a show to hear that music played, they would expect to hear certain things, since they would most likely only know the music from the old 1960s Love records. Whereas with my own bands it was the exact opposite: I would try not to play things the way I did on the record . . .
Right, but I wonder—when I go to see somebody, usually I hope to see their creativity and not just their ability to perform, and

so I hope to see whatever variants there are. The songs already mean something to me, so I wanna know why it means something, or I want that experience expanded upon. And I wonder if you had tried to overtly or subtly vary what you did just to see what it could bring out of Arthur Lee's performance; maybe there would be people who would be disappointed, but there would also be people who would be very excited by where that could take his performance.

Well, I did, in songs where that was possible. In "A House Is Not a Motel" there's a long solo at the end. I started off playing whatever is on the record and then I went off into something else. There was one show in DC where we played that song and I think I laid the guitar on the floor and was playing it with my foot, doing feedback, and Arthur got into it, knelt down, took out his lighter and started rubbing it on the strings on the fretboard. [*laughs*] Awesome.

In that same show, on a different song, I looked up after a guitar break in the middle expecting to go into the next verse, and there was no Arthur—he was out in the third row of the audience, dancing! All right! That's the way it oughta be.

Get on Jolly, **your collaboration with Mick Turner, appeared after** *Ease.* A lot of people seem to single that out and talk about the way they like that record in a more direct and heartfelt way than almost any of the other records, which is kind of neat. Mick Turner was the first person I saw play with a Boomerang [looping pedal] and make looping into something that sounded real and organic and musicianly. It sounded like an extension of improvisation, while still being, obviously, looping; which is more common now, but at the time loops were made to make a groove, or something like that, and he was the first person I knew to make it something beautiful.

I bought the book *Gitanjali* [by Rabindranath Tagore] because it looked good—a great-looking book I had found for 25 cents—and I started reading it and really liked it. Mick and I had talked about making music. He'd send me sketches, and I thought, "What kind of words could go with this? It's gotta be something kind of looped, so what else is looped and repeated?" Well, devotional kinds of things, but you don't want it strictly religious; the Tagore poems are pretty earthy and skip around. We changed it so it's not completely referential to Tagore.

Master and Everyone was recorded in June 2002. I was playing on the first session for it, at Rove [the studio at the farm in Shelbyville]; the other two guys I remember also playing were a drummer, Thomas Van Cottom, from Belgium, and a bass player, Drew Nelson, who was from Baltimore.
As I tended, or tend, to do, that was trying to repeat the formula of what worked in the session before, and usually finding out that it doesn't work that way. I was trying to do it at the farm, do basic tracking and then add overdubs as I went along. I had a

couple of people booked to come in after we did the basic tracking, so it would have grown, but [the lineup] probably wouldn't
have been as big as *Ease Down the Road*. It would have probably
been six or seven people.

**You sent me a demo of the songs, as well as a CD-R of Roger
Miller's album *A Tender Look at Love* [1968]. Frankly, at the
time I couldn't make the connection between that original
band instrumentation of *Master* and the Roger Miller album,
but I figured maybe it's just supposed to be something inspiring. But then the way the record ended up was much more true
to the atmosphere of that Miller record.**

Well, I was thinking that it would be subdued, and I have a
fondness for the Wailers records that were produced by Lee
"Scratch" Perry and that *Tender Look at Love* record. The best
way to describe it is that they sound post-apocalyptic to me, like
they would be made in the time of *A Boy and His Dog* [1975 film
directed by L. Q. Jones]. So that's what I was thinking, more
than instrumentation or anything: that to me they sound like
records that are made by people who are relearning how to make
records after a catastrophe of global proportions occurred.

**Did you ever see *Glen and Randa* [1971, directed by Jim
McBride, another post-apocalyptic movie]?***

---

* *Glen and Randa*, like *Two-Lane Blacktop*, was cowritten by Rudolph
Wurlitzer. In October 2010 WO recorded an audiobook version of Wurlitzer's
1984 novel *Slow Fade*.

No, I didn't. I just heard about it for the first time in the last two years and bought a copy off the Internet on VHS. So I own it, and you've just reminded me I haven't watched it. I really like post-apocalyptic movies, and am not looking forward to *The Road* because it seems like too formulaic a post-apocalyptic movie. It was a formulaic, post-apocalyptic Cormac McCarthy novel that Oprah liked. They put Viggo Mortensen in it, and they're trying to make something that is "undeniably great," so that you have to go to it and say, "Oh my God, that was so amazing." Which you're not supposed to do with post-apocalyptic movies . . .

When you made the demos of the songs, did you have a sequence in mind? 'Cause the sequence on the demo you sent me is similar to the final album.

Is it? It could be that I got accustomed to that sequence, but usually the final sequence is something I probably think about a little bit before the record. But during the tracking, during the overdubbing, during the mixing, and then after the mixing, decisions about sequencing are made then.

You halted the session at Rove after a day or two and relocated to Nashville. This is the first time you worked with engineer Mark Nevers.*

---

* Nevers is a producer and engineer who operates Beech House Recording in Nashville. He has worked with a large number of established country artists (Travis Tritt, Kenny Rogers, George Jones, Amy Grant, Billy Ray Cyrus), as well as indie-rock performers (Lambchop, Calexico, David Kilgour, Vic Chestnutt, Clem Snide).

It was similar to the *Days in the Wake* thing; I thought, "Gotta make a record somehow." We went down to Nashville 'cause I refused to go into the depression that came after the California abortion. I knew Nevers had sort of held David [Berman]'s hand through the making of [Silver Jews'] *Bright Flight*, and I figured this is what I want—I want someone to fuckin' hold my hand through a session. We went down there, and he brought a drummer in, and after a day and a half of playing with him, I thought, "We gotta get rid of this guy." And then I thought, "It was more than just taking away things. I don't know how to make this record, Mark's not helping me figure out how to make this record . . . I know the songs are in order, so I'm just gonna present the bare bones of the songs and try to pretty them up a little bit, and put that out as a record, even though it's not what I wanted to put out."

It sounds like there were some field recordings on "Joy and Jubilee," "Wolf among Wolves," and "Even if Love."
No, those are all trademark Nevers things, where he might say, "Let me put a mic outside," and record and/or loop something through his reverb units on the wall.

Was Marty Slayton someone that Mark had found?
One of the great discoveries of that session was, after we kicked everybody else out and Paul and I just did the tracks live, I told Mark, "It would be nice if there was a female singer on here," and he said, "Oh, I know the guy who's head of the singers' union. Tell me what kind of voice you'd like." I played him some

Dolly Parton and some Sandy Denny, so he called the singers' union and described, without mentioning names, what he thought the voice should sound like. They gave him four names and phone numbers, and the first one was this Marty Slayton woman. She came over and did everything in forty minutes; it was amazing. And that's basically why *Greatest Palace Music* was made, those forty minutes, because all of a sudden I realized, as I always imagined, that there were incredible session musicians on this planet who are good at what they do and have made records that I love, and [I was] wanting to make a record with them. I told Mark that, and he said, "Oh, totally, we could make a record like that."

You're a big fan of Kevin Coyne's 1979 album with Dagmar Krause, *Babble*.* Was that one of the things that made you think about singing more with female vocalists, which you've increasingly done in the last ten years?
Yeah, but that *Babble* record, or more specifically Royal Trux's third [album] and *Cats and Dogs*, to me, are like listening to a third person who is a composite of two other people, who are male and female. It's like a religious experience, man and woman coming together and making something that is music, offspring that is music. That's one of those records that, for me, brought up so many different emotions each time I listened to

* Bonnie covered two songs from *Babble* on a 1998 7", and in late 2010 Bonnie Prince Billy and the Cairo Gang played the entire album as their own opening act on a short tour, under the name the Babblers.

it; and I didn't know anything about the record, so there was no way of knowing where they came from. So it was all about exploring where the emotions went, and not about exploring where they came from.

I feel like I was born with some crazy male/female mix internally. It's nice sometimes to imagine that gender-neutralizing the song is actually a more accurate representation. Sometimes it feels necessary to feel like you are singing with the women as much as you are singing with the men in order to say, "Just so you know, I'm not really taking any sides here."

A lot of people interpreted *Master and Everyone* as a breakup album . . .
Hmm.

. . . but it seemed to me more about being alone and about freedom, and how to weigh freedom against being with another person. And also, having the female vocals on it made it hard for me to understand why someone would interpret it as a breakup album.
Yeah . . . and the female voice *may* have been something like calling those early songs "blues." The songs may convey a subject matter, but they are songs and not necessarily vehicles for the conveying of a subject matter.

You said once that you "value the freedom to change courses at any moment." Do you think that's something that relates to the songs on this record?

Well, definitely the "Hard Life" song. It's a little bit in *Ease Down the Road* as well. I'd probably relate it that way, in terms of being obsessive/compulsive about the freedom concept.

Freedom is the topic of "What I'd Give to Be the Wind" on that Roger Miller album.
Yeah, and it has that beautiful song "My Elusive Dreams," where the freedom is a freedom for two instead of a freedom for one.

There's a story that you played this record for a room full of friends, who found it really depressing, and you had second thoughts about releasing it after that.
I can't remember why I didn't like it, but after making it I really thought it was an unpleasant listening experience. But I can't remember, honestly, if I had played it for anybody. I played it for my lady, Sue. Then I made a six-song sequence for it to be an EP that was gonna be called *It's Expected I'm Gone*, after the Minutemen song, and I remember giving that to Agostino and Giovanna when they had a show here in Louisville and saying, "Yeah, this is the new EP."

Sara DeVincentis was supposed to come and sing on the record. She and D.V. [DeVincentis, her brother and screenwriter/producer] and her husband Jeff liked to go to Biarritz to go surfing, and I went with them that fall, for a week. She said, "I'd like to at least *hear* the songs, even though I didn't get to sing on them." I played them for her on my laptop speakers, and as we were listening it occurred to me, "Ah, this record sounds good," and that was when I figured it would come out as a record.

There was another story that when you came up with the proposed EP, you had dropped the songs you figured people would like too much.

I've heard that a bunch of times. I don't really understand it. I think the six-song sequence that I had was really good because they asked for, and would reward, a closer listen. [I was] wanting them to be six equal songs rather than five songs and a single, or something like that. So you would want to listen to all six songs every time, instead of wanting to put on one song you like.

Now you're blowing my whole comparison to John Cassavetes, who supposedly changed the ending of *Opening Night* when it got a standing ovation at a preview screening.

Are those things just legendary? I mean, having been on the other side of these decisions, I sort of imagined, when I heard that *Opening Night* story, that it was a coincidence; that he probably had heavy misgivings about the way he'd cut *Opening Night*, and saw that there was this reaction, which might have made him think even stronger, "This isn't right, this isn't right." But also just watching it in a room full of people—not that their reaction was the catalyst—but when you finish something you think it's one thing; and the first time you play it for somebody, you learn more about it just by being in the room with that person and them listening to it too.

It may have been that the reaction had no effect one way or the other, that his mind was already made up that the ending needed to change.

Yeah. Or it could have been that such a strong reception made him feel like, "You're not supposed to clap at the end of this movie in *that way*. It's not supposed to be a triumph, it's supposed to be something that you take home with you. You don't release the energy at the end of the movie, you keep it inside of you and walk outside of the theater and take it into your life."*

But there are other ways that I think you're comparable to Cassavetes, particularly in the way you use family and friends in the production of records, like he used them in the production of films. There's a story about him I've only heard once, I think in an *American Masters* TV special, so I'm not sure if it's true, but the story was that he was playing softball in the park—I think with Seymour Cassel, and it might have been Cassel who was telling the story—and they had finished the game and were leaving the park, when this guy came up to them and tried to mug them. And Cassavetes said, "What's the problem, you need money? I'll give you a job. I'm shooting a movie, show up on Monday morning." And the guy did. Cassavetes gave him a job, and the guy went on to have some kind of career in the film industry.
Wow.

---

* See p. 424 of Ray Carney's *Cassavetes on Cassavetes* (London: Faber & Faber, 2001) for Ted Allan's account of preview screenings and ending changes for *Opening Night*.

That also reminds me of ways in which you've given people jobs that they weren't necessarily applying for, as musicians or tour managers.

And I like the Cassavetes-by-extension story: it can't be credited to him, 'cause it's not him, but not too long ago there was a group of supposedly creative people, including Terrence Malick, who wanted to start a production company that made small, vital movies, and they wrote a letter to [Cassavetes scholar] Ray Carney asking for advice as to what Cassavetes might do, 'cause they had some questions about how to get funding, things like that. And Ray Carney published the letter and his response on his website, and his response was, "You know, John Cassavetes wouldn't have written this letter, wouldn't have been worried about where the money was coming from, so I can't give you any advice, because what you're embarking upon has nothing to do whatsoever with John Cassavetes." And I just thought, "Good answer!" 'Cause so often people come and want to talk about the making of something or how to do something, and they feel like there's some relationship, and it's just like, "What the fuck? I don't understand what you're doing, I don't understand . . ."

And Cassavetes's preference for capturing a performance rather than looking for technical precision is another thing I see a lot in your work. Especially on the records, there are times where the players are not coming together in the same place and the background singing is sort of loose; it almost seems like you're letting everybody follow their own breathing patterns, as opposed to getting the timing exact.

Perfecting a part is not a priority in the least, because it is generally thought that if a part is implied in a recording, then the listener has the freedom to listen to it a thousand times until it becomes a polished part. Whereas if you're listening to a record that has a polished part repeated over and over, it inhibits the desire to listen to the record again because you know exactly what's gonna come, and it's gonna come exactly the same, in a repetitive way, and have no nuance to it whatsoever.

I think in the 1990s I remember fantasizing—and that was part of my thinking when *Arise Therefore* didn't have an overall artist credit, and it may end up being true, I don't know—but my fantasy at that time was that somebody who followed [Steve] Albini's work closely, followed [David] Grubbs's work closely, followed Ned [Oldham]'s work closely, or followed my work closely would consider that record to be important in that person's work. Just as if you were a fan of Tim Carey, it's essential to watch [Cassavetes's] *Minnie and Moskowitz*, even though he's only in it for four minutes at the beginning. It's *absolutely* essential, you *have* to watch *Minnie and Moskowitz* if you love Timothy Carey.

I've also heard that both PJ Harvey and Marianne Faithfull encouraged you to release *Master and Everyone*.
That was true. At the time when I couldn't figure out what to do with the record and wasn't sure how I felt about it, I sent both of them copies of it, under the assumption that I wasn't going to release it. I had been in communication with them: PJ Harvey over a longer period of time, but Marianne Faithfull during

that eighteen-month period.* I sent it to them and they both seemed nonpatronizingly supportive of the idea of putting the record out.

You've said that "Even if Love" is "ripping off" PJ Harvey.
Yeah, well, it's sort of like a tribute song to her and the ways in which her records have been good to me.

***Master and Everyone* is another record cover with the design of "Bonnie Prince Billy" underlined and then the title underneath.**
Which started with "I Am Drinking Again." All the Bonnie Prince Billy stuff was like that.

Was that something you thought of, to give the Bonnie Prince Billy releases more consistency?
Yeah, and to say, "This is part of something, this is part of making records." [It was] another way of recognizing that it was

---

* Faithfull and BPB dueted on "Dreaming My Dreams" at the Barbican in 2002; Faithfull has also been known to cover "A King at Night." WO: "At the Barbican there was one beautiful, surreal moment backstage after the show when she was getting dressed for the after-show party. I was walking into her dressing room to say, 'Good show,' and I was talking to her in the narrow entryway while Anita Pallenberg was helping her zip up her dress. And Anita Pallenberg and I were staying at the same weird, incredible place, as if you were in the guest-house version of the *Performance* house, in Notting Hill. [I remember] in the morning going down to the front desk, and the front-desk clerk saying, 'Miss Pallenberg wants to know if you want to have breakfast' [*laughs*]."

participating in a larger system, and that wasn't always bad but could be kind of beautiful or symmetrical or peaceful. If every record cover has to be completely different, it can get exhausting; whereas if every record cover has some things that are the same, even really little things, then the things that are different become *more* interesting.

Similar to the drum machine on *Arise Therefore*.
Yes, exactly.

In the record packaging, there's the bunny and bird drawings and the Gypsy poem.
The rabbit thing was more what I had asked for. I wanted to have Sammy [Harkham] use colors instead of black and white, which was what he'd done before, and he sent me a bunch of pieces. I just thought that was really great. The bird on the back was a blue jay, and my mom did it. I asked her to do a blue jay, and she and my dad had just been to Alaska, and she was impressed by the Native American and the Russian Orthodox art that she had seen up there. So she did the blue jay in a style that sort of combines elements of both.

I was in a pen-pal correspondence with a woman called Heather Rodkey, and at one point she went to a night at the opera and sent me the program with some of her handwritten notes on it. And that's where the lyrics for "Master and Everyone" came from, that program; there was a Verdi piece called "Italian Folk Tale," and the translated lyrics were pretty close to the "Master and Everyone" lyrics. Also in that program was the

Gypsy poem, which was also sung that night. I just thought it was a beautiful artifact and nice to put in—it had something to do with a tree, right? [*laughs*]

You hadn't really returned to acting, but you made a few minor film appearances around the turn of the decade. You're in the film *Radiation* [1998], directed by Mike Galinsky and Suki Hawley . . .

It was when I was in Spain [autumn 1997]. It was a coincidence [that they were filming there]. They asked if I would come down and pretend to do a soundcheck. So I came down by myself and pretended to do a soundcheck, and just made up a song on the spot.

And you appear briefly in the beginning of Harmony Korine's *Julien Donkey-Boy* [1999]. You went out to Newark, New Jersey, for the shoot, and you were dancing with blind people.

Trying to adapt to Harmony's way of working.

Which was?

That was kind of the ultimate, even including movies that he's made since then, but I feel that he was kind of trying to make the process of directing a movie a work of art in addition to the movie. Which could be off-putting; like that day, they shot that scene, and it took five or six hours and they covered it with five or six cameras. But then they shot it again, and I left after the first time they did it, 'cause I was just like, "I don't like working under Harmony's rules." 'Cause his rules at that time were an organized chaos, with the understanding that there was a producer somewhere who was gonna be sure that everything worked out. But other than that, anything could happen.

I think when he was trying to think of a name for *Julien Donkey-Boy* we had a correspondence about titles. He was originally going to call it *The Julien Chronicles*. I knew he was a fan of writers like Donald Barthelme and John Barth, and then I found, somewhere on tour, a flyer for a donkey-adoption farm called the Donkey Sanctuary. It was kind of neat, and I mailed that to him and then suggested "Julien Donkey-Boy," like *Giles Goat-Boy* [Barth novel], figuring that he would like that relationship to that school of writers. His email used to be pricksongs@something.com, and *Pricksongs & Descants* is a Robert Coover book.

You play a surfer in Dianne Bellino's short film *Slitch* [2000]. Was that when you started surfing?
I think so, yeah, 'cause that's when I was living in Rhode Island, in the winter one year, with Dianne. I hated being up there and just thought, "I'm gonna get in the water," even though it was winter. I bought a thick winter wetsuit and a used surfboard, and would just go to the beach every day and try and teach myself to surf in the winter water.

I was thinking about what relationship might exist between the idea of surfing and the idea of riding—riding a horse, riding a wave, riding in a car . . .
Or riding a song. Singing live, at the best of times, after the recording at least, is just trying to figure out where the song is

at any given moment and stay on top of it. On those shows with Bill [Callahan, in 1996] I would play the same set every night, by myself. Every night I took one of those truck-stop herbal speed pills and drank a bottle of white wine in the ten minutes prior to playing the set, so I wouldn't really be drunk until fifteen or twenty minutes into the set, but also at the same time this herbal speed was kicking in . . . And I played the same set every night, so that it was kind of like surfing the set. And a lot of the songs went one into another without stopping. I usually didn't remember the end of the set, but I knew that I got there with confidence. I don't know if it was good, but I got there with *confidence* [*laughs*].

7

FORWARD THROUGH THE AGES

ALAN LICHT: Do you think a song is ever really finished?

WILL OLDHAM: I feel like a song is completed when the writing is done and I present it to a friend, partner, or group of musicians. Then it's completed when we record together and finish mixing. Then it's completed each and every time someone listens. I think that a song, for the most part, is completed by the listening experience. It enters into people's brains and mutates and then might get completed again—in their dreams, in mix tapes that they make, or in new listening experiences that they have. So it *isn't* ever finished because there's never going to be a definitive listening experience. I guess the idea is that I listen to certain favorite songs over and over because for some reason I just haven't finished listening to them. But in terms of concentrating on the bones of the song, that ends with the recording; in rare cases there will be arrangement modifications, but from that point on the skeleton is always going to stay the same. From then on, playing live, for me, is more like an exercise to stay in shape for writing and recording.

There's the way a song can sound when you're just playing it in a room to somebody that's going to perform it with you, and then the way it sounds in the rehearsal room when you're playing it with a band, and then there's the way it sounds when you go into a studio and the engineer is listening to it; there's an evolution of the song's identity from when it's

something that you're creating on your own to where it ultimately ends up.

Yes. Anybody who's a big music fan and plays music for people experiences this, but if you work with recorded music you can point to the differences in instrumentation or preparedness or arrangement. And you can play the same recording of the same song and have vastly different feelings about it. You could be listening to a song in your car and not enjoying it, and then someone could get in the car and all of a sudden the song becomes good, or the reverse. It seems to me that the ears that are listening make more difference than the way the music sounds. 'Cause you can also tell when you see people who are absolutely 100 percent enthralled and enjoying inarguably terrible music, and they're smart human beings; you see it happening and you realize it doesn't have anything, or far less, to do with the music itself than the listening done by the listener and the situation.

It could have something to do with the social atmosphere or where the music fits into that group of people's shared consciousness, whatever that is, at that particular time.

Yeah. And I don't know if that will ever be measurable, so that you could say, "This song is a great song when I'm with my mother; this song is a bad song when I'm with my friend Jack." 'Cause someone could convince you, even by their presence, that it's a great record, you know? I could hear a song on the radio with you in the car, and just your shift of energy could make me realize, "That's actually a really good song, I never thought of it before," and you might not even say anything about it. I like that.

Whenever you're with a group of people that love the music that's playing, it's exciting; if you're in a Mexican bar or a Jimmy Buffett concert, when people are loving the music, the music is great. In 1985 there was a group of exchange students from Massachusetts that came to our high school for a week. I remember sitting in the back of someone's car, and the Thompson Twins song "Hold Me Now" came on the radio. Everyone in the car was really excited and happy and listening to the song, and there were tons of us, so we were all pressed up against each other. They seemed to know it and love it, because they came from a normal school, whereas coming from the Brown School it was something that you might hear every once in a while, but for the most part we didn't listen to the radio or watch MTV that much. It was such a powerful feeling that for years I always had a positive association with that song, cherishing it. I've heard it in the last few years and it doesn't do anything for me whatsoever, but it's a different song that I have in my brain now than actually exists in the real world.

Country music has often been a part of the fabric of your songs, and in the last decade you've worked in Nashville a few times. Can you talk a little about country music's significance to you?
I think that a privilege of growing up in Kentucky is that it's not as hard to accept country music as a given. It's kind of a default thing. It was mixed in with the punk rock that we heard. One of the greatest things about country music is its limitations, because by limiting something a control is provided. There's a

set of rules that work, and the interpreters of those rules vary so widely in approach and ability that it can represent the picking apart of the music as a whole. People wear belt buckles and cowboy hats and pointy boots all over the world. And because they do, they get to have a relationship to the music that someone who doesn't wear those things doesn't have, either as a representative of that music or a character in the music or as a wound-up emotional machine waiting to be released by the turn of a phrase. Another nice thing about country music is that there's a relationship to musicianship, where production isn't half or more of the listening experience.

There was a quote about your music where you said, "I think it hits the hearts of people who just aren't moved by Bon Jovi or Lynyrd Skynyrd, but it hits in a way like those people."
Uh-huh. That's kind of like what we were talking about [regarding the early Palace records]. The intention was to make songs that were not, *apparently*, multilayered songs, because it would be more fun to make, and more fun to play, and more fun to sing, and more fun to record and write.

In terms of production?
Or intent, really. To try to make the songs be what they appeared to be. Putting a lot of work into them, but half the work that goes in is not to have any work evident in the songs. And that seems to be what Bon Jovi and Lynyrd Skynyrd songs are all about as well. There's a lot of things that went into making the songs, but that's not a part of listening to the songs. If you listen to the songs for

two months or six months or a year, and you really just want to get more into the life of those songs, then you *can*, because there's something to get into. But you don't have to. They're worth looking into, but that's not a prerequisite for enjoying them at all.

Do certain songs of your own or other people seem tied to one time period, or do they seem to float across the time span since they were created? And do some things sound relevant at a certain point after they were written in a way they didn't when they were first written?
I'm sure that's the case, but I don't know how relevant something was when it came out if I didn't get access to it until months or years or decades later. Something like Washington Phillips: any time I know of someone hearing Washington Phillips in the last fifteen or twenty years, that person is very moved and touched and awed and pleased by the music.* And I would guess that that probably wasn't the case so much in the 1930s, when it was released, or at least not by the audience that's getting something out of it now. For some reason, as people experienced more and more recordings of songs, this starts to stand out as a diamond. It's like, "Oh! That's actually what we listen for when we listen to music." But at the time it wasn't; it was recording a document of somebody doing something. As all records were. There was no art of recording. This seems like a very artful recording, which

---

* Phillips was an early-twentieth-century gospel singer whose song "I Had a Good Mother and Father" was covered on *There Is No One What Will Take Care of You.*

it arguably wasn't, because I don't think Washington Phillips was a recording artist; he just recorded once a year.

At the time it wasn't much more than standing in front of a microphone . . .
Right. And there may have been weird savants here and there that understood what that meant in terms of acoustics and electronics, and in terms of imagining what that would sound like in somebody's living room or in a general store that had a Victrola player. At a certain point, say, one year, five years, ten years after someone begins to listen to 78s, you could imagine that someone would think, "Oh, I would do *this* when I play, in *this* context, but if *I* were gonna sit in front of that microphone, *this* is what I would do, because I've listened to enough records." There probably were some people who were really focused in that way, even just an individual performer with one instrument and their voice who would say, "I can perform at this hour, for money, but someone might put this record on before breakfast, so I'm gonna make a record that sounds good before breakfast. Even though I can't walk into their house and play before breakfast, I like to listen to the Victrola, I like to listen to my 78s before breakfast." Who might think, "Yeah, that's the point. That's why you make a record—because it could be played any time, and what I do otherwise can only be done at night, in front of people."

How much do you go back and listen to your older recordings?
I get a lot of joy out of hearing the recordings unexpectedly. When I consciously push "play" on one of the records myself,

it's essentially like trying to tickle yourself—it almost doesn't feel like it exists. So I find I usually listen to it for a specific reason, but I can't get back into the audience position very easily. But any time I *randomly* hear a song, in a coffee shop or someone's iPod, I get a lot of joy out of that 'cause I can fully get into the experience of recording it but also enjoy it as an audience, which is how it's intended to be.

When you *do* hear things, does it ever surprise you? Do you feel like your relationship to the recordings has changed, or is it something that continues to change?

It continues to change every time I hear it. One thing that is kind of constant, although I've grown more accustomed to it now, is that I think in my mind I was always singing with a degree of fluency and expression that I didn't actually have but that I've gained more of over the years. So when I listen to something, I'll hear all these limitations. I was using my instrument to the best of my ability at the time, but I can hear the limitations now that I couldn't hear then, which was striking for a while.

You once played *Arise Therefore* in its entirety—with Dave Heumann, Thomas Van Cottom, and François Verrue at the All Tomorrow's Parties festival [in 2002].*

* All Tomorrow's Parties is a festival curated by a different artist/band every year. Heumann is a member of the Baltimore band Arboretum and toured with BPB in 2001–2; Verrue and Van Cottom performed with BPB in Brussels in 2001.

Shellac was doing one, and I love Shellac and I love Steve [Albini], and so they were like, "We're trying to allocate stuff, budget-wise. Would you do a solo thing?" I was like, "Mm, I don't really like playing solo." And then I wanted to play *Arise Therefore* because of my specific relationship with Steve on that record.

You also did *I See a Darkness* live, start to finish, years later in Louisville.
Yeah. This was before people began charging high prices to make people watch them play old records.

So the ATP performance was really ahead of the curve.
I guess so [*laughs*].

Seemed like a good idea at first . . .
Kind of . . . I mean, even when we did it that night, I was like, "This is an interesting idea, but I don't think I would do it again." And I did it again for a specific reason, part of which was it was a benefit, a tenth anniversary party for Wild and Woolly Video. The tickets were $5, and we opened for Blowfly, with Fred Armisen* playing before us, doing the drum thing. So basically it was just saying, "If you're gonna do this kind of indulgent bullshit, you need to provide other entertainment and charge

---

* Blowfly is the costumed alter ego of songwriter/performer Clarence Reid, who has been penning and recording sexually explicit soul/proto-rap songs since the early 1970s. Comedian / *Saturday Night Live* star Armisen also played drums in the 1990s Chicago indie-rock band Trenchmouth.

a lower ticket price" [*laughs*]. But I did get everybody from the record to come and play on it. Arellano came, Colin came, Pajo came up, and we added Sweeney just because I'd been playing so much with him at the time, and Pete and Paul.

Do your records in some way encapsulate what's been going on since the last record, like a yearbook?

I don't have much of a relationship to the word "yearbook," 'cause my school was too disorganized to really have a functioning yearbook. It's more in reverse, where it's presenting new ideas, lyrically and musically, and in terms of collaboration and cooperation. Not to sum up, but to begin; to gather ideas, ideas, ideas, ideas, make a record as sort of a focal point, the beginning of understanding where those ideas were going and where they *will* go. It's only reflecting back on research, or imagining what could occur. That's the crucible, and beyond that is, "OK, what have I learned from that experiment and how will that affect the year to come, the period of time to come?" There's a lot of tension and labor that goes into making a record, so when the final mixing is done and the final mastering and the final artwork, all that stuff, then it *does* feel like, "Aw, yeah!" Then I look forward to beginning this yearlong process again. In that way, it's more like movie-making than record-making.

People think of making a record as the end of something. In every way, it seems much more about the future, and part of the true excitement of making and finishing a record is thinking, "OK, this is now part of the future. Now my life is going to be moving forward in time in parallel with the life of this piece of work," and watching what happens then. Definitely not showing people what happened before. You trade off who's the control—am *I* the control or is the *record* the control in the years to come in terms of how it reverberates against and with the world?

Maybe it's an effect of making music, or maybe it's making music that makes me think this way, but I'm always considering how each moment will affect what happens in the future. In making a record or writing a song, you have to have some concept of an end in mind. Whenever they push "record" and I begin singing, when I come to the first pause I can't help but think, "Is *this* going to be the take? Is *that* going to be how I will hear that first line for the rest of my life?" And also how that will affect where I'm going and how I'll get to the end of the song.

For *Bonnie "Prince" Billy Sings Greatest Palace Music* [2004] you asked fans to select Palace-era songs to be redone, and then, in the style of *The Very Best of the Everly Brothers* album, went and re-recorded them in Nashville with some venerable session players and your own associates. You also thought of having people like Dolly Parton and Don Williams sing them.
Mark [Nevers] said he would try to get Williams and Parton, but we didn't have any luck. I think we might've tried to get Don Everly also. But we turned out to get a pretty good lineup of folks on there. I didn't want to do it with new songs because I'm obsessive with new songs, and I didn't want to obsess with these people that knew exactly what they were doing—at least not until I'd done a session with them once.

With *Greatest Palace Music*, the idea was that Bonnie could sing these songs because they already had their own lives and he didn't have to worry about creating new ones for them. All the musicians who played on that record worked with confidence that there was already something there, and there wasn't *fear* of discovery—only the *joy* of discovery. And whether it's *Charlie Rich Sings Country and Western* [1967], which is Charlie Rich singing all Hank Williams songs, or George Jones singing Leon Payne [*George Jones Sings the Great Songs of Leon Payne*, 1971], all those, I thought about that as a tradition among many that the record could fall into.

I hadn't researched who any of the musicians were in that Nashville session. There was so much history apparent in their playing, and after a few songs I realized that some of the records that are most important to me had these musicians on them. But since they were the kind of people whose names didn't appear on the records, it wasn't until we started playing and I could *hear* it that I was like, "Whoa, wait a second." I got into a conversation with Pig Robbins, who was the piano player. I started to suspect or recognize some things about his style, to the point where it was specific, and I asked him, "Do you know those Billy Sherrill / Charlie Rich records in the early 1970s?"

"Yep."

"That isn't Charlie Rich playing piano on those records, is it?"

"Nope."

"That was you, wasn't it?"

"Yep."

"Thought so."

Immediately, it occurred to me that I probably don't have anything else in common with Charlie Rich, but I've got a record with Pig Robbins playing distinctive piano parts, and that's enough for me.

The guys were happy to be playing with each other in the same room. Most of them had played together occasionally for over forty years, but had rarely, if ever, been all in the same place at once. They were hilarious. They have a funny phrase that they kick about, which is, whenever a session musician plays on somebody's final session or final show, they say they "killed" him. So one would be like, "I killed Johnny Paycheck." They'd bring that up once or twice a day.

With "I Am a Cinematographer," I said, "Can we do it with a little more swing?" Within minutes, the Bob Wills interludes were arranged, and Eddie [Bayers], the drummer, basically cut the beat in half. He kept the same beats per minute, but it felt slower. But I felt like that's what their speciality is, coming in and attacking a song based on everything they know about music, recording sessions and songs. And so I figured whatever direction I was going to give was going to take the shape of what I brought to it after the session, like all the overdubs with friends and family and other musicians, and the mixing and choosing of songs.

You said before that seeing how you could work with Nashville session people led to *Greatest Palace Music*. Did doing the session with Johnny Cash also lead to it?
I don't think so.

What made me think of it was, when I listen to *Greatest*, I feel like you're singing the songs in the same way that Johnny Cash would be interpreting someone else's song, rather than you redoing your own songs. Partially because the voice is so different in the Bonnie era than it was on the Palace recordings.

Once we did *Master and Everyone*, I had a fantasy to do a Nashville record with Nashville session musicians, and Mark was into it. For the year between, I actually spent a lot of time coming up with a list of songs to do for this session. My idea, at first, was to make a record of great soft-rock songs of the 1970s that people looked down their nose at but were undeniably great songs, including "Don't Go Breaking My Heart" by Elton John and Kiki Dee, "Two Out of Three Ain't Bad" by Meat Loaf, or some REO Speedwagon and Journey songs. I figured that the Nashville musicians would approach them in a straight, professional, and great manner, and that would be a good way of doing those songs. Only as we got closer did I start thinking how we're playing all these old songs in the Bonnie Prince Billy sets, like Danzig used to play Misfits songs in the Samhain set. But if someone buys Bonnie Prince Billy records and then goes to the show, I want them to not necessarily feel like, "What's this song, what's this song?" And also not feel like people should have to go back and *find* these [Palace] records. So I thought, "We'll make these part of the Bonnie Prince Billy group of songs by doing them." It was approached like a singer singing somebody else's songs. I didn't know how I was gonna sing until I was in the studio with those guys, and when they started playing that was the voice that came out, which blew my mind. I was surprised. I was like, "Wow, who is this person singing, singing with this kind of confidence and not too out of place with these incredible session musicians?" I didn't know that I was gonna *do* that; that's literally what happened once we started in the studio. And except for "New Partner" and maybe "Agnes, Queen of Sorrow," they're all live vocal takes. Live *with* the A-list musicians, while they were playing. Then we started overdubbing, which was really fun.

In general, how much of the vocal delivery comes to you in the moment? How premeditated is each take of a song? How much of the phrasing is something you've thought about in advance? Very little. That's one of my joys. My excitement is . . . like getting to the top of a ski jump. When the phrase is about to begin, it's like, "Let's see if I'm prepared or not; let's see what happens," and then listening as I'm going along, to some extent. [The exceptions are] one song on *Greatest Palace Music* and one on *The Wonder Show of the World*; there's probably been more, but these are two very specific, very vivid instances. On *Greatest Palace Music* there was the song "New Partner," which sometimes I have difficulty getting into and I feel kind of a burden because listeners talk about liking that song more than others. David Berman came in, and he was like my acting coach on that song. It didn't prepare the phrasing; just a character which allowed for the phrasing to come out. We did different takes, and David told me, "OK, that's good. But it's more like you've been driving this truck for sixteen hours and your ex-wife calls you around 5:30 p.m. and you still have five more hours, and it was great to talk to her but you couldn't tell if she wanted to see you again when you got back to town or if she didn't, and so that's all you were thinking about, and you couldn't find a radio station that was playing . . ."—things like that. And it clicked.

On *The Wonder Show of the World* there's a song that's based on an Italian pop song by a guy named Piero Ciampi; the lyrics are tangentially related to the lyrics of that song. After we recorded a few takes, I started to imagine this character [*laughs*], and it was really fun to imagine this older Italian divorcee, very tan with a Speedo bathing suit, waking up at twelve thirty or one in the afternoon at his rented condo on the beach, and the first thing he does is go out to watch girls walk by on the beach and smoke a cigarette. I sang this whole song like that, and Shahzad [Ismaily, multi-instrumentalist, engineer] convinced us, "That's the take."

There are a lot of guests on *Greatest Palace Music*, like [Jesus Lizard guitarist] Duane Denison, D.V. [DeVincentis]—on saxophone, which I didn't know he played—[arranger and solo artist] Andrew Bird, Sweeney, Colin Gagon, Jack Carneal, Ned, and Aram Stith.

Paul's on one song. And Dave Bird and Todd are in there somewhere, I believe. Yeah, I wanted *that* to be kind of like a yearbook thing, so the songs came from the past ten years; and then the idea that not only can the songs be in the same room with all these incredible musicians, but also all these *people* who are out doing their own thing, all over the country—*they* belong in here too. With the idea being if you love music, from any period, then you *are* a part of that music, you belong with that music, and it's not a separate existence.

The other thing to note about this record is that you added some songs that the fans had not selected to be on there.

Yeah, the fan thing was more like a checking in. It's not like they were gonna have the final say; it was more just saying, "I'm making believe that this is a best-of or a greatest hits kind of thing, but I don't really know what that means, because we don't have song sales figures or anything like that. All I know is what people shout out at the shows." So I was just curious if there were going to be any surprises. I also knew that the fans that reported in were the sort of fans who sit at their computers and look at the Internet and fill out forms like that, so I didn't imagine that was the exclusive voice or the exclusive audience. "Viva Ultra" and "No More Workhorse Blues" probably weren't in the top [choices], but I wanted to do those so we did them anyway. There was a great "O How I Enjoy the Light" that Bob did a bunch of stuff on that didn't make it on there, and "Idle Hands" and "Come In" also.

Overall, what effect do you think the audience has on your work?

I feel the value of my work is determined very precisely by the audience. What does entertainment mean, anyway, and what's the difference between that and art? I would say the main difference is that art isn't necessarily funded by the consumer, but entertainment always is. In that way, entertainment is a million times more important to me than art, and being an entertainer is more important to me than being an artist. The relationship with the audience is so direct, while the government or rich collectors are going to pay for something that is art rather than the person who is actually going to have a relationship with the piece. That's what's most important to me about what I do. I think of entertainment as being very serious and important, from Laurel and Hardy upward. It has to do with emotions of release, giving up, or extreme hilarity and absurdity.

It's rewarding when I find a broader audience that doesn't think I'm too crazy. [I'm] trying to make something for that audience to experience, also knowing that at some level I will be sharing the experience. My absolute, purest particular taste would not be something that could be appreciated on a grand scale. It just wouldn't. If I really made a record just to serve myself I would end up alone in a dark, wet room, you know? That's not really where I want to be. That's why it's more important to me to make a record that serves itself and its audience well. A good record should involve my needs, the listeners' needs, and the needs of the other people who worked on the record. If I manage that, I feel I've accomplished something; but ultimately it is the audience that holds the lion's share of determining if a record is worthwhile. The only way for my entire audience to appreciate the music is if they come to it *of their own accord* and find something in it that satisfies them as individuals. I'll do what I can do, and they'll do what they can do, and hopefully a mutual understanding can be formed.

The Palace records were sung to an imagined audience, based on a knowledge of myself as an audience member. And then, of course, I got to know the audience better, so the imagined-audience concept was no longer feasible. That's where the Palace records ended.

Do you have a sense of how your audience has changed over the years?
No. Because again, most of the music that *I* listen to I have zero relationship or contact or communication with the people who made it. Most of the music that I love the most is that way, because the people who are responsible for those musics are dead or they're foreign or they're too rich and famous. So I'm gonna assume that it's the same, that I'll never know who the audience is that is really into the music . . . I'll never know who they are or why they're into it. I listen to enough music from different times and places that it's always my hope that any records I am involved with have a chance of finding an individual or five people somewhere else in the world: they're most likely not gonna ever find the bulk of their audience here in Louisville, Kentucky. I wouldn't release a song that I don't have some love for, and I also know that if I have love for it then someone else will, but I never know who it's going to be.

But from touring do you have an idea of who's coming to the shows?
Touring is people that want to go to clubs, and I don't like to go to clubs, so I'm assuming that many of the people who are

really connecting to the music don't go to clubs. I do go to shows
sometimes, but a lot of people go a lot because they like going
to shows. So you never know what the audience makeup is; how
many people are just going to the *club*—went and saw Truman's
Water last week and whoever next week—and also how many
people are there and get something out of what occurs live as
opposed to [on record]. Hopefully there are people who don't
live in cities that you have access to that are into the music. Ideally, most people who connect to my music are going to do it
in relation to their own universe and not mine. That's why it's
mass-produced: so it can have an existence in the places that I
myself will never reach. *More people probably know about the music
than will ever get a chance to go to a show.* So I don't think of that
as a good barometer.

It was great that this Swedish guy [Magnus Bärtås], for example, wanted whatever my voice would bring to this film he was
making [*Madame & Little Boy*]. That's when I get clues, but I
don't know if they're misleading or not. The Coil guy [Jhonn
Balance], in the months leading up to his death, was reaching
out to communicate and possibly collaborate, and again it's
like, "Wow, this might be working." I can't imagine a direct line
of communication there, but a communication *is* being accomplished on some level. I like to think that I don't know who the
audience is and that the reason you're making the music, also,
is for people who are maybe inhibited—or prohibited in some
ways—in their ability to connect, and that's part of what it's for.
When people put energy into a recording, then that recording can keep giving that energy; the audience is absorbing that

energy and ideally, and most likely, recycling it in some way. And it may or may not get back to the people that made the record, the people that put out the record, the people that distributed the record, everybody who had a hand in making it available. If there's a good energy that the person gets, it might circulate back.

Or your show guarantees go up, which is another way of seeing that things are evolving. For years, Ali [Hendrick] and Boche [Billions] at Billions [booking agency], especially Ali, would lowball things, because I think we work outside of lots of news and advertising scenes, so when the tour was over and I was paying Ali the commission, she would be like, "Wow, those shows did really well!" She didn't expect them to do well because she didn't read about me in the magazines, so she just assumed that the audiences would be lukewarm or not there. But I figured that there were people who like their music not to be fed to them or filtered through other voices.

A band like Metallica, who sell millions of albums, you only see them on the cover of *Rolling Stone* maybe once every ten years. Yeah, but they seem over the last ten, fifteen years to be more participant with the machine . . . They were part of the crew of folks who were up in arms early against file sharing, which is a bad sign, I think. That implies to me a disconnect between the audience and the musician. You're making music and people are loving it: now, what's your problem? Don't have enough money? What? It seemed like the people who were the most outspoken were probably people who were out of touch [*laughs*].

Or it's just a knee-jerk response to what they perceived as being piracy.

Yeah, but what is their priority if that's where their reflexes are at that point? And maybe also at that point becoming too dependent upon advances as opposed to being dependent upon a symbiotic relationship with the audience. Like hearing from their record company, "You didn't recoup your advance."

"What? Whose fault is that?"

"Everyone's stealing music."

"Let's take 'em to court."

Take to court the people who are keeping your music alive? You want to sue 'em? That's the ultimate insanity.

Because the same people are going to the concerts, which is really what's paying their salaries.

Right, they're going to the concerts and they're keeping things like licensing fees up; that there's a demand for the music means that they can live. It also means that if they go broke tomorrow because the record companies robbed them, there's likely going to be hundreds of thousands of people that would be willing to give them five dollars or take them into their house because they love them, because they love their music. These are your people!

I've always been curious about your ideas regarding onstage etiquette. Are there certain things that you think have no place being onstage, and certain things that you think a performer should be doing when they're onstage?

When I saw Bruce Springsteen play on the *Tunnel of Love* tour [1988], I think I was probably just at the point of realization that a show like that, there's nothing off-the-cuff, no improvisation. All this talk between songs is memorized, and it's the same every single night. And I don't like that. I feel like Bruce Springsteen seems to be a kind of dishonest performer in a lot of ways, and that's one of them, because he's fooling people. It seems like he's fooling people all the time with what he does. And I love a lot of his music, you know, but then it seems like he, on some levels, lost touch between fantasy and reality and bounces back and forth a lot of times, and I don't think that's healthy for an audience.

We did a week of shows with Shannon Wright. She's a really good musician, but another thing is when people try to discipline the audience from the stage and tell them how they should be behaving, telling them to be quiet or telling them *anything*, you know? Like, "What makes you the boss?" When they come and they're paying you, *you're* not the boss, the *audience* is the boss, *they paid you. They are your boss.* You can't reprimand people from the stage for doing what they want to do with their fuckin' money that they brought in. If you can't hold their attention, then that's your problem; if you can't handle the audience acting human, then don't go play. But I don't like witnessing and I don't like being in the audience when the people on the stage get upset when people are talking.

I remember last year I went to two shows downtown at Freedom Hall: I went to see Bob Dylan, with Elvis Costello opening for him, and then saw R. Kelly. The Bob Dylan show was very bad, and the audience was distracted. It was also a third full, and whenever you see Bob Dylan over the last ten years, it's as if the musicians are all in soundproof booths. The amount of onstage communication I've witnessed in the three or four shows I've seen . . . it's just like watching player pianos onstage who probably don't know each other's middle name or what anyone's gonna do after the show. It just looks *awful*, harsh, and unpleasant. Like you're going into an H&R Block office instead of a show. And then at the R. Kelly show, everybody on- and off-stage is there for a reason, and you can feel it every moment; just full-on engagement, with the music, with each other, between the performer and the audience—really cool.

I never know when it's going to happen, but I *like* it when we have a night somewhere, or I have a night somewhere, where there is in-between-song banter that has content to it. But I never know when that's going to happen. I think that it's important, because people have been fooled into thinking that people are really talking to them from the stage, to *really talk* to them from the stage. And if you don't have anything to say, then don't say anything—don't say the same joke every night. Although seeing this R. Kelly show, everything was choreographed, and there's lots of casual moments in the show that are choreographed. But it's such an epic and elaborate production that I'm impressed with the showmanship of those moments. I'm just blown away by his ability as a performer to pull off this epic night that includes these orchestrated but sort of casual-seeming moments in com-bination with all the other things that go on over the course of the two-hour show. I don't know if that's hypocritical, but it's exciting. I was standing next to a woman who had seen the show a month before, in Memphis, and she would sometimes say, "Now watch what he does with that pair of underwear." When I told Dan [Koretzky] afterwards that the underwear gag was part of the show, he was like, "*No!*"

What about spontaneous onstage expressions that have to do with drunkenness, or band members getting into a physical altercation onstage?

I've seen very, very, very few Cat Power shows, and I've been fortunate that every one that I've seen has been a full set, but I know there was a show here in Louisville that she played, years ago, where apparently she went onstage, started a song, screamed at the top of her lungs and left, and that was the show. I'm not into it. And it's telling about my understanding of the world at large that I'm completely mystified, and I can't get to the place where I understand why someone would go to see her again. But people have, and people do. That baffles me, and maybe it's the same as people wanting to see a train wreck happen, or maybe not knowing what to expect and it's a whole new set of rubes that are laying their money down, thinking, "Oh, I'm going to a show."

She's been doing [complete] shows for the last three years, or something like that. But for that period of ten years or so where I don't know if it was half the shows she did or a quarter or two-thirds or four-fifths . . . Compare that to the Dr. Hook video—I think you can find it on YouTube—a show that they did in a European TV studio in the early to mid-1970s, where one or more of them is apparently intoxicated to a high degree. They play a full set, and it always seems like it's about to fall apart, and there's one point where he vomits and then sings into the lead mic. And another guy in the band, they have to trade off for one song and he covers the mic with a handkerchief 'cause he doesn't want the vomit smell . . . But they're so good, the harmonies; they'll sing this chorus part together, and you're just like, "Yeah!" They do the show—and it's really exciting, knowing that there are things working against the show, but they push themselves through to do it. If someone has a fistfight onstage and they keep doing the show, then that's great. To some extent, there should always be potential for every night on any given artist's tour to offer something different, and it could be *vastly* different or microscopically different.

Seeing the Mekons play in Central Park in 1991—amazing set, one of the best shows I've seen. Then they played in Asbury Park that night with Pere Ubu, and it was also a great set, but if I'd just seen that set I might not think so. Because it was just kind of dark, they were dealing with very spent tanks, you know [*laughs*], like empty energy tanks—but it was great to see people play music that I *loved*, full *and* empty. And to see them find a way to get through a song in the set, both ways. Seeing one show was great, but seeing *both* of those shows was *really great*. 'Cause it was like, "I can see how these songs can be completely different"—and the Mekons, as people and personalities onstage they can be anything, but as musicians they're not necessarily the most spontaneous group; the songs have parts and melodies and harmonies, and that's it. But the energy and spontaneity between songs and how a song might end could always be different.

You haven't toured as an opening act very much, although one of your earliest appearances, in 1988, was as an opening act for Rapeman, which involved anal breathing.[*]
I was living in Providence. It was probably the first semester that I tried to go to school, and Rapeman played at CBGB and I went to the show. Steve [Albini] either knew or suspected that I could do that, and he offered me $50 to do it. Fifty bucks was great, and also kind of a perverse thrill at knowing that he would be singing with this microphone that I had pushed up against my butt. And getting to perform at CBGB—it was my only performance there.

The Björk tour [in 2003]: she asked through Billions, and Boche seemed totally surprised that I had been invited to open. But it was an easy decision because I wanted to see her show every night. I knew at that point, after having hung out with her a little bit and followed her music somewhat, but not too much, that she had an extensive attention to detail, and I figured that the shows would be great in the way that *A Thousand Pieces of Gold* and *Matewan* were great: that the crew would be great, that the lighting people would be great, that the sound people would be great, the musicians would be great—and it was true.

---

[*] WO: "This skill developed among certain high-school peers in the 1980s in Louisville, of drawing air into your anus and pushing it out, being able to make all sorts of noise in both directions."

I don't remember what it was, but it was a respectful offer; I could afford to do it, even though I did it solo. I could afford to rent a car, fly to these places and play these shows, and then see the shows every night, which was cool because she played these outdoor venues, had fireworks every show. And [electronic duo] Matmos were on the tour, which was great, 'cause I knew Drew [Daniel] from my teenage years here. That was a nice trip. I was sort of like a little cork on the sea of Björk, just bobbing around and watching everything that happened.

PJ Harvey asked me to do a tour a year or two before, and made some kind of offer personally. Then her management said, "Actually, this is what we can afford," and I think it was like $250 a show. I talked to Boche, and he was like, "Well, that's standard for people who open for bigger acts," and I was like, "Can't do it [*laughs*], don't wanna do it." He said even if you open for bigger things, like the Rolling Stones or whatever, that oftentimes the guarantee is pathetic because the idea is that they're doing you a huge favor by having you play with them. It's to the point where you essentially are paying to play before these bigger acts.

This is one of the myths of the music industry, that somehow by opening for huge acts you're going to win new fans. For one thing, most of the time no one's even there yet.
Right. I remember seeing Sonic Youth open for Neil Young in Washington DC in 1991 and standing next to a guy, and halfway through the set he was like, "That dude playing bass has tits" [*laughs*]. That was his reaction to the Sonic Youth set. Which I

thought was an amazing set, but again, it's mostly people getting to their seats, drinkin' beer, talking to each other.

I actually like seeing a band facing a slightly antagonistic or indifferent audience; in fact, I once saw [New York noise outfit] No Neck Blues Band open for Royal Trux at Mercury Lounge, who you would think might have a sympathetic audience, but they were given a hard time, and they don't usually play regular venues anyway. I enjoyed that a bit more than seeing them play a show in their own loft, which was more like preaching to the choir.

Yeah, I think the show ends up being better all around, if you make sure there's a reason besides the traditional reason for two acts to be playing together, because the traditional reason just doesn't have any basis, I don't think. I saw Jonathan Richman [in the late 1980s], and he was great. He had an eight- or nine-piece sort of Latin-funk party band open for him. They were super fun, and I remember asking someone [who worked at the venue], "How'd they get teamed up?" They said, "His contract required that we pick a band that would make the audience happy" [*laughs*].

You were booed at the Hollywood Bowl on the Björk tour.
Yes. Extensively.

Which you've said you were into.
Yeah, 'cause I figured, from the very first, that tickets were forty, fifty, sixty bucks, and Björk was Björk, and I knew there was not

going to be a single person—and if there *was*, there might have been *a single* person at each of the shows that I played—that knew who I was or gave a shit that I was there. The goal isn't to play a great set so they don't enjoy the Björk set as much; it's *her* night, you know? That night was amazing, 'cause people were listening and booing and shouting obscene things. For me, the tour was about seeing how Björk put a tour together, and everything else was gravy; so that was delicious gravy. Being at the Hollywood Bowl was amazing, and then being onstage, having this reaction, knowing that it didn't matter *at all* since I didn't care what they thought, necessarily; I wasn't trying to get an audience from playing the tour. There was no emotional build; the whole thing would be one piece, roughly twelve songs, autoharp only. I was trying to learn the autoharp, 'cause I thought, "While I play music every night I might as well be learning something, so I'm gonna learn how to sing and accompany myself on the autoharp."

And that helped me learn to not take the autoharp out again.

8

THE WEED TREE

ALAN LICHT: Do you prefer the relative permanence of albums or recorded music as opposed to a live performance?

WILL OLDHAM: They play completely different roles. The records are just trying to get the songs across, and then live we're just trying to spend time together. It's great that records are sort of permanent or consistent, that you can listen to them again; maybe it's even just that records can apply to any aspect of life, whereas a live show can't, so they're totally different. It's nice to have the ability to experience the music however, whenever, wherever you want, or to know that there's going to be random interactions with recordings, whereas the live experience is so much more limited because it happens at a specific time, and that's it. And a specific place. You can't say, "This show's going to happen at seven thirty this Friday. Where do you want to see it?" Can't even do that [*laughs*].

The recording is a crucial part. I write a song to be recorded. And to some extent to be performed, but definitely more to be recorded than performed, because the recording will last longer than a performance. With a recording you can layer the levels of expression. You can have two live events occurring simultaneously on a recording, because you can do one live take and then throw a musician into that recording and force them to play live against it. Right then you've got two live events occurring simultaneously. Then a third level of that is when you're mixing. That's kind of a performance in and of itself, an interpretation, so that's three things. So your brain is hearing three different musical, emotional, artistic moments, and they're interrelating to each other, and it can provide for years and years and years of listening.

I like the idea of sometimes drawing attention to the fact that it's a record. Not only is it a moment in time, it's a construction. And there's something beautiful about that. There's the great *Zelig*-like publicity photo for either the Drag City Red Krayola self-titled record or *Hazel*, which was a composite photograph of everybody that played on it. I remember it as looking like an absolutely obvious, crazy sort of dinner-party scene. No two people were in the same room together when the photos were taken—which I think is the way that record was made, which is very exciting as well. He [Red Krayola leader Mayo Thompson] just sent the tapes around, with maybe [John] McEntire adding drums last of all.

Someone made the point that all films are documentaries, in that they always document something that happened, even if it was on a soundstage.[*]

Right. Though there can be more or less documentary material available to the viewer depending on how the movie ends up. Watching *Avatar*, or most James Cameron movies, you're losing that kind of documentary material because the technical side is so huge that it's impossible to get a feel for it in a two-hour movie; you can't get a feel for thousands of computer anima-

---

[*] See Richard Roud, *Jean Marie Straub* (New York: Viking Press, 1972), p. 67.

tors. Whereas if it's a two-hour movie where there's a cinema-tographer, a director, an editor, it's easier to isolate decisions. Whether or not you can understand them, you feel more like, "Whoa, there's something about that scene I can relate to, and it's not just the script and it's not just the acting"—that there's something else.

With movies and records, I like it where I can at least imag-ine that I'm hearing or watching or experiencing not just the relaying of the material but . . . that what's recorded is an actual event. And it's almost ideal if it could not be reproduced the next day. It seems like something should be going on in the studio, something should be happening in the recording pro-cess for it to feel like a special event. Either the song can be to some extent written at the time of the recording, or the guitar part, the one you hear on the record, is the first time you ever hear it played, combined with predetermined elements, so it's not just all improvisation. The first Boston record, or the R. Kelly record *Chocolate Factory*, those are two examples of where it seems to be all about the recording experience, an excite-ment going on in regard to how something is mixed or how something is produced and arranged.

It's funny to see the duping of indie bands that goes on. Peo-ple think they're going to go and record with Steve Albini and that's going to make a magical record, and all Steve does is turn on the tape recorder and show them what their music sounds like. And 90 percent of the time it's unexciting because they play like they're having band practice, and then it's over. Then they think, "This is a magic record because Steve Albini made it." The recording studio is a very special place; it's not just *being there* that makes it happen. A decision has to be made, multiple decisions. You can hear the decision that was made just prior to pushing "record" on the singer's part; you get the sense that you're hearing the brain or a body or a human or a soul experiencing what you're listening to or watching.

When you go into the recording studio there should be no preconception of what you're going to leave with. It's usually a surprise in the studio; even going in with a small group of people there's no way you can tell how it's going to sound. With *Arise* there's the same amount of people on each track as there is on the *Hope* EP, yet the *Hope* EP has this full, complicated sound. So you can never tell how things are going to come out at the end of the process. I didn't know what it was going to sound like to bring Ned, Grubbs, and the drum machine together. I had no idea. It sounds totally different than I expected.

I try to document the pure moments that occur over a month between a particular group. Part of the idea in making a record is to freeze lots of moments of learning and discovery so that it really is like every time you press "play" you are opening up this experiment again and this coming together of people. I like the records to have integrity within themselves, so that every song is dealt with the same way the other songs were. That's a fault I find with Neil Young records: during his best period, from 1970 to 1980, his records are weird because they're a hodgepodge of sessions, musicians, and producers. Whereas I like a record where the diversity of the songs comes from approaching them in the same way, so it comes from something inside the musicians or inside the songs and not with how we dealt with it. Even using the iPod as a listening device and shuffling, sometimes that can really shine a spotlight on what songs originally *were*, together as an album. If you listen to ten Thin Lizzy records on shuffle, you can understand, "Oh, that's that sound! That's when the drums sounded like *this*. That's when *this* musician was playing with them." You recognize that that's what an album is: not even necessarily a collection of songs that go together, but a record of that moment in this ensemble's history and what they sounded like, how they felt about their music, and how they felt about each other. That's the value, to me, of a record. It's a time to go over multiple kinds of songs and show yourself what's happening with all these musicians and how good you are at attacking songs. That value will never go away. Any time you record two songs as opposed to one, it's like "Oh, wow," to hear how they're related to each other in so many ways—not just thematically.

What about the experience of listening to an album multiple times? When you listen to an album once, you don't really know the songs. If you listen to it several more times you know the songs better and to some extent your relationship to them changes.

For every record, *if* it changes and the *way* that it changes is unique. There are records that you listen to and don't give a shit about or dislike that become essential to your relationship to music over repeated listens, and then there's records that you listen to and you'll be like, "Wow, I have a feeling this is going to be one of my favorite records for a long time to come." And then you might listen to it one more time and it never occurs to you to put it on again, and then you sell it three years later. That's part of the excitement—that you don't know what your relationship to a record is going to be until you're dead, because it always has the potential to change. With any record, on any given day, you could have a different relationship to it.

How important are lyrics to you as a listener and as a singer?
When I listen to a song, it seems like it can be about the relationship between the singer and his or her voice and the melody he or she is trying to sing, and I won't even notice what the lyric is. A great thing about songs is that they're not all built on delivery—certainly not to the extent that a scene in a play or a movie is—because they are also so much built on the melody and structure, along with the words. So the performance can vary if you have any faith at all in the song itself. If you can get through the melody and the lyrics, there should still be something *there*, whether or not the words make sense that night. Sometimes the words don't make sense; different songs make sense on different nights in different ways. But it's important to remember that the totality of the song doesn't lie only in the lyrical content. The song is equally instrumentation and melody and structure and just the rhythm of the lyric, the words within the lyric. Not the significance of the words, what they mean in English, but what they mean in order.

It's hard to know what a song's about sometimes. There's a Roy Harper song called "I'll See You Again." I first heard it in a bar, and it blew me away. I asked the bartender if I could borrow it. I listened to that song over and over. I became totally obsessed. When I played it for my girlfriend, she started crying, saying they were just the saddest, meanest lyrics she'd ever heard. I went, "Lyrics?" I hadn't even *noticed* what they were about. At all. And I think sometimes I have the same relationship with my own songs. The lyrics have their own existence—I knew what I was doing when I wrote them—so I don't have to worry about them anymore. When you revisit them, you're a different person.

The greatest songs are the ones you can listen to for years and years and they'll always offer up more. I have found, increasingly as I get older, that a lot of the songs that are most important to me are songs that continue to teach me things, sometimes over the course of, God knows, maybe thirty years. Songs that I can enjoy on some level on the first listen at age fifteen and then get more into at twenty-three and more into at thirty-five. And the listening experience is completely different, and I never could have gotten to this different level of listening if I hadn't started with it a long time ago. But ideally there are things put in there for your enjoyment, and things put in there ideally for your edification. If it has legs, then you can one day get to the center of the Tootsie Pop.

For the *Superwolf* album, you wrote the lyrics and sent them to Matt Sweeney, who wrote the music.
That was the experiment. Zwan had imploded by that point. Domino had asked for this show, in London, and I was trying

to think of a way to make the show interesting for myself. I called Matt: "Would you want to play this show with me, and as part of it, to make it interesting, what if we wrote two or three songs together and played them that night for the first time?" He was into the idea, and that's how we started with the *Superwolf* stuff.

You and Matt hadn't written anything together before this, even though you'd played together for a few years. Was this to encourage him to keep writing in the aftermath of Zwan?
Yeah. Zwan was very painful, for me and for a few other people that I know. It was painful losing touch with friends while they did something that I couldn't think of a good reason for them to do. And it was just confusing because there were a lot of people who were trying to be optimistic about it, which I thought was counterproductive, because there was no foundation for that optimism. Matt, whom I was starting to play with regularly, essentially dropped off the face of the earth.

Matt and I could play together, but rather than do something that's slowly inching him back into the real world, we tried to make it more intensive, more like actually jumping in full-force, going further than we did before . . . I wanted him back in the world! [*laughs*] And figuring that out of a year and a half or however long of frustration, there would be an explosion of effort and ambition and creativity, which turned out to be the case. I sent three songs to him, and it worked so well [at the London show] it was like, "How about continuing with this? Let's do a full set of songs."

What was Cockfighter? Was that an earlier name for this?

It may have been. *Superwolf* was what we named the record and ended up being what we and other people called the collaboration, but it was just the name of the record. Before that, I think we would just fuck around with different possible names, but never very seriously. We might have played a show and said, "Let's call this a Cockfighter show," instead of a Bonnie Prince Billy show—just playing around with the idea of having a name at all.

Pete Townsend drums on a little of it, but most of it is just voice and guitar. Was there talk of doing it more as a band, or was it just decided to do it that way?

To just do it that way. The parts that Pete is on, Matt said, "I really want to hear drums on this."

There was some double-tracking on the vocals, which is not usually the way you go.

Yeah. Startin' to learn [*laughs*].

What was the monologue/dialogue on "Blood Embrace"?

It's from *Rolling Thunder* [1977], which is a sort of Vietnam-veteran revenge movie with William Devane that Matt's friend, the actor Nicky Katt, was way into and pushed hard on us. I think we watched it while we were making the record, and instead of filling the space with a solo or have it be empty we had the idea, "What if we pulled that movie in?" And didn't credit it, so we wouldn't have to deal with rights or anything like that, figuring that nobody would know what it was, which was the case. We watched the movie during the session, and it seemed like some of the more painful themes were, on some level, addressed in that song: themes of circumstantial infidelity and how heartbreaking that is, when the intention is not there, on anybody's part, to be hurtful, and still it's so destructive. Damned if you do and damned if you don't.

It's also like the Joe Wise quote at the end of "Riding" and the Sam Walter Foss poem excerpt at the end of "Gezundheit": an appropriation at the end.
Right, exit music.

The album artwork is by Spencer Sweeney . . .
And Matt, actually. I think there's a couple of parts that are just Spencer, but then a lot of it Spencer and Matt did together. Then the poster was a Babyleg [Brian DeRan] wax painting—a painting made of colored wax instead of paint.

Paul Bowles's quote on drink and drugs was in the package.
That was Matt's idea. I loved the quote, and while I didn't fully understand why Matt wanted it in there, I figured he had reasons to, and as long as *one* of us has a good reason to do something cool, that's enough for me [*laughs*].

Do you find drugs useful or enjoyable, or both?
I think both, yeah. I like mushrooms a lot. I've only tripped on acid a couple of times; I thought I was really prepared to do it

again, and then my dad died, and I didn't do it. But mushrooms—
I like to play on mushrooms and do other things.

Write songs?
No, not really write. And I like pot, specifically on tour or on
a movie shoot. Marijuana's great at the end of the day to come
down off the day. After dealing with so many other people's
energies, marijuana sort of seals you off and gets you back in
touch with your own energies, and that's nice.

How do you compare it to alcohol?
It seems so much healthier. It seems like alcohol is related to poi-
soning and deadening and turning things off, *after* the second
drink. The first two drinks are great, and I recommend them to
anybody, for any reason, and I have no respect for teetotalers who
deny themselves one drink a week or one drink a day even, unless
they have an alcohol problem. But after that second drink it seems
to be about forcing the world to go away and shutting down. People who drink more than three drinks a day, it seems like a little
suicide every day, whereas marijuana seems like the opposite; like,
"I haven't had the chance to appreciate things today, so I'm going
to smoke a little marijuana. It's going to help me find my center
again on some levels." It's more about continuing the day, continuing your thoughts. For me, it's a very sensory thing.

**Are there things with music you think you appreciate more
under the influence of alcohol or drugs than you might
otherwise?**

Alcohol . . . I wouldn't say very much. But it does seem like marijuana can make for a very different listening experience. When you're recording or mixing, you can experience the time expansion, so that it's natural to listen to five seconds of a song over and over again and pay attention to those five seconds of that song. For many listeners, if not most, those five seconds are negligible, although it adds up if you spend a lot of time with every five seconds of the song. But when you get high, you can hear those five seconds, so then all of a sudden it was kind of exciting to listen to music and realize that for a good portion of the population, some part of the time, spending that effort on those five seconds of the song was actually, specifically, *worthwhile.* It wasn't just cumulatively worthwhile; it could mean something to somebody. I also do find that there's certain music that changes . . . I remember the first couple of years of listening to the Faun Fables record *Mother Twilight,* which I liked a lot, when I was straight. Whenever I would put it on when I smoked pot—and it was *always* this way, even when I could anticipate it and think, "Oh, it's not gonna be this way this time when I listen to it"—it would just be so monumentally frightening to listen to, in a serious and scary way. Like being a kid and walking into the woods by yourself without a flashlight, where it's thrilling but you actually do think that something bad might happen. I would get sort of terrified when the voice would start singing. But horrified, terrified, and attracted, because most of me, whether consciously or subconsciously, knew I was fine and safe.

I remember going to Las Vegas. There's some rides on top of a skyscraper. It was very entertaining, the emotion that I felt. I was

99 percent sure that I would die if I rode these rides. My body was revolting against this ride, but I was laughing because I knew that I would live through it . . . It's like when you put the opposite poles of magnets together and it's funny: here's two things, and you're trying to push 'em together; there's nothing between them, but they won't go together. Or if you were gonna jump off a cliff into the water and your body tells you that you can't do it; you know that you can, because it's just water, it's just distance and water, but your body is giving you a huge hurdle. Can you make your body do something that you know is fine? But I don't know how much that translates. There's so much music that we've heard that would have been impossible without intoxicants.

The live album *Summer in the Southeast* was recorded on the "Pebbles and Ripples" tour. You were traveling with someone recording [Kris Poulin], so you had a live album in mind.
Yeah, he joined after a week of shows and then recorded sixteen shows. He didn't need to be on the whole tour; I wanted him to record a lot of shows but I figured they would get better after a week or ten days.

Had you wanted to do a live album for a while?
No. In fact, I always figured there would never be a live record, and then because the two previous tours with the 'bobs [Naybob and Raybob] were so fun and communal-feeling I thought, "If we're ever gonna make a live record, let's do it now."

I wanted it to be like [the Rolling Stones'] *Get Yer Ya-Ya's Out*, 'cause I love that record. And it doesn't affect my loving of it—

in fact, it probably increases it—but I heard that they did a lot of postwork—overdubs and such.

Jagger redid vocals on it.
Yeah. So I was thinking that was how we were gonna approach it, which is why I wanted to multitrack, and then I thought we were gonna get in there and mix the shit out of it and add overdubs and all this stuff, which we didn't end up doing. I ended up, though, listening to sixteen shows over the course of a year, trying to figure out a great set to assemble. And I did mix it, but it's all the live stuff, from probably eight of the sixteen shows that were recorded. There's a song from Orlando, from Athens, Georgia, a few songs from Tallahassee. But wanting to take into account, "OK, there's no audience, there's no weather, there's no environment, so we do, on some level, have to manufacture a narrative over the course of the record that resembles how we would manufacture a narrative over the course of the night with the set."

Someone told me there was a live James Taylor album [1993's *Live*] where they took every line of every song from a different performance.
On purpose?

I think they were looking for the best delivery of every single line. I'd be curious to hear that record just to see how noticeable that is.*

---

* Peter Asher's liner note to the Taylor album is interesting in light of WO's comments on *Summer in the Southeast*: "A live James Taylor album has

Strange. This was trying to be about the whole trip. A live record from a [single] show . . . if it was a great show, it would be a coincidence that it was a great recording, because once it's on record, there's no audience, and the thing that made it great, which is everybody being in the room together, is not there. So I think that's why some great live records weren't necessarily great live shows, and vice versa, some great live shows aren't great live recordings.

It's a boisterous record; you really hear the audience getting into it too, which makes it more fun than a lot of live records where you hear the audience off in the distance.
Yeah, and that's a reason why I like that part of the United States, from the northwest to the southeast: the audiences are less reserved. I always feel like when I'm in a room with between a hundred and 1,500 people, why aren't they making their presence known? This is an opportunity to participate in this night—and in those places they did. There is audience participation all of the time, but mostly the audience doesn't realize it. I love going to the movies when people are talking or yelling at the screen.

---

been suggested, demanded, and contemplated for many years . . . For this record, a tour was planned specifically with a live album in mind. The tour played for three weeks in a variety of halls and to different kinds of audiences . . . The best performances from 14 shows were chosen, mixed, and assembled into this record. No additional recording was done and the music on this album is entirely live."

Do you think that, in turn, informs the way you sing, because especially on this album, and other live recordings that have come out here and there, you're whooping it up, as opposed to what you do in the studio, which is much more measured?

Yeah, you can't be measured, live. It's usually a proclamation of the songs, on some level. Recording is more like film acting. Live is like improvising—you are given restrictions, and to hold your own attention, as well as others', you go off from there. It's the rare occasion where I find, as a member of the audience, I can really take in a *song* by anybody live. I can really enjoy it, but really getting the full understanding of the lyric . . . It's more like, I'll get little bits and pieces, and it's more about the performance and everything. I figure that's what the records are for, that's when people can hear the songs, and this is more about being together.

It's a celebration of the song that's already been presented.

It's a celebration of the song, and the fact that we were welcome in this city, in this bar, to play.

Did some of the covers that the Minutemen did on *Double Nickels on the Dime*, like Van Halen's "Ain't Talkin' 'bout Love" or Steely Dan's "Doctor Wu," ever serve as an inspiration behind the covers that you've done of songs by bigger-name bands?

No, not at all. Not only are those not among my favorite songs on that record, but they weren't songs I was familiar with. Even though it's not as exciting a record, I liked their covers on *3-Way Tie (for Last)* more—the Blue Oyster Cult ["The Red and the

Black"], the Creedence Clearwater Revival ["Have You Ever Seen the Rain"], and the Roky Erickson ["Bermuda"]. But the Ramones was a big one—seemed like the Ramones always had a cover [version] on their first seven or eight records, and I was way, way into the Ramones. That was always a thrill, seeing what the cover was gonna be on each record.

Were those songs you knew already?
Some of them were, but most of them weren't, and that was another thing that was extremely educational: that they made a song their own, but if you looked at the lyric sheet you realized it wasn't their song, and it made me excited to get into what they were into, to find old records.

Ideally, if I choose to cover a song, it's because I think there's something I'm hearing in it that isn't obvious to other people. I wouldn't bother to cover a song if it's a great song and perfectly done. About a third of Hank Williams's most popular greatest hits I don't understand, because I've never heard anyone pull anything new out of them. They seem kind of completed. I know I could be very wrong in that, though, because I remember one of my great moments of musical discovery was driving around in Virginia once, picking up Charlottesville's radio station, and hearing someone covering a Hank Williams song. And I was feeling my mind quietly being blown open and was like, "What the fuck is going on?" And this was before the Internet; I was calling friends and asking people in conversation, "Do you know who does this Hank Williams song?" It turned out that it was Cat Power, her cover of "I Can't Help It (if I'm Still in Love with You)" on her *Myra Lee* record. She did something that I would have thought was impossible—taking something that I thought was finite and showing me that it wasn't necessarily so.

Part of what makes a song mean anything to me in the first place is the way you *sort* of cover *every song* that you *like*. When I really like someone else's song I feel as if I'm performing it. It's been like that since I was little. The songs that hit you are the ones where you somehow get inside them and make them your own as you listen to them. There are a lot of people who are better listeners to music than most people are performers. They can interpret through their listening. It seems that when you have a strong relationship with a song, it's basically because you are taking it in. You don't have a strong relationship with the people or the writer—you have no relationship with any of that. You have taken on things that were given out in the song and you've made it into something that it wasn't before. So it feels like when you sing along with a song or just when you hear it or feel like it's there, that's like playing the song.

How did the all-covers album with Tortoise, *The Brave and the Bold* [2006], come about?
It was originally supposed to be an EP; Howard [Greynolds] was ostensibly doing a series of collaborative EPs [on his label, Overcoat]. [At the 1999 Liss Ard festival in Ireland] we did this super-long set where we did musical backing for David Berman, where he would read a poem, then he might tell a joke, then we might tell a joke, then we might play a song . . . it just went around like

that for two or three hours. And that's where we did "Thunder Road," which we improvised—Matt trying to figure it out, and me trying to sing it while we were playing—and Howard heard about it. He was a huge Springsteen fan. "Would you consider recording it with Tortoise and making an EP?" So I suggested we do [Richard Thompson's] "Calvary Cross," "Thunder Road," [Elton John's] "Daniel," and [Melanie's] "Some Say I Got Devil." We went in to record those and had a blast. We decided to make it into a full-length and told Howard, which he seemed panic-stricken about. And then we took a break for two or three weeks 'cause we'd only scheduled enough time to record four songs, and it's six people with crazy schedules. But we all had time not too far in the future to do the rest, so then we had to decide what the rest of the songs were going to be. The other six songs were everyone throwing song ideas into the mix.

How were the arrangements worked up? Collaboratively?
Yeah. We all got in the room and would start something . . . Every song was different: the arrangement and the instrumentation was different on each song, who played what. Four members of Tortoise played drums on different songs.

Were your vocals recorded live, with the band?
Mm-hmm.

They really seem to sit in the mix as another instrument.
And made them [Tortoise] sing a little bit. They do some "Aahs" here and there. Some of them were saying, "Wow, I've

never sung before on a recording." It was so cool. I loved making the record.

**Someone showed me this video of Lou Reed and Pavarotti
singing "Perfect Day" together. Pavarotti takes a verse and Lou
takes a verse, and Pavarotti can't sing it really. And that made
me think, "Jeez, maybe only Lou Reed can really do this song."**
The best performances of Lou Reed songs are the ones where
he nails it in a way that nobody else could. "Perfect Day" . . . I
remember, before I heard the song, Ned and his friend singing it on the bus on the way to school, and it always seemed
to me that what they loved about it was how it was a satire of a
beautiful song. And then when I heard the song at age eleven
or twelve I was like, "No, it's just a beautiful song." Of course,
it really works either way, and there are very few people who
have that ability to express beauty and disdain at the same time.
Maybe not Pavarotti.

**To what extent have you heard other people's covers of your
songs?**
Some European metal band did a cover of the song "Black"
that sounded pretty good [Cadaverous Condition, on 2006's *To
the Night Sky*]. I really liked the Johnny Cash "I See a Darkness."
Marianne Faithfull did "King at Night," and that sounded pretty
cool. Some folks sent me a cassette or CD a long, long time
ago; they covered a bunch of songs off *Arise Therefore* but all the
vocals were sped up, and that was pretty great. I haven't listened
to it many times, but there was that tribute record that came

out, *I Am a Cold Rock I Am Dull Grass* [2006], and I remember being scared to listen to it for about a year and then listening to it one day and thinking it sounded good. But I can't remember specifically what's bad or good on there.

That's the idea, to be able to write songs and not have to go out and sing 'em. I love singing, but . . . it'd be nice to not have to play live. I had originally written "A Whorehouse Is Any House" [B-side of the "Let's Start a Family" 7"] for the Sally Timms record [*Cowboy Sally's Twilight Laments for Lost Buckaroos*, 1999], with the idea that her voice would be singing it.

And you wrote "His Hands" for Candi Staton.*
Yeah. That was *so* rewarding because as I was writing I felt like I was working in a tradition of songwriters that I'd read about, where someone says, "I want you to write a song for me," in Nashville or wherever, even Celine Dion or whoever. They would contact the songwriter and have meetings where the songwriter would try to get a feel for what works for the singer—what rhythms, what keys, what chords, but also what themes really resonate and what themes might catch the singer off guard, but off guard in an empowering way. As it was going on I felt like, "Oh my God, this song seems to be working," and

---

* Soul and gospel artist Candi Staton began touring with the Jewell Gospel Trio as a teenager in the 1950s. By the late 1960s she had switched to soul as a solo artist, and had a disco hit in the summer of 1976 with "Young Hearts Run Free." She resumed performing gospel material in the early 1980s, but does the occasional secular project; the song WO wrote, "His Hands," became the title track of one such album, released in 2006.

then sending it to her and having her dig it, and also have it be the title song for her record, that was pretty fuckin' exciting.

The lyrics concern domestic violence, something that pertained to her personal life. Since you avoid lyrics that are specific to your own personal life, it's curious that you would take that tack in writing a song for somebody else.

Well, it's a similar process because writing for her, she can then sing the song knowing that she didn't write it, you know? She knows that it's not confessional, even if it's about something that she's familiar with. And I feel like when I'm writing lyrics that I am gonna end up singing I'll do the same thing. I'll try to write about an experience that is related to something that I understand or would be able to sing about, as if I was writing for somebody else, knowing that somebody else would be able to get behind some of these lyrics.

You made a return to feature films when you played Kurt, one of the two protagonists in Kelly Reichardt's *Old Joy* [2006]. Is it true that she originally had you in mind for Mark, the character that Daniel London played?

She originally called me because she wanted to shoot in North Carolina, and she knew that I liked swimming and I liked hot springs. She wanted to ask if I had recommendations for locations, because she was having trouble finding hot springs that would suit the script. So we talked about that, and then she sent me the short story [by Jon Raymond] in book form, with the photographs, and then she sent the script. We just kept talking about it, and she asked if I wanted to play the other part. We talked about the Kurt part for a long time, and she was looking at different people. Ian Svenonius[*] was one person she talked about, Kyle Field from Little Wings was another, and then finally she was like, "I've met someone who I think would be good for the other part." But no one for Kurt. Then she asked, "Would you consider playing Kurt?" And I responded, "I think that would make a lot more sense, honestly; I *would* play the other part because I'd like to work with you and it would be a challenge, but I'm not looking forward to it. I'm not looking forward to where that part would take me. Having to identify with that character would be really depressing for me" [*laughs*]. Both characters have depressing aspects about them, but the other one, sympathetically portraying that guy, I wasn't looking forward to.

It seems like *Old Joy* is a Spinozistic[†] movie because it has elements of human plus inhuman. The burden is shared; the viewing time is equally dispersed between humans and other things, whether it's a dog or just nature. A good third of the movie is nature shots. One of the great things about *Old Joy* is that you have the sense that humans aren't everything.

You made up the story you tell in the hot tub.
Yeah, 'cause the story in the script was a story that I'd heard before, about someone finding a deer in the middle of the road,

---

* Frontman of the now defunct Washington DC indie-rock bands Nation of Ulysses and the Make Up. Currently leading Chain and the Gang and host of VBS.TV's *Soft Focus* talk show.

† That is, comparable to the philosophies of Baruch Spinoza (1632–77).

putting it in the trunk of a car and then driving on, and then the deer wasn't dead and starts freaking out. I told Kelly, "I've heard this story from a couple of people. I think it's an urban legend, I don't think it will play to a lot of people." I just started throwing ideas at her until Kelly said, "Yeah, that's a good one."

And you threw in a reference to _Jesus Christ Superstar_.
Well, that actually happened; I _did_ have this encounter with a woman at Office Depot, an Indian woman. Most of the story was true, how it plays out in _Old Joy_: I saw this guy I kept seeing come in the store, and the woman behind the counter said, "Superstar." And I was like, "What did you say?" She said, "Superstar. You said 'Jesus Christ.' " And I hadn't remembered saying "Jesus Christ" [_laughs_].

Watching _Old Joy_ again, within a day or two of watching _Matewan_, it's remarkable to see the difference in your performances, beyond the difference in age or anything else. In _Matewan_ the portrayal is very much how someone who's trained to be an actor would perform in a role; and in _Old Joy_ it seems like a more natural inhabiting of a character.
Another thing about when I stopped acting: I think my impression as a kid, in watching plays and watching movies, was that that _was_ life experience. And then I slowly realized, when I was eighteen, nineteen, twenty, that no, actors were bringing life experience to the parts, and that _wasn't_ life experience for the most part. And I thought, "I want to _do_ what the actors are doing. I don't want to act, I want to actually be part of those

things." But also I thought, "I don't have anything to put into these parts." *Old Joy* was a nice mix of both things: it was bringing everything from before that point, but also it was my ideal kind of production, where you kind of *are* there and *doing* it; you're doing what people are seeing to some extent. There's still a script, there's still direction, there's still construction, all this stuff, but there's an element of it that allows you safely to be the character.

There was a moment, when I was in London and went to see *Ulysses' Gaze*, where I thought that Harvey Keitel was doing what I imagined acting would be. It seemed like a really epic, sort of personal experience on his part, an exploration of character to the point where I was imagining that both the movie and he were benefiting from the work put into it. But I also then recognized many things: (1) that it was not the norm, at all, for an actor's life; (2) Harvey Keitel, I don't think he's good at conveying the thought and effort that he puts into a part. I don't think his performances really come off to the extent that I think he really thinks about them and puts a lot of work into them and really, really cares about them. He never seems natural; it always seems like you can kind of see the printed word when he's speaking it. And so that helped me think that I had just been *wrong*; many of the great performances are great performances because they are by great actors who are not necessarily doing things for themselves besides doing a great job. They are not necessarily getting into the development of the character or the world of the story of the movie; they're *just great actors*. From seeing interviews with him, and seeing

the breadth of his work, I sort of suspect now that Christopher
Walken might be just a really, really great actor. Whenever I've
seen interviews with him, they're so completely uninteresting to
me, and because I've seen him be great in *Pennies from Heaven*
or *Blast from the Past*, I started to think, "Wow, he must be an
incredible actor." On *Matewan*, Jem Cohen had funny stories
about Walken 'cause he worked on *At Close Range*, right before
Matewan, and he painted him as being a total nutcase. But I've
never seen anything else that corroborates that. And Jem said
that everyone on the set was in awe of him, but they were also
making fun of him because he was so wild. They would start
imitating him when he would give his performances, because
they were so strange-seeming.

There's no reason why we should suspect that somebody
reveals that much of their inner workings in any interview,
much less a performance; so it could be that he's a perfect actor
and really does live all that stuff in one way or another, and
isn't just a great actor, but doesn't care to share it with anybody,
which is kind of an ideal in many ways. Or it could be that he's
just a normal guy who's amazing at his job.

**In *Old Joy*, you're credited under your real name, Will Old-
ham, and when you were doing promotion for the film you
were only talking about the film, you weren't talking about
Bonnie Prince Billy at all.**
No, and there were opportunities to do so, to do a performance together with a screening or something like that, which
I declined. I can be an idealist or sometimes, when things are

going well, I assume the world is the world that I imagine it to be; so going into *Old Joy*, it didn't occur to me that there was going to be anything involved other than the work itself. I wasn't thinking about any sort of presentation or anything that was going to happen after we were done with it. I wouldn't have known what to do if I was put in the situation to deal with both things, so that was the motivation behind not wanting to do it. *Old Joy* was a kind of pure experience also, in that I don't think I got paid any money. I think I paid my way out there; we didn't get per diems or anything like that. It was like something that I would dream of as a kid—it was just something that you *do*. So it just didn't seem to relate to anything else that I was involved with. That's when I got a call from Mark Nevers to write a song for Candi Staton ["His Hands"], and I found that I had a part of my brain that I normally use that wasn't being used at all during that time, and so getting into making a song for somebody was very free . . . it felt like it came very naturally. And on a day-to-day basis, nobody cares that you make music when you're acting. They want you on set, and they want you to be good in your character. And so it's almost like this is the dream world where nobody cares that I make music, therefore I can make music and feel free about it.

Did it pose any difficulty in terms of putting yourself out there under the name Bonnie Prince Billy, maybe not during the filming, but after the fact, after the film came out?
It probably did . . . It surprises me when people use the name Will Oldham in any musical reference, and probably doing

things like *Old Joy* doesn't help with that. But it really does just surprise me.

I was struck by how much of your press mentions both Bonnie Prince Billy and Will Oldham.

Over in Europe it's nice if I run into a fan in the street or something and they say, "Bonnie, Bonnie!" I like that feeling. But yeah, the two kinds of work seem so unrelated. That gets back to the problem in the 1990s, the dilemma that I had in the first place, which is just that I understand things to be a certain way, and it's figuring out how that relates to how other people understand it. If I do more acting, in my ideal world people would not associate the two people together at all. Except there's also the advantage of cross-pollinated promotion, even on a word-of-mouth level . . . Financial success is always a plus, because it means you can make more stuff, do more stuff.

You also acted in *The Guatemalan Handshake*, which was filmed around this time.

That was a guy [director Todd Rohal] who had helped out Dianne [Bellino] a lot with the online editing on *Slitch*, essentially as a favor. He'd written and asked about this, and so even though Dianne and I weren't seeing each other and hadn't been for years at that point, it seemed like it would be good for all involved to do it. I think that was a week or two, in beautiful Pennsylvania countryside, so gorgeous, with a good crew and interesting other nonactors in the other parts. And it seemed like this, again, was not a standard-practice movie. *Junebug* was,

but I only had to work for a day, and it was great.* I love acting
and filmmaking, and it's just when I realized that the standard
practice was loathsome to me, depressing . . . One of the principal problems I find with movies is the lack of accountability.
Everybody has to talk to somebody in order to talk to somebody
else. It just doesn't make any sense. I don't know how to do something if somebody can't ask me directly for it. Even with making
music for movies, there'll be a music supervisor who calls you,
and they can't speak directly for the person they're claiming
to represent. It ends up creating heartache for everybody, and
worst of all it creates subliminal heartache for the poor audience, who have to suffer through a disjointed music selection.
There's a lot of bureaucracy, there's an industry, there's agents
and managers and casting directors and assistant directors and
production managers and production designers and music
supervisors and all these producers. [Director] Wim Wenders
wrote and asked about using music for a movie [*Palermo Shooting*
(2008)], and it was great because *he* wrote. If it's a lawyer or any
go-between person, it's always, "Thank you for your interest,"
and throw it in the fucking junk box. I agreed, and that was all
great in relation to the film, but then there got to be all this
weird soundtrack stuff and lawyers and contracts and music
supervisors. Easily one-third of the way through that process, I
was like, "This sucks, this was not worth it."

If I can wake up today and have a direct relationship with
somebody I'm working with, there's no reason why I would

---

* WO has a small role in this 2005 feature, directed by Phil Morrison.

choose to have an indirect relationship with somebody else. That's what most acting is, and what a lot of people turn music into as well. But it doesn't have to be that way.

Have you seen the movies you've been in with an audience, after they came out?

I remember seeing *Matewan* at its New York premiere, and *Old Joy* at its New York premiere. When *Matewan* premiered, I was told to hold a seat for Bruce Springsteen, next to me, and I was sitting near the front. It turned out that he came in after everyone was seated and sat in the back of the theater. Barbara Carr, who's his manager, was friends with [John] Sayles and had been affiliated with *Matewan*—she was an extra, for fun. But *Matewan* was too novel of an experience; too many things were going on. I couldn't really feel anything or draw any conclusions from it.

You were still pretty young then too.

Exactly, that's what I mean by "novel." But then *Old Joy* was a really great feeling. Part of it was seeing it at the Walter Reade; that's a nice theater, and I'd seen movies there. If you can find in your performance something that you can relate abstractly to the performance of somebody that you admire, it's also easy to do that when you see the movie projected in a room where you've seen movies that you like. And it was beautiful. I thought the movie looked beautiful. I could see all this *work* up on the screen—my own and everybody else's—and I thought, "*That's* what I wanted to do when I was a kid. This is a good example of what I've always wanted to do."

Something I was thinking about a year or two ago—not in relation to you, but it's something you would probably have an opinion on—is the recording of music, particularly songs: when you're recording and mixing it you have to take into account whether it's going to sound good on CD, on the radio, on vinyl, on cassette, on headphones; does it sound good in the morning, the afternoon, or night; the foreground or the background; at high volume or low volume; what it sounds like if it's translated into a different language, cover version, or arrangement; if it's in a TV show or a movie or a commercial. And then playing live, whether it will sound good in a small club, a theater, or an arena. It occurred to me that an actor might be considered in the same way: do they look good with different sorts of hairstyles—physical things—and also the contexts they're in: do they work well in comedy, drama, musicals, what their range is . . .

Or also where you see those things, whether it's on late-night cable or a Greyhound bus or an airplane or renting it or for free or in a movie theater.

Yeah. But maybe there's a parallel between the flexibility of an actor and the flexibility of a song. Would you take these things into account both when you record a song and when you were pursuing acting?

I'm sure that the relationship that I have to actors is similar to the relationship that I have to songs, because actors are their performances; they're not people who live outside of their performances, in my mind. So they become like songs. Acting is

like covering a song in a lot of ways. It has a lot to do with yield-
ing and trying to accept a lot of what's already there. There's not
as much forward energy or striving that has to go on, because
somebody else has already done that. When I was acting as a
teenager, I didn't yet understand what I was learning by absorbing music and movies and plays in all the different ways that
I was at that time. 'Cause I wasn't responsible for *making* anything at the time; I was actor-as-tool (shut up) during that time.
And then when I started to make things, and it was all music,
I started to think about how and why it could be a valuable
listening experience to somebody, and I would stop at the ways
that it couldn't, which was probably a handicap, you know? I
would sort of assume that something could translate into any
situation, and then gradually I'd realize and forget—and then
realize again and forget again that music is not necessarily the
universal language that we think it is [*laughs*], or give lip service to it being. Every once in a while a song crosses over from
one sort of listener to another, but I think that's the exception
more than the rule, for whatever reason.

9

IT'S ALL ABOUT
THE WATER

ALAN LICHT: Is songwriting something that comes naturally? And is there a lot of revision that goes on?

WILL OLDHAM: Yeah, there's a lot of revision, but with *Arise Therefore* it began to feel like I was starting to get the hang of things; it was the beginning of me trusting myself to make songs. Before that, it was always like, "Are these songs? I'm not sure . . ." So no, I don't think it comes naturally, but I think the motivation to want to make songs and to contribute songs to the canon of songs that exists comes naturally, and then the feeling that I've worked hard enough to contribute songs is more just from working.

Do you have the sensation of songs just flowing out, or is it more considered?

Considered, yeah. Part of the rest of the time, the rest of the day or the month or the week or the year, is preparation for writing the song. Knowing I was going to write a song for Candi Staton or knowing I was going to write a song for a [folk singer/songwriter] Mariee Sioux session . . . of course, there's all the preparation that led up to the moment of finding out I was going to do that, and then starting to prepare specifically, starting to focus thoughts towards making the song by just thinking about musical ideas or listening to these singers or listening to other music. Then just waiting for a time when it was gonna be appropriate to sit down, with the idea that I don't wanna sit down if I don't know what I'm doing. And after a week, two weeks, three weeks, a month, all of a sudden thinking, "What am I gonna do right now? Oh my gosh, it might be time to write that *song*"—and then sit down and write the basics of that song. Ideally, you write one line and the next line and the next line, because that's how it's gonna end up; you want it to have a relationship to how it will exist in the end, even though there will be revisions. The most satisfying songs are the ones where the *writing itself* is also a piece of time-art, in the way that the song is a piece of time-art.

"The Weaker Soldier" started off as a chord—the opening one. Then it had a line: "I once was a lonely soldier." Then it took six or eight months to put the verses together. At one point it was a twelve-chord song; now it's a four-chord song. And it had a supercomplicated melody; it was getting more and more complicated, and then some of the verses I took away, and I'd go to another set of notes, get parts for a new verse. Probably a month before recording I simplified the melody, simplified the chords, got the drum machine, started working with it, and took it into the studio to work out the final arrangement with Grubbs and Ned.

A song like "You Don't Love Me" on *Beware*, I knew it was becoming a funny song, like "The Race Is On" or "The King Is Gone," one of those George Jones songs. I didn't even have to think too hard about the situations I was describing; it was just a matter of turning the situation into something kind of humorous. All of the theme and content were there and relate to the other songs, but this time I just thought, "That's not very funny, but *this* would be, and this rhymes with that and then I have to repeat. OK, I've got these two lines and they've got this meter in this rhyme scheme, so I wanna put *that* in the second verse also." And then I just fill out the form that I created by making the first verse and the chorus; the second part of the song is just filling out the form and not even paying any attention to where the theme is coming from.

"New Partner" [from *Viva Last Blues*] I've always thought of as a very constructed song. In writing it, I felt like the verses were my version of "if a computer wrote a song," and then the choruses were like trying to mix three songs: a song called "Tony" about a rodeo that I've only heard Johnny Cash do—I don't know who wrote it; "Get Off of My Cloud"; and "Heart-Shaped Box." I was trying to make a chorus that combined those three in lyrics and/or dynamic. So when recording it I tried to build it together using the instrumentation and then the overdubs and sort of make it a constructed, beautiful song.

The Letting Go was recorded with Emmett Kelly, Dawn McCarthy, your brother Paul, and Jim White in Reykjavik in December 2005, and engineered by Valgeir Sigurðsson. Dawn, Emmett, and Valgeir were people you had wanted to work with for a while.
One of the big things about that [album] was working with Dawn, 'cause for a couple of years up until then I'd had this kind of fantasy musical relationship with her. I asked her if she wanted to participate in the record, I'm sure not even daring to hope that it would be as intensive a collaboration as it was.

I just wanted to be in the room with her making music. I sent her demos for all the songs, and she put all of her ideas on four-track and sent it back to me, and I was just like, "Wow, this is definitely going to be unlike any record that I've worked on so far." And it *is* to a great extent, thanks to Dawn. Of all the great singers in independent music and punk rock over the last thirty years, there aren't a lot of people that focus on their voice; Dawn always has been and always will be curious about how the voice works on a musical and mystical and religious and rhythmic and harmonic level.

I'd met Emmett numerous times in Chicago, but saw him play with Azita* here at Uncle Pleasant's. He was so good, and I loved the way that he loved playing with Azita, so that made me think that I'd like to see about making music with this guy. I sent him this double CD of Yugoslavian recordings [*World Library of Folk and Primitive Music, Vol. 5*] that were part of the Alan Lomax archives—although Lomax didn't do those recordings—just to think about scales and harmonies for the record, which he received enthusiastically, which was, in turn, cool.

Valgeir and I had talked about doing something together during the Björk tour, and then [during the recording of "Gratitude" for Björk's soundtrack to Matthew Barney's film *Drawing Restraint 9*] he said, "When are we gonna do some kind of project together?" I was in the final stages of writing songs for *The Letting Go*, and I was like, "Are you ready now? Are you ready to make a

* Azita Youseffi, solo artist who played keyboards with BPB in 2005, 2006, and 2007.

record in a few months?" "Yeah, sounds great." Nico Muhly and Ryder McNair also contributed; early on in the session, Valgeir and I talked about wanting strings on some songs, and eventually we decided to pick the songs that we wanted strings on, send them to Nico and Ryder, and have them both make arrangements, telling them in advance this is what we were doing, and then pick the best arrangements. We ended up choosing two of Ryder's and two of Nico's, and then on one or two songs we used both of their arrangements on top of each other.

The string arrangements remind me of classical music more than most of your other work. You've said that classical music is something you haven't spent a lot of time listening to; but then there's also the "orchestral" version of "Song for the New Breed" [from *Dream of a Drunk Black Southern Eagle*], while "Someone Coming Through" [from *Wonder Show*] reminds me of a madrigal . . .

Uh huh. But the string arrangements and Dawn's wordless vocals are these people's contributions. The string arrangements are about Nico Muhly and Ryder McNair's work, and the wordless vocal—my job in that was to not say no, or to encourage a direction. But essentially it's what they got from the song; it's not what was asked of them.

In "Then the Letting Go" you have parallel voices and lyrics. Can you talk about how you came to do the song in that way?

Dawn was inspired to add the parallel lyric. That totally came from her, 100 percent; the idea for it and every idea inside of it.

One of the reasons for putting out the *Wai Notes* record was to reveal some of the process, because I sent her all the songs and then she dug into them with her four-track and sent back what is the *Wai Notes* record. She had lyric sheets and chord sheets and the handheld cassette-recorder recordings that I sent to her. And she was so close to her ideas that there was one song—it might have been "The Seedling"—where all our instruments, for the take that we kept, wound up not being in 440 [i.e., standard concert-pitch tuning]. And then Dawn put vocal parts on afterwards, but she knew her vocal parts so well that she sang her parts in 440 and not to the tuning of the song, so then we had to modify the speed of the playback and reapply her vocals. She could hear the song, she could hear all the instruments, but her creative mind has kind of a vice-grip effect.

In the song "Wai" there's another quote from the song "Careless Love": "Oh love, oh love, oh careless love." Was that an intentional connection back to that song?
Yes, it was. Back to the song, and the record as well, and the idea of trying to blow out of the water the idea that there can be such a thing as a careless love, and that a careless love is no love at all, I guess. Running through a lot of *Ease*, minus the first song, is a striving for, or finding strength in, carelessness, or finding strength in freedom or in the individual's pursuit of happiness. In so many country songs, like Dolly Parton's "It's All Wrong, But It's All Right" or "After I Made Love to You" [from *Ease*], it's people using that expression of how can something that feels so right be so wrong, and having to learn for oneself

how and why it is. That the Ten Commandments or the Seven Deadly Sins are not writ for nothing.

Children are in "The Seedling," "Then the Letting Go," and "Cursed Sleep," and fear is mentioned in "Wai," "No Bad News," and "Cold & Wet." Were those conscious themes when you were writing those songs?
Not premeditated, no. It's just what comes out.

But did it start to feel like those themes connected them when the album was coming together?
Yeah, for sure. In some ways that's how some songs get finished and some songs get abandoned, because they begin to reveal a relationship to other songs in a group of songs being worked on. If it seems as if the songs are connected, then they stay together, and the ones that don't exhibit any connection I'll either abandon completely or maybe mine for parts of the songs that survive, or get abandoned completely *completely* or get abandoned and returned to years later, or a year later, or whatever. "Valentine's Day" was recorded when *There Is No One What Will Take Care of You* was recorded, but again, it seemed so out of place with those songs it got eliminated from that record and was put on *Lost Blues*. There's a song from *The Letting Go* that appears in some form on *Wai Notes*, and we've done it live a few times, but I think finally it will be recorded in what will end up being its final form in December [2010], which is very exciting, because [*laughs*] I've been thinking about the song for four or five years now.

I remember seeing an interview where you said the landscape and maybe the time of year had something to do with the way *The Letting Go* came out.

Well, I did some press for that record, and that's a question that everybody asked, so basically I was forced to say, "Yeah, it did." It *did*, because landscape *anywhere* does. Driving to the studio every day, it's crazy-looking; also, it was winter in Iceland, so it was dark most of the day and night, and that's great for making a record. It just meant that we were always huddled together; we found warmth with each other, in making the record. It was winter, but every day you could go to a public pool that was outside and heated. It's pitch black out, might be snowing, and you swim in an outside pool with the rest of Reykjavik, who are out there getting their exercise swimming in the pool.

And you don't feel the cold at all under the water.

No, not under water, but going from one pool to another you'd be like, "Oh, Jesus!" Or getting up on the slide and sliding down, when there's ice on the steps of the slide. And Dawn was amazing in Iceland: because we were there near Christmastime, she was taking the opportunity to interview everybody we saw about Icelandic Christmas traditions, which made us all more involved in being in Iceland. If we weren't witnessing it, she would report it at dinner, which was great.

Something else you talked about in the press were the coincidences with a Guy Waterman biography.

Yeah, it was pretty weird. I bought the book because it was called *Good Morning Midnight*, and there's a great line in a Mekons song,

"Oblivion," where Sally Timms sings [Mekons lyrics excised here due to copyright]. So I bought the book between tracking and mixing, from a table in a store that's only open at Christmastime to sell remainder books. There's one song that Dawn wrote some lyrics for that I couldn't settle on a good title for, like "Letting Go of a Little Girl, Something, Something"—stupid titles. The book's about this guy who loses two sons, separately, who disappear into the snow and are never seen again—which happens in the song as well. And Guy Waterman committed suicide through exposure, as an older man. His wife was the daughter of the guy who helped edit and bring to public awareness all of Emily Dickinson's works. That's where the title of the book came from, *Good Morning Midnight*, and at some point in reading the book, while we're mixing this fuckin' song, there's a quote from an Emily Dickinson poem, where she says, "First the chill, then the stupor"—describing freezing to death—"then the letting go." And we're working on this song that also has to do with kids disappearing into the snow, so it was then going to be called "Then the Letting Go" after this Emily Dickinson line, and the record would be called *The Letting Go*.

The record was supposed to be called *Wai*, which means "water" in Hawaiian, and it's the name of one of the songs, but I wasn't really happy with that because I knew everyone would mispronounce it, the way everyone called *Joya* "hoya," and I didn't want to throw that obstacle in there. And then the last song on the record is "I Called You Back," and someone wrote me saying, "This record's all about Emily Dickinson," and I'm like, "What are you talking about?" "You know, on her tombstone it says, 'Called Back' "—that's the epitaph on her tombstone. And *then* the reason I bought the book in the first place was because "Good morning, midnight" is a Mekons quote, and later, when I sang a couple of shows with the Mekons and started to get back into them and picked up on some records that I'd missed, [I realized] they have a song called "Only You and Your Ghost Will Know," and the chorus is: "First the chill and then the stupor / Then the letting go / Only you, and your ghost, will know." So they had also quoted this Emily Dickinson poem. Crazy [*laughs*].

The photos of Oahu on the cover—
—which most people thought was Iceland, and still do, probably. It's a place I went with Dianne called Makapu'u. At the end of our trip Dianne found a book of short stories by Ian MacMillan called *Squid Eye*, and there was a story about Makapu'u, which we read while we were there. We then went to that place, and it's since become one of my favorite places on earth, for getting in the water and being surrounded by the things you can see in there. Actually I think I went to Moloka'i—one of the [Hawaiian] islands—in the spring before the recording to finish up all the songs, but I knew that I wanted to take pictures of Makapu'u for the artwork, even though we hadn't recorded yet.

Water also appears in the photos you took for the *Western Music* EP and for Slint's *Spiderland*.
The *Western Music* front cover, I think it's Darren [Rappa] and who knows who else, Steve Driesler maybe, swimming in Laura Orr's pool. It's a long exposure, so it just looks like seals in the

water. *Spiderland* was a day where we went out and did band photos. It was probably for the album cover and/or publicity shots. Most of the photos were taken in Louisville on a quarry property, around the piles of refuse or dust and rock. At one point we were all swimming. I think I was treading water with my feet and holding the camera. I gave them all the film. It was definitely for professional use.

It was a limestone quarry, which is now, as of about two or three years ago, sort of a high-end housing development, so anyone can go there. It used to be illegal, so we were always on guard. There was one time when I was swimming there with Darren and Jennifer Vislisel [a friend]. Some guy with scuba equipment swam over to us and was like, "Do you swim here often?" We're like, "Yeah, every once in a while," and they go, "Well, that's bad news because we're supposed to arrest you." But then it turned out that they knew my uncles from the volunteer fire department, and then the crucial breaking point seemed to be when we bonded over what we agreed was the best bakery in Louisville [Plehn's]. And within ten minutes they were letting us use their emergency spare regulators to explore the bottom of the quarry, which was pretty neat. But it was a place where we'd swim daytime, nighttime—it was a really beautiful place.

You did two live albums: *Is It the Sea?* with [drummer] Alex Neilson and Harem Scarem, recorded by the BBC in Edinburgh, Scotland; and *Wilding in the West*, recorded on a tour from Chicago to the West Coast. You had something of a history with Scotland.

Our whole family went over to Scotland once, in 1982 or so. That was the first time I went overseas, actually. Nancy Sexton from the Walden Theatre organized it. We went with older folks from the theater, for the most part, and stayed at this house. John Pielmeier, who wrote *Agnes of God*, was there too, and it was when he was researching a one-man play called *Courage* about J. M. Barrie, who wrote *Peter Pan*. So Pielmeier read a draft of the play to us in the living room of the house that we rented, which was pretty exciting. I went to Scotland again a couple of years later, but mostly with younger people, including Steve Driesler and his sister Amy, 'cause Amy was involved at Walden.

Both times we rented this house. The family that lived next door and took care of this house had three boys. The middle son's name was Andy, and a couple of years later I went to Europe with a couple of friends and hitchhiked around, and at one point we split up and I went back to visit this family, and Andy happened to be around. We started talking about music, 'cause I'd made a country and bluegrass mix tape for his parents a couple of years before, and he was like, "I really liked that thing," and I told him, "I'd really like to hear some Scottish music. 'Cause I can hear all this good stuff *in* Scottish music, but what I'm hearing isn't good; it just has all these elements, and I'm *sure* there's good stuff." And he's like, "Oh yeah—there's *so* much good stuff." I didn't know what to get, and he's like, "Well, give me a couple of pounds for postage, and I'll send you a mix tape."

Six months later he sent me five ninety-minute tapes with twelve pages of notes that included "The Loch Tay Boat Song," which became "The Ohio River Boat Song," and also included at least one recording of June Tabor singing "Where Are You Tonight?" June Tabor is now one of the people I listen to more than anybody else, and we did "Where Are You Tonight?" as a three-piece [with Emmett Kelly and vocalist Cheyenne Mize] at this Italian sacred-music festival last Christmas. I remember when I got the tapes from Andy I didn't listen to anything else for *months*. Just drove around in the car and listened to them. And Andy grew up to become involved in booking and promoting music in Ireland, then in Scotland, and sat on the Scottish Council for the Arts; he arranged that tour with Harem Scarem many years later, which is kind of amazing.

Alex Neilson wasn't in Harem Scarem, right?
No. I knew I wanted to bring an ally, so I brought Alex. Somewhere in there was the making of that Alasdair Roberts record [*No Earthly Man*] in Scotland; that's where I met Alex, which was a really great encounter. We rehearsed a little bit in Edinburgh and a little bit in Birnam, which is sort of in the countryside, in an old manor house. It was with funding from the Scottish Council for the Arts, so we could have per diems and rent rehearsal spaces and things like that, which was very cool.

That was immersion into the Scottish/Irish trad scene. All these people were super involved, except for Alex—which is interesting, 'cause Alex was way into trad music, but through record collections and things like that, and not at all into the current scene and what people were doing. But we were going to sessions, constantly, in any city that we played in, or during rehearsal time, and musicians were coming to the shows. It was really nice.

That record is a real contrast to *Summer in the Southeast* because it's more of a sit-down audience concert, and the music is so recast, in that traditional vein, that it's a viable alternative to, or variation on, the studio versions as well.

We did a couple of *Letting Go* songs, but I played them the mixes of the songs prestring sections because I wanted them to make their own arrangements instead of trying to reproduce the record, and that was good. And we did this traditional song that I learned through Ali Roberts ["Molly Bawn"], as well as a Gene Watson song, "Love in the Hot Afternoon," which we had played on a *Superwolf* trip. The song was introduced to us by Ferg [Dave Ferguson], who was the engineer on a lot of Johnny Cash stuff, but was the engineer on the Rick Rubin Johnny Cash stuff as well. He was somebody that Cash brought to the session; he and Sweeney became friends, he sent us that song, and we started playing it.

Why was *Wilding in the West* only released in Australia and Japan?

Summer in the Southeast was released on Sea Note only, no P-Vine [Japanese label], no Spunk [Australian label], no Domino; *Is It the Sea?* was Domino; and then *Wilding in the West* was the other two territories, so each territory got its own live record. Paul came out and recorded four or five shows, and then we sent all the tapes to [Neil] Hagerty, who mixed it and created a couple of songs [the sound collages "Naked Lion" and "Magnificent Billy"]. There's definitely some songs that have vocals from multiple nights all on the same song, so there might be a third harmony that existed because someone sang a different part on another night, so two of the same person's voice.

In this era there were three "sea" songs—"My Home Is the Sea," "Death in the Sea," and "Is It the Sea?" Can you talk about how the sea came to figure so heavily in these songs?

Well, "Is It the Sea?" is written by Inge Thomson, from Harem Scarem, but she did write it specifically for our collaboration, in what I think is a perfect songwriter move, a perfect songwriter approach: to write a song for a singer that in form and content is related to the intended singer's life and work. I think at one point she writes, "Fifteen years have passed," and I always felt, when singing the song, for *her* it was a metaphor for touring and playing music in the way that we do. And basically when we did that song fifteen years had passed since I started making records. My reading of it was that it was a song about participating in music; she's talking about *work*, work and music, the sea being the life of someone who's out of society and working in the wilds of the sea. And then "Death in the Sea" and "My Home Is the Sea" are more tributes to both the chaos and entropy around nature that many people feel pulled towards, the chaos and entropy that we came from and, for many of us, it's inevitable that we return to. Some people crave a willful, participatory reentry, or multiple entries and exits, into those wilds, more so than, say, the order of a political system or the order of society. I believe that many people do not know their place in the order of society. I've never known my place in the order of society, and therefore have oftentimes found that it was more rewarding or relevant or convenient to associate my drives or my desires with things that exist undeniably and even that dwarf all human endeavor, whether it's the animal kingdom or our oceans. I would rather be on that team than Team Democracy or Team Society. If you're careful, you can be welcomed into natural systems, ecosystems, societal systems. But it sometimes feels like it would be more rewarding to be destroyed by a natural ecosystem than it would to be destroyed by a societal system . . . if you're going to be destroyed.

I always think that people look ridiculous when they dye their gray hairs away or get face-lifts, and in the same way, when we try to "preserve" our planet, it sometimes has the same nonnatural, uncomfortable . . . it's like denying that the planet has a life cycle. We exist within the planet and therefore are a part of its life cycle, and we most likely will be part of its destruction in one way or another.

Right—human beings didn't cause the Ice Age . . .
Yeah, right. And if there's an ice age coming up, will there be a political party that's siding for it and one that's siding against it? There seems to be now with global warming. It's hard to fathom that people will take the life and health of the planet and make a political issue out of it.

Do you think that man has to serve nature?
Nooo!

Do you think that nature has the upper hand?

I think I've always been a little mystified by the separation of man from nature, even the green movement and this idea that human beings have destroyed the world—that assumes that we are not *of* the world. That takes the position that because we can "think," we have the "responsibility." To me it seems the ultimate hubris to say that humankind is destroying the world and could save the world, as opposed to saying that we are, in every action that we do, an aspect of the world. So it's not that it has the upper hand; it's that we are a tiny subset of the natural order. Some like to say that we are even a force to be reckoned with or recognized, but I don't believe that we are. I don't believe that anything human beings do is any more or less significant than anything that a weed or a gust of wind does. I don't think humankind, throughout history, collectively has done anything that's any more valuable or important to the development or eventual destruction of what we recognize as the Earth than a sound vibration.

The *Ask Forgiveness* EP, another record of covers, was made with Meg Baird and Greg Weeks of the band Espers in 2007. Did the song choices overlap with Meg's or Greg's taste or sensibility?

No, they didn't know any of the songs. I sent them demos of me singing the songs, and while we were mixing they would be like, "All right, whose song is this?" "R. Kelly." "Ha ha, right, OK, no . . . *really*, whose song is this?" [*laughs*]

There was one time when Sweeney and I were in California to do a show for a surf-movie festival. They put us up in a hotel in Santa Monica, and we were like, "What the fuck are we gonna do tonight?" We looked in the paper and Espers was playing at McCabe's, opening for the Incredible String Band. That was the first time I went to McCabe's since I'd seen Bob Mould there in 1989, so it was kind of rediscovering the place. I'd never seen Espers, only heard about 'em, and it was *great*, they were so good. I started listening to them, and it was kind of intoxicating every time I heard the first album and the covers record, *The Weed Tree*, which is amazing.

So was that an inspiration behind trying to do a covers record with Meg and Greg?

I think so. Part of it, again, was thinking of an excuse to get to know them and be in the same room with Meg while she was singing, and so I presented the idea of doing an EP of covers and tried to choose songs that would be belly-gazing, self-reflexive, soliloquy-style songs—like, where-am-I-and-how-did-I-get-here kind of songs—but trying to cull them from different musicians who'd been important to me.

What you were saying about the Ramones doing covers was something that had occurred to me about this record anyway: that it fits seamlessly into a lot of the language of your own songs—and the way it's designed, you don't know whose song it is unless you look at the CD itself.

Actually, we only included songwriter and publisher names; didn't even include the song titles anywhere on the record artwork. Maybe if you download it, but I don't think the song titles are on the record anywhere. It's just the track numbers and then the writer and the publisher, 'cause I didn't want anyone to think of it as a covers record. I didn't want them to easily be able to look up the songs by title or to immediately say, "I think I know that song, by that person." It was just writers whom I figured most people wouldn't know, but it was enough to give credit to them, which was proper, and force people to do a little bit of research if they liked the song—they could find it in five minutes. But it would ideally be more of a *listening* experience, and then if you wanted to do more work, you could.

The title comes from "Better to ask forgiveness than permission"; I guess some of those people would want permission asked to cover their songs?

Possibly . . . and it was intended to be, with some fun, a self-indulgent record, because I was choosing all these self-indulgent songs, so it was [addressed] to the audience as well, not just to the [original writers/performers]. There was that really garish picture on the front: I found the artist's business card over in Indiana, in a coffee shop, and I was looking for somebody to do this drawing. I called him, and he turned out to be this total wallflower guy that I'd gone to middle school with, and I had no idea he was an artist. All the photos in the artwork are from my trip to India with my mom, and after she'd left, and it's all pictures from Kashmir and Ladakh, from 1987.

What made you want to include those photos on this release?

I think it was that they were pictures of kids. I was just imagining they were a lot older now . . . and partly imagining a distance that I have, for the most part, yet to cross with making music, which is: no matter how much I've done in music and how far I've traveled, none of these people have probably ever heard it, and possibly never will; but it's sort of an underlying goal, in making music—how do you find that *one* person somewhere in the world, how can you get a song to that person? The distance between me and them remains. As *well* as that distance, which will never be bridged, there's the distance between myself and Phil Ochs, myself and Mickey Newbury—because they're dead—myself and R. Kelly—I met R. Kelly, but still, I'm a fly, I'm a flea, I'm nothing to him. And it's the idea that there are some distances that probably will never be crossed. *Maybe* will, but who knows . . .

I read somewhere that you met Glenn Danzig again, and he didn't remember you from the 1985 Samhain/Maurice tour at all. But you'd thought about him every day since then.

Yeah . . . well, maybe not *every* day, but it was also great. I went there [to the Danzig/Samhain concert] because I *did* become friends with London May, who was the drummer in Samhain for *November-Coming-Fire* and the tour that I was on with Maurice, and used to be in Reptile House with Dan Higgs, and we stayed friends since then—he actually came to nursing school in Louisville. He called me, and he was like, "We're doing this show, do you want to come see the Samhain/Danzig show?" And afterwards he was like, "You gotta say hello to Glenn, you gotta say hello to Glenn." He's like, "Glenn, this is Will, do you remember him?" and Glenn goes, "Hey!" but obviously didn't remember me at all. I told him, "Great show," and he said, "Thanks a lot, man," and then, you know . . . But it reminded me of this story somebody told about being a huge Fall fan and seeing Mark E. Smith randomly in a pub in England, just drinking in the corner, and going up to him and telling him, "Mr. Smith, sorry, just a moment of your time, I really apologize. I just saw you there and I couldn't *not* tell you how important you are to me, how important your music is to me, and it is unbelievable just being in the same room with you." And Mark E. Smith just saying, "Yeah, heard it all before." And the guy turning around and exclaiming, "Yes!" [*laughs*] Like, that's what you would *want* from your heroes.

Not only did you meet R. Kelly, you appear in episode 15 of his ***Trapped in the Closet*** **video. How did that happen?**
Nicky Katt, the actor who's friends with Sweeney, was also friends with [director] Richard Linklater, and somehow Linklater got the idea to ask me to make music for his *Fast Food Nation* movie. Although it was Nicky who called me first about it, and they were talking about *Superwolf.* That was the beginning of a series of frustrations with Linklater; I was always asking him about what he wanted, 'cause he was talking about *Superwolf* but calling *me*. I was like, "So, do you want me and Matt to do it?"

"I don't know."

"Do you want songs?"

"I don't know."

"Do you want incidental music?"

"I'm not sure, I don't know."

"OK . . . I'll get started!"

At one point I ended up going to see a rough cut of *Fast Food Nation* in Austin, in which the Mexican characters in the movie were watching TV, and the TV showed *Trapped in the Closet*, just in the background. So after it was done and all the notes were given I asked Ann Carli, who was one of the producers, "Why was *that* in there?"

"How did you even know what that *was*?"

"I like R. Kelly's music a lot, and we covered one of his songs on the *Summer in the Southeast* tour, 'Ignition Part One.'"

"'Part One'?! I'll have to tell Rob [Kelly]!"

She called him and told me, "He was so touched."

Eventually I blew up at Linklater and quit. But coming out of that was the relationship with Ann Carli, who got Dan and me tickets to see R. Kelly in Chicago. We met him, he complimented Dan on his Vans, and I got his autograph—the third of the three autographs I've gotten in my life—and took his do-rag wrapper out of the garbage can of his dressing room to keep as a souvenir. Later Ann called when I was in New York, and said, "Rob wants to know if you want to play a part in the next installment of the *Trapped in the Closet* videos. It would mean coming to Chicago this weekend and shooting."

So I bought a ticket to fly to Chicago from New York instead of back to Kentucky. Got there, immediately went to a costume fitting, *immediately*, from the plane, and then that afternoon went over to R. Kelly's house to rehearse with everybody in the Chocolate Factory, which is his basement studio. Went out to a fancy dinner with R. Kelly and all the cast and crew, including the cinematographer [Jim Denault], who also shot [Kelly

Reichardt's 1993 film] *River of Grass*, and then the next day we shot all day. And it was mind-blowing.

A year later [2007] you sang three shows with the Mekons.
I felt like doing the R. Kelly thing was an unbelievable bridge to have crossed, a dream-come-true thing, also in terms of getting from being a *listener* to being a *colleague* of sorts with someone whom I never imagined that there would ever be any possibility . . . I just figured it would always be this distant thing. So when that happened I felt like, "This is amazing, dreams *can* come true." Then when I did the thing with the Mekons, it was like, "No, *this* is what it feels like for that to happen." In that Michael Jackson movie [*This Is It*] there's a scene where as part of the making of these shows they shoot something for their Jumbo-tron, for an interlude, and it's him acting in a constructed short movie, a gangster picture, with Humphrey Bogart, using all these Humphrey Bogart scenes, and I thought, "Yeah, if I had the money . . ." It's the same feeling that he probably had watch-ing himself acting with Humphrey Bogart; I was in the same thing with the Mekons, except Michael Jackson had to spend his own money and invite *himself* to do it [*laughs*].

And he wasn't actually with Humphrey Bogart.
No one wants to be *with* Humphrey Bogart; you want to be in a *movie* with Humphrey Bogart, 'cause no one knows if that's the reality.

I'd so much kind of psychically entered this Mekons space, years before. Driesler and Britt Walford were way into the Mekons, always listening to them, and I loved Britt and Steve but couldn't get into the Mekons. Right before I moved to DUMBO, I went over to Steve's house and taped all the Mekons records, and I was like, "I'm gonna give this all I've got." When I was living in New York I did LSD for the first time, and I remember I kept one of those Mekons cassettes in my pocket the whole night as my security blanket and just got so into them that I never went back. Over the course of the years I became acquainted with Jon [Langford] and Sally [Timms], and interestingly—like virtual-reality stuff—the voice that I identified with was Tom [Greenhalgh]'s. The Mekons were doing their thirtieth-anniversary tour, and Tom had to attend to the birth of his fourth child. So they were asking multiple people to come in and sing Tom songs, and asked if I would sing a Tom song or two. I said, "Yeah, of course." Still, I've never had a conversation with Tom or anything like that, except when I gave him a cassette of "For the Mekons et al." right after we recorded it. They played a show in Louisville, and I went up afterwards and told him, "I wanted you all to have this." I don't know if they listened to it; if you give someone a cassette on tour, what are the chances that they listen to it? Fifty percent? 'Cause they lose it or don't wanna listen to it [*laughs*]. Half the time when I would have an opportunity to listen to something, I would be like, "I'm gonna listen to this when I get home," and it would just gather dust.

So I went to Chicago and *oh*, it was just so exciting. For two and a half minutes here, two and a half minutes there I was filling in the Tom spot and singing these songs that I knew backwards and forwards, every inflection, *with* everybody else in the Mekons, and talking to most of them for the first time, 'cause it was only Jon and Sally that I'd had conversations with before. Back in 1989, when we first saw them, [Rich] Schuler used to do cool silk-screens, just radical, *badass* silk-screens, and in the early 1980s he had khaki pants with "Flex Your Head" rendered in silk-screen, one color. He made this Mekons silk-screen, which is from the logo that was down in the corner on the back of the *Slightly South of the Border* 10". Rich blew it up and made this thing. So when I got onstage I pulled my jacket off and I had this on and they were like, "Where did you get that?" Then I just sang my heart out. They did two shows that night, and I was one of seven or eight people singing Tom songs, but I went with them to Lafayette, Indiana, the next night, and I was the only Tom in the house! Those two shows in Chicago were electric sets, and then they did the acoustic set that they'd been doing a lot on that tour, where they sat in a semicircle.

Yeah, it's a wild feeling. When I did that show with Tom Verlaine, where Billy Ficca was playing too, I remember coming home from rehearsal and thinking, "I just played [Television's] 'Little Johnny Jewel' with Tom Verlaine and Billy Ficca, and I'm one of four people, maybe, who can say that."
Right [*laughs*]. I guess Johnny Cash, R. Kelly, and the Mekons were the three classic dreams-come-true moments. Wholly unbelievable.

But what propels you into a space where that can happen is being intensely involved with the music to begin with, where you picture yourself being part of it—
That's why it's a dream, that's why it's a dream.

—as opposed to laying back from it as just a consumer, or else it's a hobby or a diversion.

Yeah, it's something that's become a part of you, and you feel like you're a part of it, but you just assume that there will never be a physical manifestation of that. The most intensive part of my training as a person who makes records was from *listening* to records and being more than a passive member of the audience. I never felt that my relationship to records or movies was merely one of a consumer. I always felt something was going on, and I was using those feelings, those skills learned from sitting in front of a record player or movie screen, to guide my decisions.

Getting certain records, you feel like you're a part of that record's world, even though sometimes it existed before you did, but it's still somewhere you belong or feel you can belong. But most of your brain knows that there will never be an acknowledgment that that is true.

So when its creators then extend the invitation to join . . .

Yeah, when all of a sudden, you're *in* it—that's why it's like virtual reality.

10

SHUT-EYE

ALAN LICHT: Sleep is something that's frequently in the lyrics: "How can you sleep when I'm going away?" [in "Stablemate"], "We sleep more than we sleep" [in "You Have Cum in Your Hair"], "Who needs to sleep when sleeping just keeps our life undone?" [in "What's Wrong with a Zoo?"], and "I gave you a dream and you never wake from it / now I'll never go to sleep again" [in "I Gave You," from *Superwolf*]. Like many things in life, with sleep it makes a difference if you're alone or with someone else in the room, or if someone else is doing it at the same time, even though you're unconscious when it's happening—and something we've been talking about is the difference that another person's presence makes, either in listening to or making music, or in watching a film. So I don't know if I have a question or if I just want to talk about sleep [*laughs*]. Do you ever feel like you're missing things when you go to sleep? To me, part of the excitement of staying up all night is seeing what goes on during the hours when you would usually be asleep, like you haven't missed anything.

WILL OLDHAM: If I had three wishes one of them might be to have for myself a thirty-six-hour instead of a twenty-four-hour day, because I think what goes on during sleep is as exciting as what goes on when you're awake. I don't feel like I'm missing anything, but sometimes there's more that I'd like to do . . . The only time where I ever feel like I'm missing something is when I get into a cycle of waking up early, *really* early, then I realize that the early part of the day is kind of the best part of the day. To wake up at four or five in the morning on a regular basis is far more satisfying and rewarding than it is to go to bed at four or five in the morning. It's something that I forget all the time.

Yeah, that's the reverse angle: the feeling of super-early-morning rising is related to the feeling of super-late at night if you haven't gone to sleep yet.

But also, in the morning it's nice because I feel like my brain settles down overnight, and usually by the end of the day it's at its most frantic. The space is so much more open in the morning than it is at night, for the most part, unless I take a mind-clearing drug like Ritalin or something like that; then the night can be a free space, but it's not the healthiest approach.

There's also going from light to dark and then to light again, and whether or not that's in one cycle or not.

For the most part, the rest of the citizens of the Earth have ended, or will end, their day soon, and so you feel increasingly alone as the night goes on, whereas if you wake up in the morning you find that you are actually increasingly in company, which is a nice feeling: to wake up alone and, as each minute passes, more people are entering the sphere of potential interaction.

***Lie Down in the Light* was recorded in fall 2007 with Shahzad Ismaily, Emmett Kelly, Paul Oldham, Ashley Webber, and some Nashville session guys too. Shahzad and Ashley you had met, separately, on tour?**

We did a couple of shows with Dawn and Shahzad in Switzer-
land. That's where I met Shahzad. Shahzad started playing
with Alex [Neilson] and me in soundcheck, and started playing
with us in both sets as well because he played bass; he played
drums with Dawn. One of my favorite shows ever was Dawn
and Shahzad at Bad Bonn in Düdingen, which is a tiny village
next to Freiburg. It's just a small homey venue in the middle
of nowhere; if you go to their website, it says, "Where the hell
is Bad Bonn?" He'd done that bass-playing, but I also watched
him drum, hung out with him, and wanted to work more with
him. During the *Wilding in the West* tour we played a show on
Vancouver Island, and Ashley was in the opening act, in a duo
where a guy played guitar and sang and she just sang. I liked
the way that she worked with that guy, and I like people who are
dedicated singers, especially dedicated "backup" singers, which
is not a common thing in the underground indie world.

Somewhere in this time period I took a year off [roughly
summer 2007–summer 2008] from playing shows, which was
partly because I had shows scheduled when Dad died and the
record was coming out, but I felt like I needed to get back here
and see how my mom was doing and stuff like that. So the goal
of that record was to make a record that didn't have anxiety
involved with the recording of it, 'cause I was tired of getting *so*
anxious during every record, always feeling like the recording
was going to fail. I was like, "*Not* gonna do that this time. We're
gonna enjoy ourselves and be confident." There's no reason to
have anxiety. Just make a record, be confident and . . . *just make
a record*, you know? So there was still some anxiety, very, very

early on, and I was just like, "OK, how do we get this *out* of here? Let's get this out of here!"

The Wonder Show of the World was terribly exciting, with no crisis moments, because essentially it was just Emmett and myself; it's so much easier to focus and know what you're doing when there's less people. Emmett, Cheyenne [Mize], and I recorded the *Chijimi* 10" in that room upstairs [in my house]. Four songs in a day, mixed it in a day, and it was such a relief. And from then on, I thought, "*That's* how we're gonna do the next record, just like that." Whenever Emmett and I would listen to *Chijimi*, when we played it for Drag City, we were just laughing our heads off because we were so psyched about it, just so happy to listen to it. Like, *this* is how to make a record: in private, and just loose and free, with no studio hours or anything like that, coming up with stuff as you go along. I love that record. There's an engineer and they're doing stuff all the time, especially now with plug-ins. It's like, what the fuck are they doing? "*Talk* to me. What are you doing with your fucking fingers right there? 'Cause I don't want to tell you to undo that in ten minutes or in six days." It's just constant, constant twiddling; it's nerve-wracking, 'cause then you're also going, "Why doesn't the song sound as good now as it did thirty minutes ago?" And they say, invariably, "I don't know . . . I didn't change a *thing.*" You don't know if they're lying, or if they did something that to them is negligible, or if your awareness has changed over the last thirty minutes and you were excited at that moment and it's just worn itself out. And that's frustrating, because you can't access that person's brain, you know? You could take two hours off and say,

"OK, let's go over everything you did over the last thirty minutes, figure out if this is me or this is you."

Lie Down **seems like a record that's permeated by the idea of family, and obviously the three songs—"Missing One," "What's Missing Is," and "Where Is the Puzzle?"—were made in the aftermath of your dad dying. But also the idea of someone being missing, or feeling an absence, is something that goes way back in many of your other songs; it's something that runs through your music even back to the Palace records.**

Yeah, I think that's probably right. For whatever reason, I do have a reclusive, antisocial tendency, which I try to combat by working a lot, and always with friends and family, because otherwise I sometimes don't know how to engage. So probably some of the themes of the songs are about the inability to engage [*laughs*]. It's not a choice or a desire or anything like that; it's very . . . frustrating.

Some of the lyrics on *Lie Down* have to do with singing or songs: "You Remind Me of Something" has "Dancing goes on in the kitchen at dawn to my favorite song," and the chorus is: "You remind me of something, a song that I am, and you sing me back into myself / When I wake when sleeping, the song is a man and a woman and everything else." Then in "Where Is the Puzzle?" you sing, "Knowledge is born with a singing dawn . . . I want only to sing with you."

Yeah, "Where Is the Puzzle?" and "You Remind Me of Something" are both fully odes to the song, and to singing, absolutely. They're kind of devotional and/or love songs, putting either the song or the act of singing, or both, into the role of God or woman or whatever you would normally put in the place of worship.

Also, in "Teach Me to Bear You" [from *Wonder Show*] there's the lyric "sang away the name you gave to me." Are you familiar with the Dreamtime in Aboriginal culture in Australia and the idea of spirits taking a long journey where they sing the world into existence by naming all the inhabitants of the Earth in song?

Yes, I have heard about that, and I was thinking about the Dreamtime earlier when we were speaking about sleep and dreams. [Jon] Langford's making a record of a big Aboriginal country-music star down there, and I just sang a harmony on one of those songs to close *that* circle [*laughs*]. But yeah, I think it's a good concept. I think that worlds *can* be sung into existence, if the singer's right.

Were lines like "end each day in song" [in "Hard Life"], "always end the day in song" [in "The Sounds Are Always Begging," from *Wonder Show*], and "I sing the whole day through" [in "Ohio River Boat Song"] also conceived as being hymns to the activity of song? Or as an ideal, to sing the whole day through?

"Sounds Are Always Begging" is a more epic, elaborate, almost Genesis kind of story about how and why one would think of song in this way, in the way that "Where Is the Puzzle?" and "You Remind Me of Something" approach song and singing and music—why would you ever sing shit like that? And then "The Sounds Are Always Begging" is like, "Well, let's turn things back to the beginning, and here's the story of how singing became in and of itself something to be worshipped." "Ohio River Boat Song" is a traditional Scottish song—but that is my line. In the old Scottish version I think he says something like "sing honey hadoo," or something like that. So yeah, singing as a way of expressing or escaping or expelling unbearable events: if you have a thinking brain, which some of us are cursed with, you have to have *something*, and it could be singing and it could be alcohol, but it's progressive rather than regressive—you don't get better by drinking.

The idea of ending each day in song implies a kind of a ritual too.
Yeah, a ritual and a connection, 'cause even if you sing by yourself you are using things that have been given to you. The idea of singing is that it's communication from the past into the present and *right on through* to the future.

In "Keep Eye on Other's Gain" there's the lyric "sleep out in the rain," and "That's What Our Love Is" [from *Wonder Show*] mentions sleeping outside, which made me think of the camping tours, although those were a few years before these records.
Yeah, and there's also the line [Sally Timms lyric excised here due to copyright] in the Sally Timms song "Horses." In *Kinski Uncut*, whether or not he did everything he [actor Klaus Kinski] says he did in that book, he seems to sleep outside a lot in the

life that he relates to us. And it's a fantastic image, and a fantastic thing to do too. It seems like some people are given the strength, right, or privilege to sleep outside, and many people don't give a shit about it at all [*laughs*], even though it seems to be kind of the ultimate expression of freedom. It's like certain approaches to sexuality, it's a freedom from things that are human without ever wanting or needing to deny humanity, but you're not doing what it is to be civilized, what it is to be human, and if you can do that and be happy or be strong, then you've kind of got it made.

I don't feel like we ever got "Other's Gain" mixed quite right or something. I feel like it's a song with a shitload of dynamic built into it, and for some reason I didn't ever feel like we got the dynamic. On the record it's sort of a relatively even portrayal of the song, but I don't know what to do about that . . . We do a verse and chorus of it in this long medley that we've been doing this year that's kind of a tribute to an Everly Brothers medley from their live record, *The Everly Brothers Show* [1970]. They do an eighteen-minute medley of songs, and we do a twelve- or fifteen-minute medley of songs that opens and closes with the Everlys' "Price of Love." Throughout the middle is a bunch of Bonnie Prince Billy songs, and "Keep Eye on Other's Gain" is the first song we go into. It's the only song we do a full verse and chorus of, and sometimes we really hit it right. It's satisfying to get to where we couldn't get in the studio.

That song and "Missing One" have chord progressions that I feel emulate my older brother [Ned]'s chord progressions, which was a kind of tribute and a kind of absentee collaboration.

"You Want That Picture" has an interesting structure, where Ashley sings after the first two lines and then you sing together in the chorus, and she sings another two lines and then you sing the rest. Was that her contribution?

No, that's written as a duet. It opens with the male character describing a situation and presenting it to her to comment on, then she comments on it, and then we sing the chorus together. Then *she* describes *her* situation, and then *he* comments on it. So it was written as a dialogue, kind of inspired by a great Patty Loveless song called "You Don't Even Know Who I Am." A single character sings the song, all in the third person, but the first verse lays out one situation from the female's point of view, and then the second verse is all from the male point of view, so the idea was to present the male and female voice in a similar kind of situation. I think it was after the "Kiss" song and other duets with Scout Niblett* that I started writing these songs and started to realize some of the satisfaction of duets. And some of my big talisman records are some of those early Conway Twitty / Loretta Lynn records, so I thought, "I wanna try to write some proper duets." I'd had the experience with Dawn of two strong personalities singing together, but only when she wrote the parallel narrative in "Then the Letting Go" did I start to think, "I should write some parallel narratives or some dialogues into a song."

* WO sings with Niblett on "Do You Want to Be Buried with My People?," "Kiss," "River of No Return," and "Comfort You" on her 2007 album *This Fool Can Die Now.*

On "Willow Trees Bend" there's the line "I will never lay down for every man alive," which reminded me of the line "servant to all and servant to none" in "Master and Everyone."

"Willow Trees" is inspired by one of my favorite songs of all time, which is a song that Johnny Cash and June Carter Cash sing as a duet ["The Pine Tree"], and at one point they sing about trees, willow trees versus oak trees: [Johnny Cash lyrics excised here due to copyright]. There's another song that bears a very close resemblance to it, in concept but not in execution, on that record—"For Every Field, There's a Mole." On both of those I feel like I was trying to recall some of the different ways that Bryan Rich's songwriting always inspired and mystified me.

In "For Every Field" you sing a line, "every king a crown," which is also in "Willow Trees Bend," so that's an additional connection.

Yeah.

There's not a lot of drum kit on this record, but there are a lot of hand drums.

I don't think there was ever really a drum kit. I think it was all percussion and hand drums. I've always had a hard time with drums.

Too loud?

Kind of . . . It's just that it's a person surrounded by their instrument that makes a lot of noise, therefore your communication has this obstacle. And because the thing is so big and involved

and noisy, sometimes I worry that the drummer has the potential to become lost in their instrument and lose track of how the
song might be changing as it goes along. With some people, like
Jim [White] or Alex Neilson or Chris Freeland,* it's not an issue.
A lot of drummers, their strength is in creating something that
everybody else can depend on, but I like it when a drummer's
always aware and anything can happen over the course of the
song. It also meant that when we tracked we could all be in a
tiny space, all be together, 'cause there's no kit.

The front cover is by my mom; the back cover is a self-portrait
cell-phone photo from when I was touring with Richard Bishop,
maybe. My mom used to draw Jacob wrestling with the Angel a
lot, and she would draw it based on a Gauguin painting, where
that's featured small, off to the side of the painting. I liked that
idea, and Annabel [Mehran, photographer] had turned me on
to that Courbet painting, *The Origin of the World*. It's a close-
up of a vagina. I was looking through this Courbet stuff and I
found these two wrestlers, and I was like, "Mom, would you do
Jacob wrestling with the Angel based on these two wrestlers,
but using a Gauguin-style palette or unrealistic colors?" And
she did. I wanted to do a photo reproduction of *The Origin of
the World*, so I put an ad on Craigslist to try to get female models to exactly match this painting, which was such a challenge.
It was embarrassing, difficult, and unpleasant. There were so
many obstacles; I ended up doing two sessions, and neither one

* Freeland drummed for Baltimore bands Long Live Death and the Oxes,
and toured with BPB in 2003.

302 WILL OLDHAM ON BONNIE "PRINCE" BILLY

worked out, and it was so painful doing those sessions that I was just like, "I'm gonna abandon this idea."

There's sort of a link to the next record, which wasn't by design, in the line "Heed this word: Beware" [in the title track].
That was one of the last lyric revisions. There's no touring in between those two records, and I started working on the writing of *Beware* not long after that. It's hard to say, 'cause every time we've played that song, "Lie Down in the Light," live, I always think about that [*laughs*], that that record was coming, or had come then. It definitely wasn't when the line was written, but I can't remember how long after that I knew the next record was gonna be [called] *Beware*.

In the last three months of that year of not playing shows, I was away from everything:* I was away from my friends, away from family, and I was in a kind of wilderness where I could wake up and nothing attacked me, and I could let music be the first thing that happened in the day. And part of what that did was give me this space to think ahead about the songs, as opposed to letting certain things happen and then figuring out, "Why is this song being written this way?" *Beware* was more, "What if I tried to write a song this way?" I had a lot of time to myself, and I would listen to a lot of music—mostly music that I knew fairly well and had a relationship with. And I'd think, "Well, what is it that I've never been able to do that this person

* During a three-month residency at the Headlands Center for the Arts, Sausalito.

or people are able to do with this song? Why haven't I been able to do it, and what can they do that I wish that I could do?" And then I'd try to do that. I'd start each day getting into the songs, and I'd think about how I might get closer to this music that I love but hadn't been able to make before.

If you follow the records from one to another it will establish a *kind* of reliability or trustworthiness in the narrator/protagonist's voice, in Bonnie's voice, and I feel like *Beware* kind of pulls the rug out. If there was a trajectory of positivity and growth and evolution, this record was showing that things don't necessarily always move forward, ideas don't move forward; imagining that if we have a variety of things at our disposal, then following the path outlined by the singer Bonnie Prince Billy, as exemplified by the record *Beware,* is probably not the best way to go.

Does "I only ask that you close your eyes that you won't see me" in "You Are Lost" speak to that as well?
Yeah, exactly, so as not to be drawn in, suckered in, conned by the vulnerability costume that the P. T. Barnum Bonnie Prince Billy is wearing. It's a Venus flytrap, I guess.

The image of eyes being shut or eyes closing is also in "I Won't Ask Again" ["I'll ask you where I'll go when eyes are shut"] and in "Give Me Children" [from *Arise Therefore*; "closed her eyes saying quietly as she went to sleep, don't let anyone see us"].
I think it's common, but I don't know; I think I have a specific relationship to vision, the out of sight, out of mind idea. It seems like every part of the world is so full that if your vision

is shut down, even for a moment, things immediately flood in to fill the void that is left by the absence of visual information. So if thine eye offends thee, don't pluck it out, just close it, I guess. You can find alternate realities are immediately at your disposal.

If you close your eyes you can still hear things that are going on around you; it's a way of drawing into yourself, but at the same time on another level you're still conscious of what's going on. Right, except vision is always available. Even when my eyes are closed I think I still rely on the visual. I don't close them and then immediately create a three-dimensional picture of my surroundings based on sound; instead I start to picture other worlds, other things, and maybe even forget about the sound.

Sometimes the sounds themselves are unidentifiable. There's also the line "cursed eyes are never closing" in "Cursed Sleep" [from *The Letting Go*]. Yeah, those cursed eyes, they're never sleeping, they're never closing . . . always *looking* at things, seeing, taking in.

In "I Don't Belong to Anyone," the line in the chorus—"it's kind of easy to have some fun when you don't belong to anyone"—kind of reminded me of "Death to Everyone," where death "makes hosing much more fun." The melody for that began as a borrowing from "It's All in the Movies," the Merle Haggard song, and originally it was a fully different melody and a significantly different lyric for most of the song. It was more like a Sir Douglas* kind of melody and a Glenn Danzig kind of lyric. But I couldn't get it to where I felt like it was believable, so it became what it is now. It's super fun to play, a superfun song to sing. It has a joyful, collaborative sound to it, but the lyric is kind of devastating, and pathetic, and *negative*, essentially. Most of the songs on the record have this kind of weird negativity to them.

But that's always been a trait: in "West Palm Beach" you've got the slick-sounding 1980s keyboard sound, but the lyrics are "sun is a festering red" and "sky is threatening black and grey," while "Cold & Wet" is an old-timey song that's kind of goofy about water, and then there's the line "watch them die impaled on balsa spears."

It seems like in "Cold & Wet" the singer is singing from a position of reacting against the world at large, whereas in "I Don't Belong to Anyone" it seems like the negativity comes more from inside. "Death Final," actually, is maybe one of the more optimistic songs on the record; maybe because it's about the end of existence, or the potential end, but then it not being the end but an opportunity for renewal.

When you recorded *Beware* you used the same band from a tour you did just before the recording sessions.

We rehearsed and then toured, with the idea that that would be the band for the upcoming recording, for the first time doing

* That is, Doug Sahm, leader of the 1960s band Sir Douglas Quintet.

something that way. Which was all right. Don't think I'd do it again [*laughs*].

The *Beware* recording sessions had a lot of guests; you've said that they were there for very specific purposes.

Yeah, 'cause we tracked everything with the band. Basically, on the last day of the tour, or a week later, I gave everybody all the songs. Then we tracked, and then Jennifer [Hutt, violinist] flew back to France, and Josh [Abrams, bassist] went on tour, but he was in and out of the studio, and [percussionist Michael] Zerang probably went on tour and was in and out of the studio, just checking in, saying hi. So from then on it was just listening to the songs, thinking where they could go, and then thinking who could play on them—mostly Emmett and I. Rob [Mazurek, cornetist] was in town for the Chicago Jazz Festival, so we thought, "It would be amazing if Rob could do this here and this here." Whereas before I would be thinking of musicians before the session, this was thinking of musicians once we recorded the basic tracks, with the exception of Greg Leisz, who was a guy that Emmett had known for a long time and had admired for his steel playing, and Emmett, in advance, had said, "What do you think about this guy coming out and playing for a couple of days?" But we didn't know what he would do, at all, until we'd already tracked.

***Beware* was another instance of a record being recorded by a studio's house engineer [Neil Strauch].**

All the times I've worked with house engineers in studios, whether it's Stone Room and Acme for *Hope*, or the two 7"s we did at the Bates Brothers recording studio that the Bates Brothers actually engineered, or the CRC guy for *Joya*, or this session with Neil Strauch, it's always a joy . . . like working with sound guys in clubs, you know? People that know their room and have to sit through band after band, session after session, show after show, watching musicians who don't give a shit and are no fun to work with, and also not getting listened to because they're not *their* soundperson or not the chief engineer, 'cause the band brings in an engineer or a soundperson, and then all of a sudden have someone be like, "You know what? You probably know this board, you probably know this room, you probably have some good ideas about recording. Let's do this record." And Neil slid into that role so naturally, so well, it was really cool.

You've said there were "similar emotions to the first album in relation to how we were working."
Huh. I don't know [*laughs*].

And that *Beware* was "the most conscious record in terms of where it sits in my catalog."
Yeah, I was aware while writing it and while recording it that I was gonna attempt to do promotion for it in traditional ways, and also that there was a group of musicians who were prepared far in advance, so there was a constant feeling of being roped into a big thing, as opposed to feeling like anything could change at any moment two weeks before the session. So there was this consciousness that was a little constraining at times. After putting it out, I changed the record cover, which

is now changed on the digital version; once we run out of print it will be changed on the hard-copy versions, as well as taking the last two songs off the record. So it's an eleven-song record now, which I think is better. I feel like on some level—with all due respect to Emmett and Josh, whom I spoke to mostly—I was trying to sequence the record and was saying, "Probably this should be cut, probably this should be cut," with them saying, "Aw, but I like that song, aw, man, you can't." But I think putting all thirteen songs that we recorded on there was a mistake.

"I Am Goodbye" is the new last song on *Beware*, and the idea of "I Am Goodbye" is that it's supposed to be like a vaudevillian guy with a cane and a straw boater prancing off the stage, whacking the cane from side to side as the curtain closes, saying, "It's just a *show*, you know, all the records are just a show. We were throwing these terrific images at you, with *style*, and we did it with pizzazz, we did it with vim and vigor and with fists in the air and voices raised high, and *now we're off*! To another town." 'Cause yeah, we've always got to leave 'em laughing.

[*laughs*] Right. Do you ever play it last in a set?
Yeah, we played it last in the set a bunch, about a year ago. We would medley into a chorus of a Demis Roussos song called "Goodbye My Love, Goodbye." He has been, over the last forty years, an extremely popular romantic pop singer, of Greek origin. He was in Aphrodite's Child, a sort of Moody Blues–influenced band, and they had a number of hits. He started making solo records in the early 1970s and had hits in German,

Italian, Spanish, Greek, and then lots of hits in English, and one of his biggest songs was "Goodbye My Love, Goodbye." He has this really huge, incredible voice; you could say that it's operatic because of the range that he gets, the emotional range, except that it's not as formal-feeling. It doesn't sound like Freddie Mercury, but it's similar in the way that Freddie Mercury had a kind of classicism and incredible control over his voice, and yet it's very, very personable. I think that's why Demis Roussos had so many fans, because he makes these unbelievably bombastic songs into something that feel like he could be the guy at the next table at the restaurant singing to you.

What is the Jeff Hamilton cover being replaced with?
The poster image. For the poster, Dan O. [Osborn] had the Jeff Hamilton image, and I was like, "Now, for the poster, if you could build a city on top of my head, build a road to the city in primary colors and put pilgrims on the road . . ." So we worked on that idea, and that became the poster, and I was like, "Actually, this is a better record cover than the one we have." The cover was sort of a conscious weird hybrid of *Master and Everyone* and *I See a Darkness*.

That was another thing that made it interesting, as the next record after *Lie Down in the Light*: that the cover image is dark and the title is foreboding.
Right, and the song titles were all pretty harsh. Even as I was making it and it was all happening, I was like, "Why, why, why, why? That was the whole *point* of *Lie Down in the Light*, to *change*

things and make things *better*, and why is this record like this?" I was upset, but there was nothing I could do about it. It was happening [*laughs*].

With *Arise Therefore* I thought, "We're gonna make this rich-sounding, really warm record. It's going to be really inviting to people and it's got this really optimistic-sounding title." And even while making it, it was so exciting when the sounds would come up, Ned's and Grubbs's parts. I was like, "This is so exciting, so *positive*." And then I started to listen to it and realized . . . or other people listened to it and said, "There's nothing positive about *that*" [*laughs*].

On *Beware* there's echo effects on the voice—for I think the first time on one of your records.
I was never happy with how conservative I was with vocal effects. I usually would try to put effects on the vocal, and then always back off, like, "Never mind, just take some of that off, less of that, less of that, less of that."

"It's gone."

"OK, that sounds good."

Lie Down in the Light, actually, was the first time I said, "There's gonna be reverb on the voice." So Mark used his reverb thing, and it's still pretty subtle, but it's there, I think, more than on any other record, although there's some delay on "Madeleine-Mary" on *I See a Darkness*. But then with *Beware*, I was like, "OK, Neil and Emmett, hold my hand and guide me through effects on the voice, 'cause there's been enough clean, dry voice. It's time to learn how to use effects."

In January 2009 you did a slew of interviews for *Beware* to prove to Drag City that press makes no difference to album sales. What was the result of that experiment?

Dan [Koretzky] and I are in agreement that press is not the place to put money and energy into in order to sell records. The thing that was making me sick while I was doing a lot of it was that I was feeling like it was actually going to *hurt* record sales. Because with interview after interview, most people doing the interview don't really prepare, don't care, and what this is doing is providing a lot of lukewarm, empty, quasi-interesting content in relation to this record, which will also then be related to other records, which is canceling out any efforts that had been made before to try to have only stuff that's *considered* and thought about be associated with the records. And here we are, doing all this bullshit, and people will be like, "Oh, it's just the same old bullshit that everybody does. It's just bullshit, it's just a lot of garbage, magazine-filler bullshit." I thought, "We'll never get anyone's confidence back, or it will take years to get the confidence back of people who suspect or realize that the whole publicity machine is vile and corrupt" [*laughs*].

Being interviewed can be like talking to your high-school guidance counselor, where they don't really know you and are trying to find out about you, and they're looking at a press release instead of looking at your report card; like, "Oh, it says here blah blah blah. What do you think about that?"

Right. "You're a member of the chess team. Is there anything you want to do with that in college?"

"Why, do *you* know how to play chess?"

"No, I've never played, but . . ." [*laughs*].

Every once in a while you meet somebody whom you *do* communicate with; there can be shorthand, there can be a conversation that develops, and you can only hope that it comes across. But usually if the conversation develops it seems like the writer is so surprised by it that they don't want to include any of it in the piece. They think that was the icing on their hour of time and had nothing to do with the content of the piece.

So for *Beware* you did all this press and toured for three solid months. Did the extra touring also seem to make no difference to the album's sales?

I don't know, because we're also dealing with a different music economy. And with all my finances, whether it's utility bills or tour income, I try to look at it, but not too closely. I look at my utility bill every month or my phone bill, and only if it seems really weird do I think about it; otherwise I'll just look at it for a second, pay it, and throw it away. And the same when I get royalty statements. I'm still making a living, but I don't know if I'm making a living because *Beware* has sold well or because anything else has sold well in this past year and everything else has dropped. The shows went great so, unfortunately, that's a reliable way of making a living [*laughs*].

11

A PIRATE PREVAILS

ALAN LICHT: With all the traveling you do, how important are possessions?

WILL OLDHAM: I buy books when I'm traveling, books that I just don't think I'll encounter again, and then I keep them because I don't know how to get rid of them responsibly. If I travel by car, I like to have a good blanket, a good pillow, a good book, but oftentimes, if I lose something that I'm not using, it's a relief. I don't really understand my own relationship to possessions. Having possessions seems like something to do because you might as well. It's nice every once in a while to be able to access old records, but if I didn't have 'em, there's enough music you can find to fill your head with. It's nice to have space to put clutter in, because when you come back from traveling there's a lot of clutter that pops out of the suitcase, and it's nice to have a place where you can put people up or work in. But yeah, it seems for the most part that when you're traveling and you want or need something, you get it, and then you're stuck with it, even though you only have a temporary use for it. If there were libraries for musical instruments and for furniture, that would be great. Just to have something for a while, and then be able to let it go again. I'm not in accumulative mode normally when I'm in one place, so it's safe.

Is there anything you can say about the different places you have lived—your experience of them or the way you think back on living in these different towns and cities?

Part of it is feeling like if I don't keep moving around I'm going to get isolated, because that's the only way to find *all* the different people that you have things in common with and can relate to. Rather than sticking in one place and gradually alienating yourself from everybody because of the differences, just keeping moving so you're reminded, "I'm *not* the only one who thinks this or likes this or feels this or appreciates this or hates this or can't stand this." I've never known what to say about a lot of places because . . . just like when you tour, you can say, "I've played Paris," or "I've played Grand Rapids City," but there's an extent to where it isn't quite honest to say you've been to those places just because you've played them. And the same goes with living in places: if you live nowhere longer than three weeks over the course of a year, did you live anywhere? I don't know what the honest way of saying that is. Spending extended periods of time in Madison, Virginia, north of Charlottesville and then Charlottesville, Baltimore, Iowa City, Sausalito, living in Los Angeles for six months, living in New York for six months, at different times: did I *live* in those places or was it an extended visit? Or Birmingham, which was also kind of a three-season thing. Or being in and out of Rhode Island, from 1988 to 2000, the longest period being probably nine months, the shorter periods maybe one week; but it wouldn't be a deep experience of the *place* because it would be with Dianne [Bellino]'s family or we would be with Bob Arellano.

In New York, at the beginning of the day you set out to get somewhere, and by the end of the day you end up nowhere near that place. It's like being on a university campus. You do have

all the access to art and music, but art and music—unless you
are a full-time employed artist or musician—isn't really life.
Everyone's struggling to afford to live there and juggling all the
cultural activities, but at a certain point aren't all the cultural
activities supposed to be a *fraction* of our existence and *enrich*
our existence, but not *be* our existence? So you find a place like
Louisville, where people's existences are dominated by necessi-
ties, not by how to afford frivolities. I always think of the music
as pretty metropolitan music—big-city music that we make in
smaller cities because we can do things at our own pace. Baltimore's a fairly unpredictable place. There was one time I was
robbed a couple of nights in a row, and I'm pretty sure it was
my neighbors that did it. They were an older, poor, probably
Appalachian-rooted family that had been there for decades.
The patriarch of the family—I think everyone just called him
"Gramps"—didn't have a nose; it had fallen off from some sort
of cancer. The little girl would come over, and we'd set up some
makeshift karaoke thing in my living room.

Everybody has their own specific relationship to place; I
think I tend to get more into a place than many people would.
It's not a coincidence that, not counting Colin, the people that
I became close to in my time in Rhode Island were Bob, who
was beginning his relationship with Rhode Island but was there
for fifteen years, Dianne, who was a local, Paul Greenlaw, who
was a local, the Udas brothers [friends], Richard Manning [the
film archivist at Brown]—those were the people that I bonded
with, people who had a relationship to the place. I liked being
in Providence more than I liked being in school, and I got a

pizza-delivery job and loved it, loved driving around and listening to the radio and checking out the neighborhoods, going to churches, movie theaters, restaurants all over town, record stores, beaches—everything.

The song "West Palm Beach" in particular was about having specific sets of memories of family and friends in a place where you do not live all the time. My father's side of the family spends time near there, in Delray. It's been a place that we've visited for many years; each trip you're the same person, but also a vastly different person, especially if it's an annual thing that begins at a young age. Your relationship to the place goes through these changes with you, and that was the idea of trying to put into a song the intensity of the sporadic relationships. And the sporadic relationships with that community of people as well—the other people who have sporadic relationships with the place, and also the people who have a permanent relationship with the place.

That's different from when I look around here on my block in Kentucky, where people are used to things staying the same. It's a different mindset when the population is shifting constantly in both big and little ways, and I think it's something a Floridian goes through much more often than a Kentuckian. And in general, whenever I get someplace, I don't start into my own normal routine; I start to explore, I try to figure out what my relationship to the place is going to be, as much as possible.

Being in a country where I don't speak the language very well always helps with language, because it forces my brain to use English in a different way. Rather than being able to vomit out words, they all get stuck in your head, turn around like a blender, feed off of each other. And also having to force yourself to express yourself, that's always good, either in whatever limited English the person you're talking to has or whatever limited Spanish, say, that I have. It just makes me think, "OK, how do you say this word, and then how do they put this? They put the verb in front of that."

One thing that's been interesting about looking at the timeline of your tours, and who was playing on them, is that there always seem to be certain people involved who were related to where you were living at the time.

Most definitely, yeah. That seems to be a part of being part of a place, that any tour or record should not ignore geography. Whether you're passing through or beginning and ending somewhere, there should be a relationship to the place as much as possible, at all times, whether it's a recording, a tour, or anything.

Baltimore, maybe, had the most musical community to draw on.

New York also, though, 'cause of [Mike] Fellows, Sweeney, [Live Skull / Chavez drummer] James Lo, yourself . . . And then also I was in and out of Chicago a lot, including staying extended periods of time at Drag City, when Dan lived there, and from there came relationships with Josh Abrams, Azita [Youseffi], Emmett, [Jim] O'Rourke . . . you know, anyone who passed through there. For a time Grubbs was living there, [Bastro /

Gastr del Sol / Tortoise drummer John] McEntire . . . so many people. But mostly it comes from being in a place and interacting with folks. It's always nice working with people who have a sense of place and a sense of self. That's really important for me, that they're bringing *their* world in, with a degree of natural confidence, 'cause I feel like that will make the music make more sense to an eventual listener. There's no direct equation, but I just have a hunch that it works that way.

In the last few years, in trying to become somewhat positively resolved about being here in Louisville, I've found that I can also see there's a good chance that being in a place where I have deep roots and deep understanding could contribute to the music, as having more going on. I don't know if that's the case, but starting to look at different writers, musicians, directors, actors who aren't *from* where they achieved their success, and to watch their work becoming diluted over a period of time . . . it probably has as much to do with being successful, or beginning to feed off the work itself and the politics of work itself, but it probably also feeds off the fact that they've lost all connection with the beginning part of their life. So their work from a certain point begins to be about [their experiences] from age twenty-five on. That *can* be really interesting, but it can be a huge handicap to certain kinds of work.

You've said that you feel at home anywhere or everywhere, which maybe connects back to the idea of community.
It does, and it also comes from that moment in New Delhi when everything fell apart and had to be put back together, and being

on the other side of the world there's no quick fix to not feeling at home, except to feel at home. And then, just by being pretty transient, certain things take the place of what someone might feel is routine comfort. For me, routine comfort is always a little surprise, and I never know where to expect it; it could just be opening a hotel-room door or turning a corner in Champaign, Urbana, and just being, "Ahhh," you know? *Why*, I don't know, but all of a sudden I wished I didn't have to leave Main Street, Urbana, because I felt so safe, and excited at the same time.

In addition to living in so many different places, just the sheer volume of your work is notable. Given the frame of mind, the time, and the situation, can you write five songs in a day?
I wouldn't think so, no. I'm sure I've never written five songs in a day.

Are you writing ideas down in a notebook day by day, and then going back and reviewing them and coming up with lyrics?
It's different if it's for a record versus a song. As soon as I knew the session with Mariee Sioux was gonna happen I started thinking about the song, and at different times I could have my little memo pad, notebook, or business cards and write ideas for that song on the back and stick 'em in my wallet. And you can record little things on your *phone* now, or there's a really easy program on the computer called Audio Recorder, where it opens, you push "record," push "stop," and it saves it as an mp3 file on your desktop.

My sense of community and human interaction overall has

to do with music, and sometimes with acting, so it's just part of what goes on. I know that days and days and days and days go by without working on a song, although no days go by without thinking about them. When I see the volume of things, I guess it kind of seems like a lot, although the music and the movies that were the first things that I fell in love with, say, up to the age of fifteen, would have been classic Hollywood, primarily from the 1940s, and music of the 1940s, 1950s, and early 1960s, and most of the people involved with that output were people who worked every day at what they did. If you look at their discographies or filmographies, they're immense, 'cause that's what you *did*. You were expected, and allowed, to make two, three, or four records a year. A singer like Loretta Lynn probably put out three or four full-length records a year in the 1960s; they weren't even all good, much less great, but there would usually be a good song or two on them, and it meant working every day.

But she wasn't writing all her own material.

Right, exactly. But then how many movies did John Ford make, and with what frequency? It always seemed to me that in order to get better at what you do, you *do* it. People have asked questions that have to do with the volume of songs, and I've never quite known how to respond, just because it seems like that's what a person would *do* if one had the opportunity to put energy towards making songs and records. I think in the 1980s, looking with sort of a sidelong glance at the Michael Caine movies that came out, the variety of them—the apparent quality of some of them being high and others being low—just thinking,

"What the fuck is that all about?" And now thinking that that was a good way for him to have worked; he stayed *good* because he kept doing things, and doing all different kinds of things.

When you mentioned John Ford, it occurred to me that a better analogy would be Rainer Werner Fassbinder or Werner Herzog in the 1970s, when they were making so many movies a year.
I think I've only watched one Fassbinder movie from beginning to end, so I don't know . . .

I wouldn't make the comparison between the content of his films and that of your music, but more in terms of his working almost nonstop on the writing and realization of films. And the way that Herzog would do short documentary films in between the longer features reminds me of all the 7"s and EPs you've done between albums.
My single strongest emotional memory of a Herzog film is *La Soufrière* [1977]. There's many of his movies that I like, both short ones and long ones, but for some reason that one I think of as kind of a moment that I just had a pure experience of. I liked the South Pole documentary [*Encounters at the End of the World* (2007)]; I know a lot of people who loved it. He seemed to make it in cooperation with Henry Kaiser, because Kaiser has a coproducer credit on it; after watching the movie I started to think that it was probably more Kaiser's thing, like he said, "Oh, you should check this community out, you should check out this world up here. I can introduce you to

this person, I can introduce you to that person"—'cause in addition to being a musician, his other career is Arctic diving, scuba diving, which I didn't realize. And maybe the thing that I loved most about it was he [Herzog] was able to go to Antarctica and make a movie with his friend, Henry Kaiser—and that was thrilling, just thinking about that kind of collaboration being possible, with a friend and colleague, and that there's an audience for it.

When and where did the idea to do *The Wonder Show of the World* collaboration with Emmett Kelly come from?
Emmett's been essential and close and important over the past few years of making music. I've talked a lot about music with him in all ways—writing, recording, performing—and I wanted to extend that collaboration. It's credited to Bonnie Prince Billy and the Cairo Gang, which is his musical name, and so maybe it made people more aware of the specifics of how this person has been involved with these records. That was kind of the idea, to deepen our collaboration, and also we would have something to show for all the energy we've put into the last few years, besides memories. We didn't have any kids or anything.

In that way it seems somewhat similar to the *Superwolf* project.
The *Superwolf* process was three songs as an experiment, and then the rest as one big block. I gave Emmett the lyrics first, three songs at a time. There were gonna be twelve in total; I gave him the three songs I was most confident about first, and then would revise, rewrite, or redecide what the next three songs

would be, based on different things. Sometimes it would be something that would happen on my side; sometimes it would be something based on what he sent to me. For *Superwolf* we met up a few times to go over rewrites together, where Emmett and I did everything remotely, over the phone or texting. There were a lot of revisions done through texting.

Emmett went to Berklee [College of Music, Boston] for a little bit, but I don't think he got much out of it. I think that's how his mind works, it just sort of naturally goes toward . . . he understands music theory, I think it's sort of innate. So those were some of the new challenges, singing melodies against chords that had a strong theory background. Matt [Sweeney] was creating things built on top of rock, and other things, but that kind of tradition. There were a bunch of challenges in there, but even when we first started working on the songs I felt more confident that Matt was writing for this collaboration—which Emmett was too, but since his language is more foreign to me, it was harder for me to appreciate that. Understanding that he is, actually, patronizing me [*laughs*], but it's still complex. It's like, "Can't you dumb it down for me a little more?" There were times when we'd be recording a song, and I'd be thinking, "Doesn't he realize I'm just not that good? [*laughs*] Why didn't he just make a simple, repetitious song?"

Some of the chords he uses are slightly more sophisticated than on your other records—major sevenths and so on . . .
I've used major sevenths before [*laughs*]! No, he knows his way around chords much more than I do, inarguably. It's kind of

interesting also, because the whole time listening and then recording and now in the aftermath I've been thinking that I'm not sure if there are any of these songs that I'll be able to play *without* Emmett; like if ever I did a show with other musicians or solo, I might have to not do these songs [*laughs*].

When we were listening to the Frank Sinatra record [*Only the Lonely*], you were talking about how the songs don't really stay in the same musical time. I think that's something that's happening on this record also: some of them slow down or stop. There's a different sense of rhythm than in your other records. Yeah, the first recording I did with Emmett was "Ebb Tide," which is on *Only the Lonely*, and we've listened to it a lot, that record. But we've also talked about songs that have that free meter, free tempo, free something or other.

Is that something Emmett has done before as a songwriter, or is it unique to this project? Maybe unique so far, but with the idea that there's a lot of records to come on his part. There's maybe more of a sense of drama that he allowed himself to explore, relating to starts and stops, and peaks and valleys, relating to dynamic, which might have to do with the freedom of working with someone else's words rather than one's own.

The vocal harmonies seem very developed, more so than your other stuff. Is that something both of you were interested in exploring?

Yeah, definitely. Recordings that I gave him prior to embarking on this, for ideas, were the Glen Campbell / Jimmy Webb record [*Reunited*]—not for singing, but for the relationship of writer to singer—and then a bunch of Skeeter Davis. Her first popular recordings were done as the Davis Sisters, with another woman who died in a car crash, and from then on Chet Atkins produced her and got her to harmonize with herself, so the harmonies were super close and pretty much ubiquitous on her songs for ten or twenty years. We talked a lot about a guy named Darren Benitez, who's around forty years old and was born in Hawaii to Puerto Rican parents who, I think, came to Hawaii to work on the sugar plantations. He has three records that he's put out over the course of the last fifteen years or so in which he has these kind of insane close harmonies that he does with himself. Some of them almost sound like harmony effects, because he does all these little trills, and the harmony voice does them precisely. It could be a harmonizer, but he's made three records in fifteen years, so he could be just an obsessive-compulsive guy.

We've done a lot of singing together over the years. There's one song called "Someone Coming Through" that has these elaborate vocal-harmony arrangements, and I know the idea for it being like that, and the basic harmonies, were Emmett's, and then when we were together we embellished them.

When you think about early rock and roll, the voice is really the primary instrument, and even in the 1960s the lead and background vocals were still a big part of the music.

And it has been, as a listener, interesting and frustrating that in my lifetime—the 1970s, 1980s, 1990s, and even the present—it doesn't seem like the voice is as utilized an instrument in popular or underground music. It's more like something that people put in there as an element or ingredient, but there's not a lot of . . . whatever you want to call it, good *singers* or vocal stylists. It's almost like you have to have a guitar or bass in your hand in order to be a legitimate member of a band.

Maybe in country music the voice is still a primary instrument? It is, but in most country music, say since 1990 or so, and to some extent before that, but specifically in the last twenty years, like most R&B music you just can't tell anymore how good the singer is. You could listen to the R. Kelly record *Untitled*, and if you only knew this record you wouldn't be able to tell that he's a great singer, because he chooses to fit in with the radio and have Auto-Tuning effects, and his performances, whether or not they *are*, sound like fully edited performances, like most of those you hear on the radio and country radio. When we were making *Lie Down in the Light*, there's a studio about a half mile from Mark [Nevers]'s house that he has a relationship with, where we mixed *Master and Everyone*. We went over to borrow a Rhodes [electric piano], and there was an engineer in there by himself doing a session. He was listening to a line of music. We were over there for fifteen minutes and we heard this line, maybe between six and twenty words, over and over and over again over the course of those fifteen minutes. The line gradually moved forward, by seconds, and as we were leaving, I was like, "Can I ask you what it is you're *doing*?" "I'm tuning Alan Jackson's vocal." And Alan Jackson is a well-respected, sort of traditionalist, huge country star, and this guy is going through word by word and tuning his vocal. People recognize and admire his voice, and like him because of it, but no one's gonna be able to listen to that and *connect* with the voice; obviously he doesn't want, and thinks his fans don't want, to *hear his voice.* So even in country music, and even among the established traditionalists, the voice might be important, but singing isn't.

And unfortunately it feels like the motivation behind that is one of deception. I don't mind T-Pain, and I don't mind the huge Cher single years ago—I don't have anything against Auto-Tuning—but when it's Auto-Tuning with the idea that you're making the audience think that it's your voice, your singing, I tend to think that's a little weird. That's sort of like being gay and pretending to have a relationship with a woman or having a wife or a husband and kids, but essentially you're lying to yourself and your family. Not that that's inherently evil, it's just unfortunate; it fosters more confusion in the future generation, in the kids, because there was so much deception going on in their household. In a movie music swells and brings emotion to you, and once you get to a certain age you think, "The only reason I cried was because of the music," "The only reason I was tense was because of the music." But you're *not* gonna get to a certain point and realize, "The only reason I thought Alan Jackson was a good singer was because someone was tweaking every fucking syllable he did"—people aren't going to find that information out.

No Direction Home, **the documentary on Bob Dylan, shows a lot of performances by the reigning folk people of the early 1960s. They all have very strong singing voices, and then Dylan comes on and it's this raspy, thin-sounding voice. You always heard that he was the guy who "couldn't sing," but this puts it into context, compared to Odetta or Harry Belafonte. It illustrates how it was the kind of voice that would not be considered a good singing voice at that time, but has since become more acceptable as an instrument of expression.**

Yeah, I think he's a really great singer, and one reason is that he developed the only style he could, even though most people recognized it as a nonsinging voice. Then, because it was successful and popular, it was very imitated, but his voice continued to change and evolve and become a new kind of voice that was oftentimes less popular but still unique. On a record like *Street-Legal*, that's a singing style that I've never heard anybody imitate, and I think most people wouldn't even accept it as decent or listenable. It's not a very popular record. But on that and then on into the crazy 1980s style, like on *Knocked Out Loaded*, you've only heard people sing that way when they're making fun of Bob Dylan, but it still always has a relationship to melody and to the song, and it doesn't seem indulgent, for the most part. Every once in a while it would: *Infidels* seems to be on the outer edges of relating to melody in a way that I sympathize with. But then he came back as an older man with some new stylizations that I don't think anybody had done before; on *MTV Unplugged* there was a "Desolation Row" where he pulls off some vocal things that are really exciting.

Do you think your delivery of lines has evolved over the years?
Yes. First of all I've always had ideas about singing and how it
should be, but they were always limited by the control I had
over my voice and my understanding of how the voice works,
which improves, of course, with practice and experience. I
think it's kind of neat; say on the first Palace Brothers record,
I'm using my voice to its maximum potential at that time, which
was severely limited, but I feel like I knew *how* it should work.
I just couldn't *do* it. I think I struggled during the recording
of that, on the microphone, to use tiny tics and twitches and
inflection to express what I wished I could express in a larger
melodic way or in a larger, vocally flexible way. The movements
are tiny, because there's no facility. I felt that at least if I gave a
little hint or clue as to where my voice could be going, that that
could be read. It surprised me a bit unpleasantly when people
would remark about the voice cracking and that being some
sort of strange defect or something, because at the time I really
thought I was singing the best I could and didn't notice those
things . . . I was just going for it. In recording, sometimes I
pull something off and I get just *giddy*, because I imagine that I
move closer to a place alongside vocalists that I revere.

**Then does the evolution of the singing style inform the evolu-
tion of the songwriting?**
Yeah, for sure. Knowing that I can write a song around certain
kinds of singing, knowing that the potential is there for styl-
izing things responsibly makes me feel like I have greater freedom in writing the songs that I want to write. And trying to

be concerned, at times, that they aren't the "This-is-the-thing-I've-always-wanted-to-do" great stylistic disasters that so many people who make records or movies do when they get really successful, you know? I want to feel free to stylize but not to go too far into it, to where the style becomes the content, or more of the content than what's in the theme, but the theme is still more than half of the content as opposed to just this experiment in genre or whatever. It's also fun to experiment with style in writing the song, knowing that both the musicians I'll be working with and the audience that will be hearing it won't be aware there's an experiment going on, that I'm writing something in the style but that won't be part of their experience at all.

In talking about various things, about the relationship you have to music from listening to records, seeing Ben Chasny in a small place versus seeing Prince in a big place, your different acting experiences, and the *Chijimi* and *Wonder Show* records, it seems like one thread that goes through all this is the idea of intimacy.

The stuff that I got out of movies and music had to do with intimacy, so that is why it's valuable to me. And I think that that is significantly different to a lot of people, whether it's performers or audience members, who seem to really treasure the idea of performance. The whole success of the video games that are coming out now, *Rock Band* and *Guitar Hero*, which I only know from reading about them . . . it's so alien to me. It's like when you see people advertising having tits and a fully functional cock in the back of newspapers in New York, and think, "Hmm, what the fuck would you want that for, what's that all about?" Like, why would you want to be onstage in front of a lot of people?! It's so bizarre and foreign; I don't understand it, and I don't understand wanting to go to big shows, to huge shows. I don't have any understanding of what's positive and valuable about those things. The only reason I want to be onstage is because that usually means that I will be making money that I can use to make records and live life and work with people. And then I eventually made it usually mean that I *was* working with people, and it was a valuable experience—and that's what I liked about being onstage.

There's enough interaction, by learning and interpolating, when you're listening to a record or watching a movie or reading a book. In addition to taking in lessons and experiences and vicarious emotion, you're also watching people work; and especially if you see three interpretations of the same song or the same piece of work, or if you see one actor doing three different roles, or if you listen to three different records by one person, you start to see, "Oh, that's how this relates to this, and that's how this relates to this." And probably for many people in the world these can be, for great periods of our lives, some of the most valuable interactions that you have. But also, when you listen to a record, you're free to have any relationship you want to the music, and that's the most important thing. You can listen to music from anybody in the world, any time, and you can be their friend, their enemy, their colleague, their master, their servant, their husband. It's owner's rights: if they pay for the song the listeners can do anything they want with it.

So I never made the jump to where I understood just the *idea* of a show, or going to see Prince on the *Purple Rain* tour. It seems like if you're going to be involved in that relationship of writer–performer–audience, in any position, it seems important that your position has *value* and that it is, essentially, recognizable as a *relationship* and a communication. And of course there needs to be a little realism in there; you need to realize that it's a different kind of interaction, you know? New aspects of the interaction are not gonna be immediate. I can't sit here and write a song and get a reaction from an individual in Spokane; I can't record a song and get a reaction from an individual in Spokane; I can't even *perform* a song and get, really, a reaction, *unless* the performance is done like that Six Organs set—that's the closest you can come to having an interaction with the audience. The smaller the audience, the closer you can come to something you could call an interaction, that actually begins to approach communication.

Unfortunately, as I've learned how to tour in such a way that I get a lot out of it—I say "unfortunately," and it's retarded and ironic—the music has gotten more successful, and it's harder to convince booking agents *that* I would and *why* I would want to play smaller places. Once you get over a certain number of people, it seems like there's too many forces at work. I started to think about presenting an idea to Boche [Billions], asking if he'd be willing to consider booking a tour that would be an unamplified tour, that would require the spaces to be both small enough and acoustically friendly enough. And the other idea was to do a standing gig, probably here in Louisville, where

I would rent or purchase a space and do between one and eight hour-long sets a day, with an audience capacity in the room of maybe ten people. Like a movie theater: whether or not anybody showed up for the 2:30 set, you still do the set, between 2:30 and 3 or 3:30, but also have it where you could book your spot, so if you knew you were going to be traveling through Louisville on your way to Chicago from Nashville and you were gonna be there from 3 to 4 p.m., then you could go to the 3 to 4 p.m. set and book that two or three months in advance. So people would tour to see the music rather than the music tour to see the people. It would cost fifteen bucks, ten bucks, something like that, and it would be an hour-long set, but the set would also include communication, where people could make requests. You could play a song twice, you could play a song three times, you could talk some, and the musicians would change as well, but the idea would be you'd be seeing Bonnie Prince Billy solo or with other musicians. It could be anything: one set could be all requests, one could be all instrumental music. But the performance would be *unique* to the time that it happens and *dependent* upon the individuals that watched it, and no two would really be the same. You might take two days off a week and a month off in the summer or a month off in the winter . . . I don't know if it will happen, but it's an idea that I've been thinking about over the last six months or so.

The paradox of recorded popular music is—and this is maybe true of movies also—that when you're experiencing it, ideally the rest of the world sort of melts away and you feel like you're

having a one-to-one relationship with it; that someone is speaking to you, and you're receiving and responding to that, even though they don't know the response. So, when you have something that's extremely popular, you have a large number of people that are having that experience—maybe or maybe not quite that intensely—but then, as the listener/viewer, how much do you feel like you have to or want to share that experience with other people? And then, with everything you've said, how much, as a performer, do you recognize that this is something that people are going to want to bond on?

I *do* recognize that, but I think that, for example, the audience behind the popularity of *Guitar Hero* is an audience with a different motivation altogether. And that's an audience that's more about adulation and power, and a mix of those things. That's just something that I don't sympathize with at all, and I don't understand it. I feel uncomfortable in a room where the audience is all about worshipping a performer, or the performer is all about being worshipped at that moment. That's not music, to me, that's not my idea of music. But that's a lot of people, and I think that's *most* people who are public enjoyers of music. The other side of it is something that's essential, that's tremendously valuable, if not *the* most valuable thing: that music is about the corroboration, the creation, the recognition of a relationship between people. And communities, but sometimes it can be just a community of two.

When the groups of people get bigger at any gathering, any club or venue, you're starting to straddle the line to where you might be teetering over the edge into this other kind of thing, which is, to me, unrelated, although intertwined for sure. Because I can have an intimate relationship with *Darkness on the Edge of Town* and then feel uncomfortable at a Bruce Springsteen show, or uncomfortable seeing him with a Kennedy Center Honor medal hanging around his neck standing next to Robert De Niro—I don't *get* that, I don't get the value of that necessarily. But I *do* get the value of listening to *Darkness on the Edge of Town*. And recently a Norwegian guy who lives in Canada whom I've been communicating with has been sending me these *Masters of Cinema* DVDs, and recently he sent me some *Darkness on the Edge of Town* outtakes and demos, and things like that. And we never talk about Bruce Springsteen, but when I got those I was just like, "This is amazing." We communicate every once in a while, and it's usually about movies, and he sent me these recordings, and I was really happy to get them. And *that* was a crucial illustration of what's valuable about music, once it becomes something that resembles being public; that's the public manifestation that I like, and not the *other* thing, which I don't understand.

It's amazing, I feel like every time I buy a record I'm communicating to the artist or artists, to the record company, and to the world at large, something. Tiny little thing, big thing . . . *something* is being communicated. Even if it's a used record, even if it's a record from the library, it's communicating to someone, because the person at the counter might say, "A guy came in and bought this Helen Reddy record. I've always seen it there, and I just assumed no one was going to buy it." And they might forget it forever or they might mention it to somebody, but every little decision you make in relation to listening to music has the potential to put something back into the world of making and listening to it.

I've found that whenever my tastes are in tune with large groups of people, it makes me feel very happy. 'Cause I feel like my interests are perverse at times, and . . . it does feel good to listen to great music and know that other people like it *somehow*, whether it has to do with the marketplace or the economy, or whether it's more universal music. I don't know, still, why some great music everyone loves and why everyone loves some bad music, and why other, superior music very few people like.

I want to find the songs that 3 million people love and see if there's one I love too. That way we're all together with this one thing at least. I went and saw *Total Recall* [1990] in one of those weekend sneak previews the week before it opened, and I was like, "I love this movie, and this feels great." I love a movie that millions of other people like. It makes me very happy, even though they probably like it for a different reason. But my fantasy is, even if they *do* like it for another reason, that there's a relationship *and* the beginning of the ability to communicate with other people about something: we can talk about *Total Recall*.

There's also the additional excitement of seeing it right when it originally appears too. A lot of the stuff we've been talking about required going back and digging it up, or experiencing it after the fact of it being initially brought into existence.
But sometimes when something is old and well-loved it's even *more* exciting, though. It's cool to know that people are into Black

Sabbath or Led Zeppelin by the millions; they're great records. Of course, I didn't hear Led Zeppelin or Black Sabbath when they came out because I was four, or I didn't dig it, or whatever, but that feels great, to become a part of a huge community of people who are into something that's awesome. Even though you missed it the first time around, you're part of it. That's exciting.

They're perennials.
But they're perennials because they're good. That's exciting, to share that with other people, because more often there's great music that doesn't get recognized by many people at all. That seems to be more the standard case. I'm sure we've both had the experience of, say, a band like Dinosaur Jr., who put out a really good first record, a great second record, really good third record, and *then* their [audience] booms and the records aren't as interesting. I don't know exactly why that is, whether there was more money put behind them or if it was just the groundswell of interest based on the first three records, whatever . . . That's a regular occurrence when people get into something: it's not as good as it was.

If the general public welcomed one of my songs, people would be buying my next record based on the acceptance of that one song, and it would create a disappointment that isn't a part of the process now. It would affect the other audience members who have a strong relationship with my music; it would be harder for them to enjoy because the audience would have changed and there would be that dynamic of anticipation and disappointment entering into the music.

There is going to be vitality in somebody who is young and personally, but not popularly, successful. When somebody gets older, they're going to lose that vitality. When somebody becomes popularly successful, they'll also lose vitality, because their internal motors are going to be saying to them, "You don't need to do this anymore, you've succeeded." When that happens, there's no reason for you to be vital or interesting or important to anyone but yourself and those close to you.

Sometimes I'll hear things like the last few Neil Young albums, where I feel like he's not so much writing an album of new songs as making an album of more "Neil Young songs." It seems like after a certain point, when someone becomes as established as Neil Young, or if Singer-Songwriter X is on the treadmill of album/tour, album/tour every year or every other year, they might sit down and say, "I have to write some 'Singer-Songwriter X' songs," self-referentially.

Yeah, I think that's one of the things that makes both Merle Haggard and Leonard Cohen songwriters that I look up to, because as they've gotten older and older and older, and made more and more records, the approach feels the same. Even with Merle, he can be self-referential sometimes, but a new batch of songs seems to have the same energy and perspective as older batches. Or Leonard Cohen, at least through *Ten New Songs* [2001]—and since then there's only been that record *Dear Heather* [2004], which seems like a strange patchwork of songs— but for whatever reason they just haven't gotten self-referential, I guess. It seems like what comes out are things that are new to them. That's why you write songs, and it sometimes makes me question someone like Neil Young or possibly Nick Cave, who seems to write "Nick Cave songs." Why do they write songs if what they're writing now is "Neil Young" and "Nick Cave" songs? I get angry and sometimes resentful, and part of it is because I don't understand why they would do that, and I get really upset [*laughs*]. It just makes me feel so wrong about [*laughs*] what I think about the world and about life and about music, especially with those two, who have made a significant number of records that meant a lot to me.

Although it is true that it's a mistake to think that, as individuals, we're always on an emotional progression or building upon our experiences, necessarily; we can become diverted or sidetracked. Just because we're moving through time like everybody else doesn't mean that we're moving in a *straight line* through time, at least in terms of how we see the world. And it could be a physical thing; it could be that someone loses a part of their brain [*laughs*], and we try to say that that's the same person, right there, that wrote that song, but it isn't the same person that wrote that song anymore; it's a related person, but a different one. So I'm guessing that Neil Young and Nick Cave have a lot of brain damage or something [*laughs*].

In rock and pop music, at least, a lot of songs are a reaction to another song; someone hears a song and says, "I could do something like that." In Neil Young's case, when he was writing "Lotta Love" he was supposedly trying to write a Fleetwood Mac–type song, 'cause he heard "Dreams" on the radio.

Although I don't think Merle Haggard is still writing songs based on listening to the current top forty . . .

I think to some extent he was, though, and I think Merle Haggard will always be writing songs with the idea that they will stand up with the best Jimmie Rodgers songs, the best Bob Wills songs, the best Lefty Frizzell songs. I think he still thinks that those times and those artists and those songs are the best that American music had to offer, in some ways, and he wants to write songs that belong there. I don't think he ever thinks, "And now I've succeeded and so I'm going to start writing 'Merle Haggard songs.'" I think he still thinks, "Shit, I need to come up with another song that might one day stand alongside these other songs." And Leonard Cohen, to some extent—I think he gets into some weird music [*laughs*]—but I don't think he's ever thought, "I've cracked the code." I think he's someone who's in a complex relationship with satisfaction: satisfaction with himself and with his work and with his understanding of a spiritual reality, and the songs are always a part of what he uses to process and participate and include himself.

I do it for a living. Sometimes people equate the phrase "doing something for a living" with just economics, but taken literally it means you do it for a *living*: you get paid for it, but you also do it to *live* . . . it's like breath, you need it. Money is a symbol of food and shelter and the ability to exist, which is legitimate. The reason I write songs and create music has nothing to do with motivations or reasons. It's just that, to me, it doesn't seem like there's any other way to exist, to live. It's a way of communicating things in a way I'm comfortable with. It's beyond writing a song to get something off my back for cathartic purposes. I'm passionate about music, but it's even beyond that. It's not even a question of should I write a song or not. It's a necessity.

So there's no point at which you see retiring from music as a possibility?
After *Arise Therefore*, on some level I was like, "Well, that was that. I mean, why make another record?" And I think it's kind of neat when somebody stops, and stops *forever* . . . but when you peak, God doesn't turn the light off, you know? If you can't guarantee yourself that you're going to stop forever, then you shouldn't stop at all because you're not going to be *good* when you try to do it again 'cause then you won't have practiced. People run into dead ends all the time, and they say, "I just did what I could with this," or "There's no more good music," or whatever people say to say that it's an end to something, and there's no *reason* for there to be an end to something until your consciousness is at an end. Frank Sinatra ended it two or three times, and so did David Bowie, but it didn't end. I think about all the finalities I *could* pronounce for myself and then think, "Why bother? I'll just keep those finalities for myself."

A COSMOLOGICAL TIMELINE

1778   Captain James Cook discovers the Hawaiian tradition of surfing during an expedition to the Pacific

1875   First Kentucky Derby held in Louisville on May 17

1890   Erskine Hazard lays out and draws first town map of Matteawan, West Virginia (name later changed to Matewan by residents)

1939   Vogue Theater movie house opens in Louisville

1942   Joya sodas introduced in Monterrey, Mexico

1945   First edition of *Cannery Row* by John Steinbeck published

1950   Dolly Parton begins composing music at the age of four

1958   Henrique Prince begins teaching himself to play the violin at the age of nine

1959   Paul Bowles, accompanied by Christopher Wanklyn and Mohammed Larbi, travels across Morocco recording examples of traditional music

1963   Warner Brothers cartoon studio closes

1966   Haskell Wexler comes to the set of John Cassavetes's *Faces* as an extra, and ends up shooting a five-minute tracking shot in a bar scene (uncredited in the final film)

1967   Marianne Faithfull becomes the first person to say "fuck" in a feature film ("Get out of here, you fucking bastard"

to be precise), in *I'll Never Forget What's 'Isname*, directed
by Michael Winner

First Peel session (by the band Tomorrow) broadcast
on the BBC on September 21

Producer Felton Jarvis invites Jerry Reed to play guitar
on Elvis Presley's cover of Reed's song "Guitar Man"

1968 Johnny Cash proposes marriage to June Carter onstage
in London, Ontario

1970 Cat Stevens scores Hal Ashby's film *Harold and Maude*
after Ashby's original candidate, Neil Young, drops out

1971 Meat Loaf plays the role of Ulysses S. Grant in a touring
production of *Hair*

1972 Lou Reed's "Walk on the Wild Side," produced by David
Bowie and Mick Ronson, hits the US top twenty

Frank Stanford moves to New York City "to go to the
movies"

1973 Timothy Carey shoots director Francis Ford Coppola
with a blank during his screen test for *The Godfather
Part II*

1974 The Ramones play their first show

1975 Robert Bresson's *Notes on the Cinematographer* is published
in France

1976 Nancy Niles Sexton founds Walden Theatre in an abandoned log cabin in Jefferson County, Kentucky

1977 Nick Cave drops out of the Caulfield Institute of Technol-
ogy to concentrate on music

1978 Bob Dylan undergoes "born again" religious conversion
after a fan throws a silver cross onstage during a concert
in San Diego

1979 Final season of US TV series *Emergency!*

First Virgin Megastore opens in London

Mayo Thompson records the Fall's "Fiery Jack" / "2nd Dark Age" / "Psykick Dancehall #2" 7" in October

1980   D. Boon and Mike Watt form the Minutemen in San Pedro, California; the Misfits release the *Beware* EP (both in January)

Babylon Dance Band appear on the cover of the *Village Voice*, the first recognition of the Louisville underground rock scene in a national publication

1981   Steve Albini buys his first drum machine, a Roland TR-606

Lightning over Water, Wim Wenders's documentary portrait of Nicholas Ray, opens

1982   Rick Rubin makes first release on Def Jam, a 7" by his band, Hose

1983   John Cougar adds his real surname, Mellencamp, to his stage name

1984   Merle Haggard fan Robert Duvall wins the Oscar for Best Actor for his performance in *Tender Mercies*, a film some believed to be based on Haggard's life (a claim refuted by both Duvall and director Gary Hertz)

1985   Boche Billions books first tour, for Angry Red Planet

John Sayles shoots Bruce Springsteen's "Glory Days" video at rock club / restaurant Maxwell's, Hoboken, New Jersey

1986   Venom P. Stinger (with Mick Turner and Jim White) record their first album, *Meet My Friend Venom*

1987   Prince cancels the release of *The Black Album* in December, allegedly convinced it was evil after a bad experience with the drug ecstasy

1988   Bastro (at this point a duo of David Grubbs and Clark
          Johnson, plus a drum machine) releases debut EP *Rode
          Hard and Put Up Wet* on Homestead

1989   "Hero Zero / Love Is . . ." by Royal Trux becomes the
          first release on the Drag City label

          The Ramones play Louisville for the first time

1990   Dinosaur Jr. leave SST Records for Sire Records

1991   The Mekons' *Curse of the Mekons* is rejected by the
          band's label, A&M, as "technically and commercially
          unsatisfactory"

          Kelly Reichardt works as property master on Todd
          Haynes's film *Poison*

1992   Todd Brashear replaces Phil Ochs in the Sundowners

1993   Jimmy Buffett starts his own label, Margaritaville
          Records, distributed by MCA

1994   Björk writes the song "Bedtime Story" for Madonna

          Frank Sinatra gives final public concert at Fukuoka
          Dome, Japan, in December

1995   5th Lollapalooza tour, including Sonic Youth, Pavement,
          the Jesus Lizard, Dirty Three, and Mike Watt

1996   Ordained as a Zen Buddhist monk, Leonard Cohen takes
          the name Jikan ("silence")

1997   Royal Trux re-sign with Drag City after Virgin Records
          release them from their contract

          R. Kelly signs on to play pro basketball with the Atlan-
          tic City Seagulls

1998   *Hollywood Salutes Arnold Schwarzenegger: An American Cin-
          ematheque Tribute*, including guests such as James Cam-
          eron, Jon Bon Jovi, and Jonathan Richman, is broadcast
          on US television

1999 *My Best Fiend*, Werner Herzog's documentary about his friend and colleague Klaus Kinski, is released

2000 Kramer begins studying directing under Arthur Penn

2001 Harmony Korine writes lyrics for the song "Harm of Will" on Björk's album *Vespertine*

2002 Tower Records' *Pulse* magazine ceases publication

2003 Johnny Paycheck dies in Nashville on February 19

2004 Jandek makes debut live performance in Glasgow, with Alex Neilson on drums and Richard Youngs on bass

2005 Silver Jews embark on first-ever tour
  Guitar Hero video game released by RedOctane

2006 Ben Chasny, Matt Sweeney, and Baby Dee tour Europe as members of Current 93

2007 WO designs vol. 11, issue 1 of Francis Ford Coppola's magazine *Zoetrope: All-Story*
  Drag City releases *Woke on a Whaleheart*, Bill Callahan's first release under his own name (rather than Smog), in April

2008 Solomon Burke's album *Like a Fire*, which includes songs written specifically for Burke by Eric Clapton, Ben Harper, Jesse Harris, Keb' Mo,' Meegan Voss, and Steve Jordan, is released

2009 David Berman announces his retirement from music
  Actor Michael Caine claims *Empire* magazine misquoted him when it reported that he said that *Harry Brown* would be his last lead role in a film

2010 Limited edition of Bonnie Prince Billy wooden bottle stoppers, made by Scott Millar, released in conjunction with *The Wonder Show of the World*
  Jackass 3D, which includes a brief appearance by WO,

becomes highest-grossing film in the US on its opening weekend

2011   Jennifer Herrema changes the name of her band from RTX to Black Bananas

DISCOGRAPHY

This discography is in five sections: full-length albums, singles and EPs, compilation tracks, appearances on others' recordings, and group participation outside of the Palace/BPB/WO names. Album, single, and EP entries are listed by title, artist credit, formats, track titles, label and matrix number, and year of original release. Compilation entries start with the song title, followed by artist credit and release title. WO's contributions to other artists' recordings are also specified (e.g., "vocal" or "guitar").

Albums

There Is No One What Will Take Care of You (Palace Brothers) CD/LP/cass.: "Idle Hands Are the Devil's Playthings" / "Long Before" / "I Tried to Stay Healthy for You" / "The Cellar Song" / "(I Was Drunk at the) Pulpit" / "There Is No One What Will Take Care of You" / "O Lord Are You in Need?" / "Merida" / "King Me" / "I Had a Good Mother and Father" / "Riding" / "O Paul"
Drag City (DC34), Big Cat (ABB50CD), 1993; Domino (REWIG 8), 2001

Days in the Wake (originally untitled, or self-titled Palace Brothers) CD/LP/cass.: "You Will Miss Me When I Burn" / "Pushkin" / "Come a Little Dog" / "I Send My Love to You" / "Meaulnes" / "No More Workhorse Blues" / "All Is Grace" / "Whither Thou Goest" / "(Thou without) Partner" / "I Am a Cinematographer"
Drag City (DC50), Domino (WIG 8), 1994

Viva Last Blues (Palace Music) CD/LP: "More Brother Rides" / "Viva Ultra" / "The Brute Choir" / "The Mountain Low" / "Tonight's Decision (and Hereafter)" / "Work Hard" / Play Hard" / "New Partner" / "Cat's Blues" / "We Us, All Three, Will Ride" / "Old Jerusalem"
Drag City / Palace Records (DC65/PR4), Domino (WIG 21), 1995

Arise Therefore (credited as Palace on shrink-wrap sticker only) CD/LP/cass.: "Stablemate" / "A Sucker's Evening" / "Arise, Therefore" / "You Have Cum in Your Hair and Your Dick Is Hanging Out" / "Kid of Harith" / "The Sun Highlights the Lack in Each" / "No Gold Digger" / "Disorder" / "A Group of Women" / "Give Me Children" / "The Weaker Soldier"
Drag City (DC88), Domino (WIGCD 24), Toy's Factory (TFCK-88785) (Japan; adds "Black/Rich Tune" as final track), Cortex (CTX050CD) (Australia) 1996

Songs Put Together for "The Broken Giant" (Palace Soundtrack) CD/12": "Organ: Watch with Me" / "Do What You Will Do" / "The Risen Lord" / "Organ: Allowance" / "Allowance" / "Black/Rich Tune" / "Organ: Black/Rich" / "Guitar: Do What You Will Do"
Drag City (DC100), Domino (RUG46 CD), CD, 1996 (available only with initial CD pressing of *Arise Therefore*); Shock Records (Austra-

lia), CD, 1997 (available only with initial CD pressing of *Lost Blues and Other Songs*, and credited to "Will Oldham and Friends")
Rereleased as *Black/Rich Music* (Will Oldham), Drag City (DC100), 1998

Lost Blues and Other Songs (Palace Music) CD/2LP: "Ohio River Boat Song" / "Riding" / "Valentine's Day" / "Trudy Dies" / "Come In" / "Little Blue Eyes" / "Horses" / "Stable Will" / "Untitled" / "O How I Enjoy the Light" / "Marriage" / "West Palm Beach" / "Gulf Shores" / "(End of) Traveling" / "Lost Blues"
Drag City / Palace Records (DC110/PR16), Domino (WIG LP/CD 33), Shock Records (Australia) (CTX072CD), 1997

Joya (Will Oldham*) CD/LP: "O Let It Be" / "Antagonism" / "New Gypsy" / "Under What Was Oppression" / "The Gator" / "Open Your Heart" / "Rider" / "Be Still and Know God (Don't Be Shy)" / "Apocalypse, No!" / "I Am Still What I Meant to Be" / "Bolden Boke Boy" / "Idea and Deed"
Drag City (DC107), Domino (WIG LP/CD39), Shock Records (CTX088CD), 1997

I See a Darkness (Bonnie "Prince" Billy) CD/LP: "A Minor Place" / "Nomadic Revery (All Around)" / "I See a Darkness" / "Another Day Full of Dread" / "Death to Everyone" / "Knockturne" / "Madeleine-Mary" / "Song for the New Breed" / "Today I Was an Evil One" / "Black" / "Raining in Darling"
Palace Records (PR22), Domino/Labels (72438469420) (Europe),

---

* Now credited to Bonnie Prince Billy.

Spunk (URA001) (Australia), P-Vine (PCD-23010) (Japan: adds two tracks, "I Am Drinking Again," "Ode #2"), 1999

Guarapero / Lost Blues 2 (Will Oldham) CD/2LP: "Drinking Woman" / "The Spider's Dude Is Often There" / "Gezundheit" / "Let the Wires Ring" / "Big Balls" / "For the Mekons et al." / "Stable Will" / "Every Mother's Son" / "No More Rides" / "The Risen Lord" / "Boy, Have You Cum" / "Patience" / "Take However Long You Want" / "Sugarcane Juice Drinker" / "Call Me a Liar" / "O Lord Are You in Need?"
Drag City / Palace Records (DC111/PR15), Domino (WIGCD74), P-Vine (PCD-24012), 2000

Ease Down the Road (Bonnie "Prince" Billy) CD/LP: "May It Always Be" / "Careless Love" / "A King at Night" / "Just to See My Holly Home" / "At Break of Day" / "After I Made Love to You" / "Ease Down the Road" / "The Lion Lair" / "Mrs. William" / "Sheep" / "Grand Dark Feeling of Emptiness" / "Rich Wife Full of Happiness"
Palace Records (PR26), Domino (WIG CD/LP 89), Spunk (URA041), P-Vine (PCD-24054, with bonus track, "Carolyn"), 2001

Get the Fuck on Jolly Live (Bonny Billy and Marquis De Tren, featuring the Monkey Boys: Paul Oldham and Jim White) CD: "XXV" / "II/XV" / "LXXXI" / "LXXXVI" / "LXIV" / "XIII" / "CII"
Monitor/Palace (MAP001), 2001 (limited edition tour-only release)

Master and Everyone (Bonnie "Prince" Billy) CD/LP: "The Way" / "Ain't You Wealthy, Ain't You Wise?" / "Master and Everyone" / "Wolf among Wolves" / "Joy and Jubilee" / "Maundering" / "Les-

sons from What's Poor" / "Even if Love" / "Three Questions" / "Hard Life"
Drag City / Palace Records (DC233/PR29), Domino (WIGCD121), Spunk (URA081), P-Vine (PCD-23356, with bonus track, "Forest Time"), 2003

Bonnie "Prince" Billy Sings Greatest Palace Music (Bonnie "Prince" Billy) CD/2LP: "New Partner" / "Ohio River Boat Song" / "Gulf Shores" / "You Will Miss Me When I Burn" / "The Brute Choir" / "I Send My Love to You" / "More Brother Rides" / "Agnes, Queen of Sorrow" / "Viva Ultra" / "Pushkin" / "Horses" / "Riding" / "West Palm Beach" / "No More Workhorse Blues" / "I Am a Cinematographer"
Drag City (DC252/PR31), Domino (WIG140), Spunk (URA121), P-Vine (PCD-24155), 2004

Superwolf (Bonnie "Prince" Billy and Matt Sweeney) CD/LP: "My Home Is the Sea" / "Beast for Thee" / "What Are You?" / "Goat and Ram" / "Lift Us Up" / "Rudy Foolish" / "Bed Is for Sleeping" / "Only Someone Running" / "Death in the Sea" / "Blood Embrace" / "I Gave You"
Drag City (DC179/PR33), Domino (WIG 150), Spunk (URA140), P-Vine (PCD-23584), 2005

Summer in the Southeast (Bonnie Prince Billy) CD/2LP: "Master and Everyone" / "Pushkin" / "Blokbuster" / "Wolf among Wolves" / "May It Always Be" / "Break of Day" / "A Sucker's Evening" / "Nomadic Revery" / "I See a Darkness" / "O Let It Be" / "Beast for Thee" / "Death to Everyone" / "Even if Love" / "I Send My Love to You" / "Take However Long You Want" / "Madeleine-Mary" / "Ease Down the Road"
Sea Note (SN11), 2005

The Brave and the Bold (Tortoise and Bonnie "Prince" Billy) CD/LP: "Cravo é Canela" / "Thunder Road" / "It's Expected I'm Gone" / "Daniel" / "Love Is Love" / "Pancho" / "That's Pep!" / "Some Say (I Got Devil)" / "Calvary Cross" / "On My Own"
Overcoat Recordings (OC027), Domino (WIG 167), Spunk (URA173), 2006

The Letting Go (Bonnie "Prince" Billy) CD/LP/DVD-A: "Love Comes to Me" / "Strange Form of Life" / "Wai" / "Cursed Sleep" / "No Bad News" / "Cold & Wet" / "Big Friday" / "Lay and Love" / "The Seedling" / "Then the Letting Go" / "God's Small Song" / "I Called You Back" / (hidden track) "Ebb Tide"
Drag City (DC420/PR36), Domino (WIG LP 182, WIG CD 182, WIG DVDA 182), Spunk (URA190), P-Vine (PCD23822, with bonus track, "Signifying Wolf"), 2006

Little Lost Blues (Bonny Billy) CD: "Little Boy Blue" / "His Hands" / "Black Dissimulation" / "Southside of the World" / "I Confess" / "Less of Me" / "Barcelona" / "Let's Start a Family (Blacks)" / "Little Boy Blue 2" / "I Am Drinking Again" / "Cryin' in the Chapel"
Domino (WIGCD182x), 2006

Wai Notes (Dawn McCarthy and Bonny Billy) CD: "Then the Letting Go" / "Strange Form of Life" / "Lay and Love" / "God Is Love" / "The Signifying Wolf" / "The Seedling" / "I Called You Back" / "Wai" / "Cursed Sleep" / "God's Small Song"
Sea Note (SN14), 2007

Wilding in the West (Bonnie "Prince" Billy) CD: "O Let It Be" / "Little Small Song" / "Then the Letting Go" / "The Gator" / "Master and Everyone" / "No Such as What I Want" / "Naked Lion" / "No

Bad News" / "Wai" / "Three Questions" / "Weaker Soldier" / "I Called You Back" / "Magnificent Billy" / "Is It the Sea?" / "My Home Is the Sea"
Spunk (URA239), P-Vine (PCD93080), 2008

Lie Down in the Light (Bonnie "Prince" Billy) CD/LP: "Easy Does It" / "You Remind Me of Something (the Glory Goes)" / "So Everyone" / "For Every Field, There's a Mole" / "Keep Eye on Other's Gain" / "You Want That Picture" / "Missing One" / "What's Missing Is" / "Where Is the Puzzle" / "Lie Down in the Light" / "Willow Trees Bend" / "I'll Be Glad"
Drag City (DC367/PR41), Domino (WIGCD222, WIGLP222), Spunk (URA243), P-Vine (PCD24206), 2008

Is It the Sea? (Bonnie "Prince" Billy with Harem Scarem and Alex Neilson) CD/2LP: "Minor Place" / "Love Comes to Me" / "Bed Is for Sleeping" / "Arise Therefore" / "Wolf among Wolves" / "Ain't You Wealthy? Ain't You Wise?" / "Cursed Sleep" / "Molly Bawn" / "Birch Ballad" / "New Partner" / "Is It the Sea?" / "My Home Is the Sea" / "Master and Everyone" / "I See a Darkness" / "Love in the Hot Afternoon"
Domino (WIGLP213, WIGCD213), EMI Music (24279727), 2008

Beware (Bonnie "Prince" Billy) CD/LP/Ultraload: "Beware Your Only Friend" / "You Can't Hurt Me Now" / "My Life's Work" / "Death Final" / "Heart's Arms" / "You Don't Love Me" / "You Are Lost" / "I Won't Ask Again" / "I Don't Belong to Anyone" / "There Is Something I Have to Say" / "I Am Goodbye" / "Without Work, You Have Nothing"* / "Afraid Ain't Me"*

* Deleted after initial release.

Drag City (DC666), Domino (WIGCD233, WIGLP2333), Spunk (URA279), P-Vine (PCD-24220), Love Da Records (LOVECD58), 2009

Unfinal Call: A Sum of Bonnie "Prince" Billy Work (Bonnie "Prince" Billy) CD: "The Way I Am" / "Another Day Full of Dread" / "Wolf among Wolves" / "After I Made Love to You" / "Only Someone Running" / "The Brute Choir" / "Strange Form of Life" / "You Want That Picture" / "Master and Everyone" / "I See a Darkness" / "66"
Palace Records / Drag City, 2009 (all selections drawn from previously released albums)

Funtown Comedown (Bonny Billy and the Picket Line) LP: "Ohio River Boat Song" / "May It Always Be" / "Hemlocks and Primroses" / "The Glory Goes" / Wolf among Wolves" / "We All Us Three Will Ride" / "Easy Does It" / "Lay and Love" / "Rider" / "Rambling Fever" / "You Want That Picture" / "Idle Hands Are the Devil's Playthings"
Sea Note (SN17/PR44), 2009

The Wonder Show of the World (Bonnie "Prince" Billy and the Cairo Gang) CD/LP: "Troublesome Houses" / "Teach Me to Bear You" / "With Cornstalks among Them" / "The Sounds Are Always Begging" / "Go Folks, Go" / "That's What Our Love Is" / "Merciless and Great" / "Where Wind Blows" / "Someone Coming Through" / "Kids"
Drag City (DC2012/PR45), Domino (WIG257), 2010

Wolfroy Goes to Town (Bonnie "Prince" Billy) CD/LP: "No Match" / "New Whaling" / "Time to Be Clear" / "New Tibet" / "Black Cap-

tain" / "Cows" / "There Will Be Spring" / "Quail And Dumplings"
/ "We Are Unhappy" / "Night Noises"
Drag City (DC502/PR049), Domino (WIG286), Spunk (URA383),
2011

The Marble Downs (Trembling Bells and Bonnie "Prince" Billy)
CD/LP: "I Made a Date (with an Open Vein)" / "I Can Tell You're
Leaving" / "Ferrari in a Demoltion Derby" / "Excursions into
Assonance" / "Ain't Nothing Wrong with a Little Longing" / "My
Husband's Got No Courage in Him" / "Lord Bless All" / "Riding"
Honest Jon's Records (HJR064), 2012

Singles/EPs

"Ohio River Boat Song" / "Drinking Woman" (Palace Brothers) 7"
Drag City (DC25), Big Cat (ABB51s), 1994

"Come In" / "Trudy Dies" (Palace) 7"
Drag City (DC37), 1994

"Horses" / "Stable Will" (Palace Songs) 7"
Drag City (DC47), 1994

An Arrow through the Bitch (Palace Brothers) CD/12": "Come In" /
"Horses" / "Stable Will" / "Trudy Dies"
Domino (RUG 21T), 1994

Hope (Palace Songs) CD/EP: "Agnes, Queen of Sorrow" / "Untitled" / "Winter Lady" / "Christmastime in the Mountains" / "All
Gone, All Gone" / "Werner's Last Blues to Blokbuster"

Drag City (DC57), Domino (WIG LP/CD 18), 1994

"O How I Enjoy the Light" / "Marriage" (Palace Songs) 7"
Drag City / Palace Records (DC64/PR1), 1994

"West Palm Beach" / "Gulf Shores" (Palace) 7"
Drag City / Palace Records (DC61/PR2), 1994

"The Mountain Low" / "(End of) Traveling" (Palace) 7"
Drag City (DC71/PR3), 1995

Mountain (Palace) CD/EP/12": "The Mountain" / "(End of) Traveling" / "Gulf Shores" / "West Palm Beach"
Drag City / Palace Records (DC71/PR3), 1995

"Gezundheit" / "Let the Wires Ring" (Palace) 7"
Hausmusik (12), 1995

"Black/Rich Tune" / "You Have Cum in Your Hair . . ." (Palace
Music) 7"
Domino (RUG 39), 1995 (demo versions, included with initial LP
pressing of *Viva Last Blues*)

"Every Mother's Son" / "More Brother Rides" (Palace) 7"
Drag City / Palace Records (DC83/PR9), 1996

"For the Mekons et al." / "Stable Will" (Palace Live) 7"
Palace Records (PR13), 1996

"Little Blue Eyes" / "The Spider's Dude Is Often Here" (Palace
Music) 7"

Drag City (DC91), 1996

"Patience" / "Take However Long You Want" (Will Oldham) 7"
Drag City / Palace Records (DC118/PR 16), 1997

Little Joya (Will Oldham) CD single: "Prologue" / "Joya" / "Exit Music (for a Dick)"
Drag City (littleDC107/DC107x), Domino (WIG39CDX), 1997; included with first 1,000 copies of *Joya* CD; rereleased 1998

Western Music (Will Oldham) CD/EP: "Always Bathing in the Evening" / "Western Music for J.L.L." / "Three Photographs" / "Jump In, Jump In, Come In, Come In"
Ovni Records (Aff. 002) (Spain), 1997

"I Am Drinking Again" / "Dreaming My Dreams" (Bonnie "Prince" Billy) CD single
Domino, 1998

"Black Dissimulation" / "No Such as What I Want" (Bonnie "Prince" Billy) 7"
All City Nomad, 1998 (500 copies on black vinyl, 500 copies on purple vinyl); issued as a CD single with *I See a Darkness*, available at FNAC stores in France, under the title *Either She or Me*, by Domino, 1999

Bonnie Prince Billy Performs the Songs of Kevin Loyne [*sic*] (Bonnie "Prince" Billy) 7": "The Sun Shines Down on Me" / "I Confess"
Lowfly (LF075), 1998 (600 copies included with Portuguese magazine *CRU* #4, 600 available otherwise, plus a later limited edition of 20; both songs were originally written and recorded by Kevin Coyne)

"One with the Birds" / "The Southside of the World" (Bonnie "Prince" Billy 7"
Palace Records (PR20), 1998

Blue Lotus Feet (Bonnie "Prince" Billy CD/EP: "One with the Birds" / "The Southside of the World" / "When Thy Song Flows through Me" / "I Am the Sky" / "Blue Lotus Feet" / "Polestar of My Life" / "Door of My Heart"
Domino (RUG81), 1998

Dream of a Drunk Black Southern Eagle (Bonnie "Prince" Billy) CD/EP: "One with the Birds" / "The Southside of the World" / "I Am Drinking Again" / "Dreaming My Dreams" / "Song for the New Breed (orchestral)"
Domino/Labels (VISA 4562), 1999 (giveaway to *Libération* subscribers, France only)

"Let's Start a Family" / "A Whorehouse Is Any House" (Bonnie "Prince" Billy) 7"
Sub Pop (SP 462), 1999

Ode Music (Will Oldham) CD/12": "Ode #1" / "Ode #2" / "Ode #3" / "Ode #4" / "Ode #1a" / "Ode #1b" / "Ode #2a" / "Ode #5" / "Ode #3a" / "Ode #4a"
Drag City (DC183), 2000

"Little Boy Blue" / "Little Boy Blue II" / "Blue Boy" (Bonnie "Blue" Billy) 7"
Western Vinyl (West009), 2000

More Revery (Bonny Billy) CD/EP: "Someone's Sleeping" / "Sweeter than Anything" / "Same Love that Makes Me Laugh Makes Me Cry" / "A Dream of the Sea" / "Strange Things" / "Just to See You Smile"
Temporary Residence Travels in Constants, Volume 7, 2000; remixed version issued 2001 (TRR37)

All Most Heaven (Will Oldham and Rian Murphy) CD/12": "Fall Again" / "Fall and Raise It On" / "Song of Most" / "Song of All"
Drag City (DC123), Domino (RUG117), P-Vine (PCD-3954), 2000

Get on Jolly (The Marquis de Tren and Bonny Billy) CD/12": "2/15" / "25" / "81" / "86" / "64" / "66"
Palace (PR24), Domino (RUG 109), Spunk (URA026), 2000

"What's Wrong with a Zoo?" / "I Send My Love to You" / "Stable-mate" (Bonnie "Prince" Billy) CD single
Domino (WIGCD89), Labels (visa 6435), 2001 (included with initial CD pressing of *Ease Down the Road*)

"Just to See My Holly Home" (Bonnie "Prince" Billy) CD single
Domino (RUG 125CDP), 2001

"Forest Time" (Will Oldham)
Artimo (01), 2002 (one-sided 10", packaged with *Forest Time*, a book of photography by Erik Wesselo)

Slitch Music (The Continental OP) 12": "Faster" / "La La La" /

"Glock" / "Heavy Minor" / "Fantasy" / "Acoustic Minor" / "James Tired" / "Magnifico" / "..."*
Drag City (DC195), 2002

"We All, Us Three, Will Ride" / "Barcelona" (Will Oldham) 7"
Isota Records (SODY005), 2002 (500 copies gray vinyl, 500 black vinyl with hand-screened sleeve; second pressing of 1,000 in regular sleeve, all black vinyl)

"Happy Child" / "Forest Time" (Bonnie "Prince" Billy) CD single
Drag City (DC232/PR28), 2003

Seafarers (Will Oldham) CD/12": "Sapele" / "Lars" / "Bogo" / "Emmanuel"
Drag City (261), 2004

"Agnes, Queen of Sorrow" / "Blokbuster" (Bonnie "Prince" Billy) 7"
Drag City (DC278/PR30), Domino (RUG 135), 2004

"Agnes, Queen of Sorrow" / "Blokbuster" / "Pussyfooting" (Bonnie "Prince" Billy) CD single
Drag City (DC278/PR30), Domino (RUG 135CD), 2004 (also includes video for "Agnes")

"No More Workhorse Blues" / "The Color of My Dreams, if I Had Dreams"† (Bonnie "Prince" Billy) 7"
Drag City, Domino, 2004

---

* Unlisted track.
† Alternative title for "Ruby."

"No More Workhorse Blues" / "Ruby" / "The Kiss" (Bonnie "Prince" Billy) CD single
Drag City (DC285/PR32), Domino, 2004 (also includes video for "No More Workhorse Blues")

"I Gave You" / "Four Screams" (Bonny/Sweeney) 7"
Drag City (DC298/PR34), Domino (RUG 209)

"I Gave You" / "My Circle" / "Four Screams" / "Birch Ballad" (Bonny/Sweeney) CD single
Drag City (DC298/PR34), Domino (RUG 209cd) (CD includes video for "I Gave You")

"His Hands" (Bonnie "Prince" Billy)
iTunes single, 2006

"Cursed Sleep" / "The Signifying Wolf" / "God's Small Song" (Bonnie "Prince" Billy) CD single / 12"
Drag City (DC316/PR35), Domino (230CD, 230T), 2006

"Cold & Wet" / "Buried Treasure" (Bonnie "Prince" Billy) 7"
Drag City (DC318/PR37), Domino (RUG237), 2006

"Cold & Wet" / "The Way" / "Buried Treasure" (Bonnie "Prince" Billy) CD single / 12"
Drag City (DC318/PR37), Domino (RUG237), 2006 (CD single includes video for "Cold & Wet")

"Lay and Love" / "Goin' to Acapulco" (Bonnie "Prince" Billy) 7"
Drag City (DC329/PR38), Domino (RUG246), 2007

"Lay and Love" / "Señor" / "Goin' to Acapulco" (Bonnie "Prince" Billy) CD single / 12"
Drag City (DC329/PR38), Domino (RUG246), 2007 (CD single includes video for "Lay and Love")

Bonny 2007 (Bonny) 7": "John the Baptist" / "Strange Form of Life"
No label tour release, 2007

"Strange Form of Life" / "The Seedling" (Bonnie "Prince" Billy) 7"
Drag City (DC337/PR39), Domino (RUG248), 2007

"Strange Form of Life" / "New Partner" / "The Sun Highlights the Lack in Each" / "The Seedling" (Bonnie "Prince" Billy) CD single / 12"
Drag City (DC337/PR39), Domino (RUG248), 2007 (CD single includes videos for "Strange Form of Life" and "Ebb Tide")

Ask Forgiveness (Bonnie "Prince" Billy) CD/12": "newbury" / "bjork/sjon/von trier" / "danzig/erickson" / "ochs" / "oldham" / "throckmorton/haggard/mekons" / "caldwell" / "kelly"
Drag City (DC354/PR40), Domino (WIGCD212, WIGLP212), Spunk (URA238), 2007 (songs listed solely by author; song titles are "I Came to Hear the Music" / "I've Seen It All" / "Am I a Demon" / "My Life" / "I'm Loving the Street" / "The Way I Am" / "Cycles" / "The World's Greatest")

"Notes for Future Lovers" / "¿Donde Esta Prufrock?" (Bonnie "Prince" Billy) 7"
Gold Robot Records (GRR006), 2008 (numbered edition of 500 copies, blue vinyl)

"One Day at a Time" (Bonnie "Prince" Billy with Bewarers)
iTunes single, 2009

Chijimi (Bonnie "Prince" Billy) 10"/download: "How about Thank
You" / "Hey Little" / "Champion" / "Face Him"
Drag City (PR42U/ULTRADC666), 2009

Susanna and Bonny Billy Sing . . . (Susanna and Bonny Billy) 7":
"(I'll Love You) Forever and Ever" / "In Spite of Ourselves"
No label tour release, 2009

"Stay" / "People Living" (Bonnie "Prince" Billy) 7"
Drag City (DC422/PR43), 2009

"Midday" / "You Win" (Bonnie "Prince" Billy and the Cairo
Gang) 7"
Drag City (DC2012X/PR45X), 2010 (included with initial LP
pressing of *The Wonder Show of the World*)

"Without Work You Have Nothing" / "Afraid Ain't Me" (Bonnie
"Prince" Billy) download single
Drag City (DC666X/PR42X), 2010

"New Year's Eve's the Loneliest Night of the Year" (Bonnie "Prince"
Billy and Trembling Bells) 7"
Honest Jon's Records (HJP51), 2010

"Island Brothers" / "New Wonder" (Bonnie "Prince" Billy and the
Cairo Gang) 10"
Drag City (DC468/PR46), Domino (RUG395), 2011

"Must Be Blind" / "Life in Muscle" (Matt Sweeney and Bonnie "Prince" Billy) 10"
Drag City (DC481/PR47), Domino (RUG400), 2011

The Mindeater EP (Bonnie "Prince" Billy and The Phantom Family Halo): "The Mindeater" / "Roki for Now" / "I Wonder if I Care as Much" / "Suddenly the Darkness" 10"/CD
Sophomore Lounge Records & Tapes (SL030, 10"), Partisan Records (CD), 2011

"There Is No God" / "God Is Love" (Bonnie "Prince" Billy)
Drag City (DC483/PR48), Domino (RUG421), 2011

Haggard Harper Bonnie 7" (Bonnie "Prince" Billy): "Because of Your Eyes" / "I'll See You Again"
Spiritual Pajamas (Spiritual000), 2011

"Mother Nature Kneels" (Bonnie "Prince" Billy) download
Long Haul Productions, 2011

"Quail and Dumplings" / "Black Ice Cream" / "E lesu / Maik'ai No" (Bonnie "Prince" Billy) digital single
Drag City (DC506/PR050), Domino (RUG442D; RUG442CDP is a promo-only CD version containing album and radio edit versions of "Quail and Dumplings"), 2011

"I Am a Floozy" / "Remember the Terror Time" (Bonnie "Prince" Billy) 10" packaged with *Afternoon*, a book of paintings by Ashley Macomber
Black Tent Press (BTP008), 2012

Bonnie & Mariee (Bonnie "Prince" Billy and Mariee Sioux) 2x7":
"Not Mocked" / "Bird Child" / "Love Skulls" / "Mad Mad Me"
Spiritual Pajamas (002), 2012

The B-Sides for Time to Be Clear (Bonnie "Prince" Billy) 7" EP: "Time
to Be Clear"* / "Whipped" / "Out of Mind"
Drag City (DC515/PR51), 2012

Compilation Appearances

"Don't I Look Good Today" (Palace Brothers) on *Louisville Sluggers
Vol. 3* double 7"
Self Destruct (16), 1993

"Two More Days" (Palace Brothers) on *Love Is My Only Crime* 2CD
Veracity/Intercord (IRS 973.402), 1994

"For the Mekons et al." (Palace Brothers) on *Hey Drag City* CD/2LP/
cass.
Drag City (DC20), Domino (WIGCD16), 1994

"I Am a Cinematographer" / "Meaulnes" / "I Send My Love to
You" / "You Will Miss Me When I Burn" (Palace Brothers) on *The
Drag City Hour* CD
Sea Note (SN2), 1996. Versions recorded live on WMBR, July 1992.

"More Brother Dub" (Ice vs. Palace) on *Organised Sound* CD/2LP

* download only

Jazz Fudge Recordings (JFR CD005), 1996 (remix of "More Brother Rides")

"More Brother (Inbred Version)" (Ice vs. Palace) on *Macrodub Infection Vol. 2* 2CD
Virgin (AMBT14, 724384176426), 1996 (remix of "More Brother Rides")

"Little Blue Eyes" (Palace Brothers) on *Sourmash, a Louisville Compilation* CD
X-Static / Boss Snake (9606-2), 1996. Version "recorded in the basement."

"Ebb's Folly" (Will Oldham and Jim O'Rourke) on *Dutch Harbor: Where the Sea Breaks Its Back* soundtrack CD
Atavistic (ALP85CD), 1997

Untitled track on *Sounds of the Geographically Challenged Vol. 2* (Continental OP) 12"
The Temporary Residence (TRR05), 1997; *Sounds of the Geographically Challenged* CD, 2000

"In My Mind" (Will Oldham) on split 7" of David Allan Coe songs with Rising Shotgun
Palace Records (PR18), 1997

"Big Balls" (Palace Contribution) on *Sides 5–6* 7"
Skin Graft / Gasoline Boost Records (GR26/GB13), 1997. AC/DC tribute compilation spread out over several 7"s.

"Blokbuster" (Live Palace Music) on *Felidae—A Benefit for the Cedar Hill Animal Sanctuary* CD
Last Exit (lastexit-one), 1997. Live version recorded at Lounge Ax, Chicago, November 1995.

"What's Wrong with a Zoo?" (Bonnie "Prince" Billy) on *Quelque Chose d'Organique* soundtrack CD
Virgin France (7243 846935 2 7), 1998

"Watch with Me" (Bonnie "Prince" Billy) on *Methods of Intimate Plumbing* CD
Blue Bunny Records (#002), 1999 giveaway with *Flygirl* magazine, issue 8

"Song for the New Breed (acoustic version)" (Bonnie "Prince" Billy) on *Louisvillesonicimprint—Vol. 1* CD/2LP
Ghetto Defendant (6), 2000

"Today I Started Celebrating Again" (Bonnie "Prince" Billy) on *At Home with the Groovebox* CD/2LP
Grand Royal Records (GRO68CD), 2000

"The Eagle and the Hawk" (Bonnie "Prince" Billy) on *Take Me Home* CD
Badman Recording Co. (BRCD 995), 2000, John Denver tribute album

"Brother Warrior" (Bonnie "Prince" Billy) on split 7" of Kate Wolf songs with rainYwood

Palace Records (PR27), 2002

"Early Morning Melody" (Bonnie "Prince" Billy) on *Shellac Curated All Tomorrow's Parties 2.0* CD/LP
ATP (ATPR3CD), 2002

"Don't Cry Driver" (Will Oldham and Alan Licht) on *You Can Never Go Fast Enough* CD/2LP
Plain Recordings (Plain103), 2003, *Two-Lane Blacktop* tribute album

"There's Something about What Happens When We Talk" (Mary Feiock and Bonnie Billy) on *Louisville Is for Lovers 3* CD
Double Malt Music (dbm03), 2003

"All These Vicious Dogs" (Bonnie "Prince" Billy) on *All the Real Girls* soundtrack CD
Sanctuary Records / Combustion Music (06076-84605-2), 2003

"Lessons from What's Poor" (Bonnie "Prince" Billy) on *Now Who's Crazy* CD
Drag City, 2003. Alternate version from Rove recording session.

"Antagonism" (Bonnie "Prince" Billy) on *Comes with a Wide-Awake Crescent-Shaped Smile Volume 10* CD (CWAS smile 10), issued with *Comes with a Smile* magazine #14, 2004. Live version recorded at the Casbah, San Diego, April 2003.

"Brokedown Palace" / "Babylon System / I Can't Live without You" / "Lullaby of Spring" (Bonny Billy) on *Pebbles and Ripples* split tour CD/EP with Brightblack (BPBBB2004), 2004. Cover songs suggested to BPB by Brightblack (flip side is cover songs suggested to Brightblack by BPB).

"Demon Lover" (Superwolf) on *Sprout* soundtrack CD
Brushfire Records / Record Collection (48985-2), 2005

"My Home Is the Sea" (Bonnie "Prince" Billy and Matt Sweeney) on *Drag City A to Z* CD
Drag City (DCAZ), 2005. Live version recorded in Athens, GA, June 2004.

"Song for Doctors without Borders" (Bonnie "Prince" Billy) on *Not Alone* 5CD
Durtro Jnana (1963), 2006

"Monolith Lamb" (Bonnie Billy and Oscar Parsons) on *Spacemoth 5th Anniversary Compilation* 2 CD-R
No label, 2006

"Love Is Pleasing" (Bonnie "Prince" Billy) on *Louisville Is for Lovers 6* CD
Double Malt (dbm07), 2006

"Wouldn't It Be Nice" (Oldham Brothers) on *Do It Again: A Tribute to Pet Sounds* CD
Houston Party Record (HPR135), 2006

"Get Your Hands Dirty" (Bonnie "Prince" Billy) on *Louisville Is for Lovers 8* CD
Double Malt Music, 2008

"Torn and Brayed" (Bonnie "Prince" Billy and Matt Sweeney) on
Palermo Shooting soundtrack CD
City Slang (SLANG 1051892), 2008

"The Girl in Me" (Bonnie "Prince" Billy with Cheyenne Mize) on
Louisville Is for Lovers 9 CD
Double Malt Music (Dbm14); 2LP Karate Body Records, 2008

"Rich Wife Full of Happiness" (Bonnie "Prince" Billy) on *TFF
Rudolstadt 2008* 2CD/DVD
Heideck (HD20083), 2009. Live version recorded at Rudolstadt
2008 festival.

"Poor Shelter" (Bonnie "Prince" Billy) on split 7" with Young
Widows
Temporary Residence (TRR151), 2009

"New Wedding" (Bonnie "Prince" Billy) on *The Present* soundtrack
CD
Brushfire Records (B0013107-02), 2009

"My Only Friend" (Bonnie "Prince" Billy) on *Stroke-Songs for Chris
Knox* 2CD
A Major (AMAJ002), Merge Records (MRG367), 2009

"John the Baptist" / "Beautiful Star of Bethlehem" (Bonnie
"Prince" Billy) on *Face a Frowning World—An E. C. Ball Memorial
Album* CD
Tompkins Square Records (TSQ-2288), 2009

"Love Comes to Me (live)" (Bonnie "Prince" Billy) on *Does Your Cat Know My Dog?* 12"
Three Four Records (TFR004), 2010. Live version recorded in "Central Coastal California," 2006.

"Beware Your Only Friend (live)" (Bonnie "Prince" Billy) on *It Happened Here* 12" and 7"
St. Ives (SAINT42) 2010. Live version recorded March 2009. Released for Record Store Day, 2010.

"Love in the Hot Afternoon" (Matt Sweeney and Bonnie "Prince" Billy) mp3 as part of *Adult Swim Singles Program* and on 2CD *Dear New Orleans*
Adult Swim, 2010

"Simple Man (Hombre Sencillo)" (Bonnie "Prince" Billy) on *Be Yourself (A Tribute to Graham Nash's Songs for Beginners)* CD/LP
Grassroots Records (GRRCD117/GRRLP001), 2010. Sung in Spanish, lyric translation by Bob Arellano.

"Bertrand My Son" (Bonnie "Prince" Billy) on *Sing Larry Jon Wilson* 7" split with The Black Swans
(LJW-01), 2010

"All the Trees of the Field Will Clap Their Hands" on *Seven Swans Reimagined* download
On Joyful Wings, 2011

Contributions to Other Artists' Recordings

Briana Corrigan: "Simply Beautiful" on *When My Arms Wrap You Round* CD
Eastwest (0630-14271-2), 1996 (vocal)

Briana Corrigan: "I Put My Arms Out for You (Acoustic)" on *Love Me Now* CD single
Eastwest (0630-14696-2 EW 041 CD1), 1996 (vocal)

The Anomoanon: "Tom He Was a Piper's Son" on *Mother Goose* CD
Palace Records (PR19), 1998 (backing vocals)

The Anomoanon: *Summer Never Ends* CD/EP
Palace Records (PR21), 1999 (backing vocals)

Papa M: *Papa M* CD single
Temporary Residence Travels in Constants Volume 5, 1999 (lyrics to untitled song)

The Anomoanon: *Songs from Robert Louis Stevenson's "A Child's Garden of Verses"* CD
Palace Records (PR23), 2000 (harmony vocals, guitar, keyboards)

Johnny Cash: "I See a Darkness" on *American III: Solitary Man* CD
American (500986 2), 2000 (backing vocals)

Tweaker: "Happy Child" on *The Attraction to All Things Uncertain* CD
Six Degrees / Ryko (657036 1055-2), 2001 (vocal, lyrics)

Papa M: *Whatever, Mortal* CD/LP
Drag City (DC194), Domino (WIG LP/CD 104), Spunk (URA057),
2001 (bass, electric guitar, piano, backing vocals)

Papa M: "How Can I Tell You I Love You?" on *Sonic Youth Presents All
Tomorrow's Parties 1.1* CD/LP
(ATPRCD 2), 2002 (backing vocals)

Nicolai Dunger: *Tranquil Isolation* CD/LP
Delores Recordings / Virgin Records (Dol114DIGIDGVIR182/
COOL23), 2002 (vocals, acoustic guitar, electric guitar, piano;
coproduction with Dunger and Paul Oldham)

The Anomoanon: "One That Got Away" on *Asleep Many Years in the
Woods* CD/LP
Temporary Residence (TRR54), 2002 (backing vocal)

Brightblack: *Ala.Cali.Tucky* CD
Self-released, 2003; reissued by Galaxia (glx20), 2004 ("high ghost
singing")

Bobby Bare Jr.'s Young Criminals' Starvation League: "Valentine"
on *From the End of Your Leash* CD
Munich Records (MRCD253), 2004 (backing vocal)

Tweaker: "Ruby" on *2 A.M. Wakeup Call* CD
iMusic/Waxploitation, 2004 (vocal, lyrics)

Sage Francis: *Sea Lion* 12"
Epitaph (E86752-1), 2005 (vocal, guitar)

Red: *Nothin' to Celebrate* CD
Universal Music (982 599-3), 2005 (vocal on "He Was a Friend of Mine"; backing vocals on "Don't Create a Ditch" and "Nothin' to Celebrate")

Alasdair Roberts: *No Earthly Man* CD/LP
Drag City (DC283), Spunk (URA 147), 2005 (vocals, bass, piano, production)

Songs for the Young at Heart (with Bonnie "Prince" Billy): "Puff the Magic Dragon"
Lucky Dog (03) 7", 2005 (later included on *Songs for the Young Heart* V2 CD, 2007) (vocal)

Carrie Yury: *Mutter* CD/EP
No label, 2005 (vocals, guitar)

Björk: "Gratitude" on *Drawing Restraint 9* soundtrack CD
Polydor (9872853), 2005; LP Ten Little Indians (TPLP459), 2005 (vocal)

Silver Jews: *Tanglewood Numbers* CD/LP
Drag City (DC297), 2005 (guitar)

Wrinkle Neck Mules: "Lowlight" on *Pull the Brake* CD
Shut Eye Records (SE101K), 2006 (vocal)

Current 93: "Idumaea" on *Black Ships Ate the Sky* CD/2LP
Durtro Jnana (2112/LP2112), 2006 (vocal, banjo, tamboura)

Homesick Hank: "Leave It Behind" on *Leave It Behind* CD

Playground (HT002), 2006 (vocal)

Pink Nasty: *Mold the Gold* CD
No label 2006 (vocal and "additional playing" on "BTK Blues,"
"Danny," "Don't Ever Change")

Charlie Louvin: "Knoxville Girl" on *Charlie Louvin* CD
Tompkins Square Records (TSQ1042), 2007 (vocal)

The Soulsavers: "Through My Sails" on *It's Not How Hard You Fall,
It's the Way You Land* CD
V2 (VVR1045532), 2007 (vocal)

Current 93: "Idumaea" on *Birdsong in the Empire* CD
Durtro Jnana (462005), 2007 (vocal)

Soy un Caballo: "La Chambre" on *Les Heures du Raison* CD
Matamore (mtm09), 2007 (vocal)

Valgeir Sigurösson: *Ekvilibrium* CD/LP
Bedroom Community (HVALUR3CD/LP), 2007 (vocal and lyrics
on "Evolution of Waters" and "Kin")

Scout Niblett: *This Fool Can Die Now* CD/LP
Too Pure (pure208cd), 2007 (vocals on "Do You Want to Be
Buried with My People?," "Kiss," "River of No Return," "Comfort
You")

Baby Dee: *Safe Inside the Day* CD/LP
Drag City (DC351), 2008 (vocals, coproduction with Matt
Sweeney)

Sun Kil Moon: *April* CD
Caldo Verde (CV006), P-Vine (PCD24203/4); LP Caldo Verde /
Vinyl Films Records (VFR-2008-1), 2008 (vocals on "Unlit Hall-
way" and "Like the River")

Dosh: "Bury the Ghost" on *Wolves and Wishes* CD/LP
Anticon (ABR0084), 2008 (vocal)

Numero 6: "Da Piccolissimi Pezzi" on *Quando Arriva la Gente Si
Sente Meglio* CD/EP free download
Green Fog Records, 2008 (vocal)

The California Guitar Trio: *Echoes* CD
(INK7716), 2008 (vocal on "And I Know" and "Freebird")

Holly Throsby: "Would You?" on *A Loud Call* CD
Spunk (URA244), 2008 (vocal)

Susanna: *Flower of Evil* CD/2LP
Rune Grammofon (RCD 2080 / RLP 3080), 2008 (vocals on "Jail-
break" and "Without You")

Black Nasty: "Eazy" on *Shark Tank* CD
No label, 2009 (vocal)

Cheyenne Mize and Bonnie "Prince" Billy: *Among the Gold* 10"
Karate Body Records (KBR002), 2009 (vocal)

The Soulsavers: "Sunrise" 7"
V2 (VVR710890), 2009 (vocal)

Brian Harnetty and Bonnie "Prince" Billy: *Silent City* CD
Atavistic (ALP190), 2009 (vocals and lyrics on "Sleeping in the
Driveway," "And under the Winesap Tree," "Some Glad Day")

This Immortal Coil: "Ostia" on *The Dark Age of Love* CD/2LP
Ici d'Ailleurs (IDA060), 2009 (vocal)

Angie Hart: "Little Bridges" on *Eat My Shadow* CD
ABC, 2009 (vocal)

Nuala Kennedy: "The Waves of the Silvery Tide" on *Tune In* CD
Compass Records (COM4534), 2010 (vocal)

Brett Eugene Ralph's Kentucky Chrome Revue CD
Noise Pollution (Noise36), 2010 (vocals)

Hot Chip: "I Feel Bonnie" 7"/12" (remix of "I Feel Better")
Parlophone (R6799), 2010 (vocal)

Coliseum: *A House with a Curse* CD/LP
Temporary Residence (TRR175), 2010 (backing vocal on "Perim-
eter Man," "additional vocals" on "Skeleton Smile")

Anna Ternhaim: *The Night Visitor* CD/LP/2CD+DVD
Universal Music (060252783226) (backing vocals and additional
production on "Bow your Head" "Walking Aimlessly," and "All
Shadows"; additional production on "Come to Bed")

This Must Be the Place soundtrack CD
Indigo Film (IND001) (lyrics on "Lay & Love," "Open Up," "You

Can Like It," "If It Falls It Falls," and "The Sword Is Yours." Music written by David Byrne; songs performed by The Pieces of Shit)

Other Group Participation

Box of Chocolates: *Fearful Symmetry* LP (Mickey Hawaii [aka Mike Howe], Wayne Olephant [aka Will Oldham—vocal and songwriting on "Garbage Barge" and "The Ephant"], Brute Rake [aka Bryan Rich])
Mad Entropic Carnival (HB 001), 1990; CD (MEC-103), 1999

Goat Songs (The Sundowners) 7": "Turkey Vulture" / "Tonight Will Be Fine" / "Punk Rock" / "Goats" / "Pozor" / "Tallulah"
Sea Note (SN4), 1994

The Boxhead Ensemble: *The Last Place to Go* CD/2LP (Edith Frost, David Grubbs, Ryan Hembrey, Charles Kim, Michael Krassner, Fred Lonberg-Holm, Julie Pommerleau, Will Oldham, Rick Rizzo, Scott Tuma, Mick Turner, Ken Vandermark, Jim White); WO is listed as playing harmonica on "Introduction" and "Far Gone / Big Sky," melodica on "Coastal Border," and vocals on "Black Dissimulation" and "Send in the Clowns" (both only on bonus CD)
Atavistic (ALP96CD; limited edition bonus CD ALP96CD-X), 1998; 2LP Secretly Canadian (SC22), 1998

Havanarama: *Fish & Crabs* CD-R (Robert Arellano, Paul Oldham, Will Oldham, Pete Townsend): "Playa West Palm" / "Soy el Diablo" / "Carcel de Folsom" / "Rancho Grande" / "Saludo Para la Viuda" / "Cancion Urgente Para Mi Hermana Cubana"

No label, 1999; issued as *Greetings from Providence R.I.* CD with extra tracks ("Valle de Vinales," "Doble Dosis," "My Father") by Foss Records (FossCD-901), 2000

Havanarama: *Rock the Blockade: 2000 Incorruptible* CD (adds David Pajo to lineup): "Valle de Viñales" / "Rancho Grande" / "Madeleine-Mary" / "No Gold Digger" / "Carcel de Folsom" / "Simpatia Para el Diablo" / "Eso Es Lo Que Dijo Ella" / "Doble Dosis" / "Chupacabra" / "Space Killer" / "Stairway to Heaven"
Secret Eye (AB-OC-2), 2003

Amalgamated Sons of Rest: self-titled CD/12" (Jason Molina, Will Oldham, Alasdair Roberts): "Maa Bonny Lad" / "My Donal" / "The Gypsy He-Witch" / "The Last House" / "Major March" / "Jennie Blackbird's Blues" / "I Will Be Good" (unlisted bonus track)
Galaxia (glx-16), P-Vine (PCD-4267), 2002

Audiobook

Rudolph Wurlitzer, *Slow Fade* 5CD, read by Will Oldham with D. V. DeVincentis
Drag City (DC449CD), 2011

INDEX